Books from QED

Database

Migrating to DB2
DB2: The Complete Guide to Implementation and Use
DB2 Design Review Guidelines
DB2: Maximizing Performance of Online Production Systems
Embedded SQL for DB2: Application Design and Programming
SQL for DB2 and SQL/DS Application Developers
Using DB2 to Build Decision Support Systems
The Data Dictionary: Concepts and Uses
Logical Data Base Design
Entity-Relationship Approach to Logical Data Base Design
Database Management Systems: Understanding and Applying Database Technology
Database Machines and Decision Support Systems: Third Wave Processing
IMS Design and Implementation Techniques
Repository Manager/MVS: Concepts, Facilities and Capabilities
How to Use ORACLE SQL*PLUS
ORACLE: Building High Performance of Online Systems
ORACLE Design Review Guidelines
Using ORACLE to Build Decision Support Systems
Understanding Data Pattern Processing: The Key to Competitive Advantage
Developing Client/Server Aplications in an Architected Environment

Systems Engineering

Quality Assurance for Information Systems: Methods, Tools, and Techniques
Handbook of Screen Format Design
Managing Software Projects: Selecting and Using PC-Based Project Management Systems
The Complete Guide to Software Testing
A User's Guide for Defining Software Requirements
A Structured Approach to Systems Testing
Storyboard Prototyping: A New Approach to User Requirements Analysis
The Software Factory: Managing Software Development and Maintenance
Data Architecture: The Information Paradigm
Advanced Topics in Information Engineering
Software Engineering with Formal Metrics

Management

Introduction to Data Security and Controls
CASE: The Potential and the Pitfalls

Management (cont'd)

Strategic and Operational Planning for Information Services
Information Systems Planning for Competitive Advantage
How to Automate Your Computer Center: Achieving Unattended Operations
Ethical Conflicts in Information and Computer Science, Technology, and Business
Mind Your Business: Managing the Impact of End-User Computing
Controlling the Future: Managing Technology-Driven Change
The UNIX Industry: Evolution, Concepts, Architecture, Applications, and Standards

Data Communications

Designing and Implementing Ethernet Networks
Network Concepts and Architectures
Open Systems: The Guide to OSI and its Implementation

IBM Mainframe Series

CSP: Mastering Cross System Product
CICS/VS: A Guide to Application Debugging
MVS COBOL II Power Programmer's Desk Reference
VSE COBOL II Power Programmer's Desk Reference
CICS Application and System Programming: Tools and Techniques
QMF: How to Use Query Management Facility with DB2 and SQL/DS
DOS/VSE: Introduction to the Operating System
DOS/VSE: CICS Systems Programming
DOS/VSE/SP Guide for Systems Programming: Concepts, Programs, Macros, Subroutines
Advanced VSE System Programming Techniques
Systems Programmer's Problem Solver
VSAM: Guide to Optimization and Design
MVS/JCL: Mastering Job Control Language
MVS/TSO: Mastering CLISTS
MVS/TSO: Mastering Native Mode and ISPF
REXX in the TSO Environment

Programming

C Language for Programmers
VAX/VMS: Mastering DCL Commands and Utilities
The PC Data Handbook: Specifications for Maintenance, Repair, and Upgrade of the IBM/PC, PS/2 and Compatibles
UNIX C Shell Desk Reference

The PC Data Handbook

Specifications for Maintenance, Repair and Upgrade of the IBM PC, PS/2, and Compatibles

Stanley Shell

QED Technical Publishing Group

Boston • Toronto • London

TRADEMARKS

Many manufacturers claim as trademarks the designations used to identify their products. Where the author and publisher have used these designations, and were aware of a trademark claim, these designations have been identified. Any omissions are unintentional.

Registered Trademarks
AutoCAD by Autodesk, Inc.
MS-DOS, XENIX by MicroSoft Corporation
PC-DOS, PC/XT, PC/AT, PS/2, IBM by International Business Machines Corp.
INTEL by Intel Corporation
SideKick by Borland International
UNIX by American Telephone and Telegraph Corporation
WORDPERFECT by WordPerfect Corporation

LIMITS OF LIABILITY AND DISCLAIMER OF WARRANTY

The author and publisher of this book have used their best efforts in preparing this book. These efforts include the research, compilation, and assembly of the data presented herein. This book is sold *as is*, without a warranty of any kind, either expressed or implied respecting the contents of this book, including but not limited to implied warranties for the book's quality, performance, merchantability, or fitness for any particular purpose. Neither the author nor the publisher or their dealers or distributors shall be liable to the purchaser or any other person or entity with respect to any liability, loss, or damage caused or alleged to be caused directly or indirectly by this book nor for incidental or consequential damages in connection with, or arising out of, the furnishing, performance, or use of this book, the data contained in it, and the documentation of the data.

Library of Congress Catalog Number: 90-19543
International Standard Book Number: 0-89435-343-8

Printed in the United States of America
92 93 94 10 9 8 7 6 5 4 3 2 1

Library of Congress Cataloging-In-Publication Data

Shell, Stanley.
  The PC data handbook: specifications for maintenance, repair, and upgrade of the IBM PC, PS/2, and compatibles / Stanley Shell.
    Includes index.
    ISBN 0-89435-343-8
    1. Microcomputers—Maintenance and repair. 2. Microcomputers—Upgrading. 3. IBM Personal Computer 4. IBM-compatible computers.
I. Title
TK7888.3.S528   1991
621.39'16—dc20
                                                        91-19543
                                                            CIP

Contents

List of Figures

List of Tables

Preface

"The Chinese editor is wiser—he leaves his readers the supreme satisfaction of discovering a few typographical mistakes for themselves."

Lin Yutang (1895-1976)

There are close to fifty million IBM and clone personal computers (XT's, AT's, and PS/2's) in use today. They are based on the Intel microprocessors 8088, 8086, 80186, 80286, 80386, and 80486 and their corresponding numeric data (mathematics) coprocessors. But, what makes them tick? Immediately, you answer, "The SOFTWARE, of course!" We all know it's the MS-DOS, the UNIX, the XENIX-System V, the language assemblers and compilers, and the thousands of utilities and application programs.

However, the day arrives when we push that button on the panel and the prompt "C:>" or that user-friendly menu that was installed so many months ago does not appear. After trying "CTL-ALT-DEL" a few times, sheer panic sets in. Your eyeballs roll over like dollar signs on a five-column slot machine while you consider the repair bill.

This collection of data is designed to give you a clue as to the first-echelon maintenance and to assist you, as a minimum, in generating a coherent explanation as to what is wrong. It will not, however, convert you into a service engineer or a PC repairman.

Whether you are a rank amateur or a skilled professional, you will find the information in this collection to be useful. This information has been extracted from a vast collection of documentation that never seems to be at hand when you need it. It has been gathered together to provide you with an insight into how and why the PC works. The intention is that this document is to be used as a reference rather than as a textbook to be studied chapter by chapter. Nevertheless, it is expected that you will comprehensively scan each section if for no other reason than to broaden your understanding of PC operation.

In addition, as you delve further and further into the intricacies of the PC you will probably build a personal library to expand upon the information herein. To this end, a list of references has been provided that will supply many details not included in "The PC Data Handbook."

I wish to extend my gratitude to Dan Custer and John Forster for their enthusiastic encouragement and support in the creation of this book as a convenient, quick reference tool.

We would appreciate hearing from you regarding suggestions for improvement, correction of errors, or additions to the contents of this document. We hope you enjoy perusing "The PC Data Handbook" and that you find its contents useful.

Stanley Shell

My Personal Computer

Complete the following charts for each machine that you own. They will serve to document your configurations and reduce confusion when you modify your systems.

HARDWARE

Category	Example	System #1	System #2	System #3
System Type	XT	_____	_____	_____
Manufacturer	IBM	_____	_____	_____
Serial Number	xxxxxx	_____	_____	_____
Date Acquired	1/11/89	_____	_____	_____
Purchased From	NYNEX	_____	_____	_____
Processor	8088	_____	_____	_____
Processor Speed	8 Mhz	_____	_____	_____
Memory Size	640 K	_____	_____	_____
Chip Speed	100 nsec	_____	_____	_____
Extended Memory Size		_____	_____	_____
Extended Memory Mfg.		_____	_____	_____
Math Coprocessor	8087	_____	_____	_____
Coprocessor Speed		_____	_____	_____
BIOS Manufacturer	IBM	_____	_____	_____
BIOS Version		_____	_____	_____
Keyboard Type		_____	_____	_____
Monitor Type	B/W	_____	_____	_____
Monitor Size	12 Inch	_____	_____	_____
Monitor Manufacturer	IBM	_____	_____	_____
Monitor Serial Number	xxxxxx	_____	_____	_____

Category	Example	System #1	System #2	System #3
Disk				
A: Type	1.2 Meg Floppy	_____	_____	_____
A: S/N	xxxxxx	_____	_____	_____
A: Manufacturer	Shugart	_____	_____	_____
B: Type	360 K Floppy	_____	_____	_____
B: S/N	xxxxxx	_____	_____	_____
B: Manufacturer	NEC	_____	_____	_____
C: Type	20 Meg Hard Drive	_____	_____	_____
C: S/N	xxxxxx	_____	_____	_____
C: Manufacturer	Seagate	_____	_____	_____
D: Type		_____	_____	_____
D: S/N		_____	_____	_____
D: Manufacturer		_____	_____	_____
E: Type		_____	_____	_____
E: S/N		_____	_____	_____
E: Manufacturer		_____	_____	_____
F: Type		_____	_____	_____
F: S/N		_____	_____	_____
F: Manufacturer		_____	_____	_____
Video Card Type	VGA	_____	_____	_____
Serial Number	xxxxxx	_____	_____	_____
Manufacturer	Paradise	_____	_____	_____
Port COM 1	Modem 1200 Baud	_____	_____	_____
Serial Number	xxxxxx	_____	_____	_____
Manufacturer	Vadic	_____	_____	_____
Port COM 2	Plotter	_____	_____	_____
Serial Number	xxxxxx	_____	_____	_____
Manufacturer	H. P.	_____	_____	_____
Port COM 3		_____	_____	_____
Serial Number		_____	_____	_____
Manufacturer		_____	_____	_____
Port COM 4		_____	_____	_____
Serial Number		_____	_____	_____
Manufacturer		_____	_____	_____
Parallel Port 1	LPT 1–FX-80	_____	_____	_____
Serial Number	xxxxxx	_____	_____	_____
Manufacturer	EPSON	_____	_____	_____
Parallel Port 2		_____	_____	_____
Serial Number		_____	_____	_____
Manufacturer		_____	_____	_____
Parallel Port 3		_____	_____	_____
Serial Number		_____	_____	_____
Manufacturer		_____	_____	_____

Category	Example	System #1	System #2	System #3
Accessory Type #1	IEEE	_____	_____	_____
Serial Number	xxxxxx	_____	_____	_____
Manufacturer	National Inst.	_____	_____	_____
Accessory Type #2	Watch Dog Timer	_____	_____	_____
Serial Number		_____	_____	_____
Manufacturer		_____	_____	_____
Accessory Type #3	A/D Card	_____	_____	_____
Serial Number		_____	_____	_____
Manufacturer		_____	_____	_____
Accessory Type #4	D/A Card	_____	_____	_____
Serial Number		_____	_____	_____
Manufacturer		_____	_____	_____

SOFTWARE

Name #1	MS-DOS	_____	_____	_____
Version	3.3	_____	_____	_____
Serial Number	xxxxxx	_____	_____	_____
Manufacturer	MicroSoft	_____	_____	_____
Date Installed	1/11/89	_____	_____	_____
Resident	Yes	_____	_____	_____
Name #2	AUTOCAD	_____	_____	_____
Version	10	_____	_____	_____
Serial Number	xxxxxx	_____	_____	_____
Manufacturer	AutoDesk	_____	_____	_____
Date Installed	12/1/89	_____	_____	_____
Resident	No	_____	_____	_____
Name #3		_____	_____	_____
Version		_____	_____	_____
Serial Number		_____	_____	_____
Manufacturer		_____	_____	_____
Date Installed		_____	_____	_____
Resident		_____	_____	_____
Name #4		_____	_____	_____
Version		_____	_____	_____
Serial Number		_____	_____	_____
Manufacturer		_____	_____	_____
Date Installed		_____	_____	_____
Resident		_____	_____	_____

GETTING STARTED

If you are an experienced user of IBM, clone, or IBM-compatible computers and the MS-DOS or PC-DOS operating systems, you may skip the next few paragraphs. However, if using the computer is new to you, a few suggestions are in order.

Starting your system, whether for the first time or for casual use, is a relatively easy process.

1. Apply power to the video monitor. This is done first because the monitor usually requires a minute or two to "warm up" and, as the messages of the initiating processes are supplied to the screen, you should try not to miss any.
2. If you are "booting" from a floppy drive, ensure that the correct disk has been inserted properly into drive A: and the latch is closed.
3. If you are "booting" from a hard drive, ensure that *no* disk has been inserted in the floppy drive and that the latch is open. This is one of the most common problems, particularly to new users. Often the disk found in the floppy drive was one left by the last user of the computer. A more obscure problem of failure to "boot" as expected is that an incorrect partition has been selected on the hard drive.
4. If you have neither a hard drive nor a floppy disk, BASICA "boots" up on IBM computers from ROM.
5. Apply power to your computer and watch the "boot" proceed on the screen.

No Prompt—
What to Do

This chapter describes a first-echelon maintenance procedure to be performed when your PC will not boot. The first twelve steps listed should be performed at least twice before considering the removal of the cover.

Remember: "If it ain't broke, don't fix it!"

1. Turn off all the power and give the PC (and yourself) a 5-minute rest.
2. Check to see that the power cord is in good condition and is inserted correctly into the wall socket and into the PC.
3. Is there power at the wall socket? Plug in a lamp to see if it turns on; perhaps the circuit breaker or the primary power fuse has blown.
4. Are there external fuses or circuit breakers on the PC, the monitor, the printer, the modem, and so forth?
5. Are the peripheral interconnecting cables in good condition, or are there broken, frayed, or loose wires?
6. Are the floppy disk heads clean?
7. Is the floppy disk drive door closed when no disk has been inserted in the drive?
8. Does the floppy diskette have a boot on it?
9. Is there a diskette in the floppy disk drive when you are really trying to boot from the hard disk?
10. Does the PC feel very warm to the touch? Is there a thermal shutdown?
11. When the PC was last running, did you hear strange noises? Is it the fan? Is it the floppy? Is it the hard drive?
12. During winter or periods of low humidity (very dry) have you used Static Guard Spray?

Keep the area where you work clean. Dirt is the enemy of the computer. Keep the pets away. Cover the computer when it is not in use. Don't eat or smoke near the computer.

Occasionally, you come across a new program that you have not used before, or perhaps a program that you have not used frequently, and this program will not run at all or will not run as expected. Do not jump to conclusions. Possibly, the copy of the program is defective. Try to obtain another copy, or if that is difficult, at least attempt to run the copy you have on another CPU. A second approach might be to re-boot the CPU from a copy of the original DOS distribution kit and then attempt to run the program again. The reasoning behind this suggestion is that a number of programs, such as SideKick, ProKey, and SuperKey, stay in memory after you run them. Such programs change the way your CPU performs, and utilize system features available only to assembly language programs. Surprising as it may seem, this is a very common problem.

When all else fails consult the instruction manual.

The final question before proceeding to the next list is: IS THE COMPUTER OR ITS PERIPHERALS WITHIN THE PERIOD OF THE MANUFACTURER'S WARRANTY? Check with the store where you purchased the computer; there may be updates to the ROM's or other recalls. If so, do not void the warranty. Return the equipment to the store where you bought it or to the manufacturer in accordance with the terms of the warranty.

A few more words about warranties (or guarantees, which are pretty much the same thing) are probably in order at this point. Prior to purchasing any equipment or software, the salesperson should be willing and able to supply a copy of the warranty coverage.

If it is in writing it is called an expressed warranty. If it is verbally presented it is called an implied warranty. Clearly, an unlimited warranty (which even covers accidental damage) is better than a limited warranty. However, be forewarned; unlimited does not include consequential damage (in most cases), which means that if your computer fails you can get it fixed, but no responsibility for lost data or lost business is assumed. Consequential damage is when the power supply burns up and the fumes asphyxiate your Siamese cat. For loss or damage to your cat you should have had insurance. A limited warranty is also known as a parts and labor warranty, generally for some fixed period of time such as one year. Most limited warranties only pay for the shipping in one direction when the equipment is returned to the repair location.

An optional extended warranty can be purchased in some cases to extend the warranty period or perhaps enhance the coverage (for instance, from walk-in service to on-site service). Most automobile dealers now offer optional extended warranties on the automobiles they sell.

In fact, regardless of whether you have a written statement from the vendor or manufacturer of the equipment, every item you buy is covered and that coverage is enhanced by both federal and state laws. "Lemon laws" may even provide for replacement of systems with chronic problems.

The terms of the warranty should be considered now, before something has failed, because they can better be studied in a calmer environment. Remember, not all warranties are alike. In some cases the selling organization assumes the responsibility, in others the manufacturer provides the remedy. If the manufacturer is "offshore" the turnaround time can be extensive.

When initiating your request for warranty repair or replacement, the place to start is the Customer Service Department at the location where you purchased the item. It is best, of course, to have a sales receipt, showing the date of purchase and the date of delivery of the item for which coverage is requested, and any other documentation obtained when the item was received. A problem is sure to arise if you approach the matter with "You remember me, don't you? I bought. . . ." It is encouraging to note that support and service is improving in the PC business.

A warranty (with the exception of those items purchased with an American Express Card?) will generally not cover those items that have been subjected to abuse or those for which the warranty has been accidently or deliberately voided (such as attempting unauthorized repairs or operating under conditions considered to be beyond normal use). Many times the vendor or manufacturer will require that you obtain an "RMA number" (Return Merchandise Authorization) prior to returning the item to the service location for disposition. This number is for identification purposes. Don't keep it a secret. Write it on the box and tag the part. Keep good records.

Many vendors now provide some sort of telephone support, some with toll-free (800) numbers, some with information by FAX, and occasionally with 24-hour-a-day response for those late-night, emergency jobs. Often this assistance can supply exactly the help necessary to solve the problem or can provide a "work-around" to get the job done.

Other vendors will send out replacement parts prior to receiving the defective ones if they receive an authorizing purchase order or a credit card number. This will speed up the repair process. Be sure to get an RMA number so that proper credit may be applied when the defective part is returned. Be specific about what you need. The vendor does not have a crystal ball. Keep in mind that overnight replacement is not next-day repair but a promise to ship by an overnight express service.

The next step is to remove the covers from the equipment.

1. Work in an area where you have plenty of room and is well lit.
2. Unless you are testing something that requires power, turn off all the switches and remove the plugs from the wall.

3. Remove all rings, watches, and bracelets from your hands. I have a good friend who is missing a finger who did not follow this advice.
4. Be very careful when working with the power on.
5. If you take things apart, make notes as to how you removed the parts or connectors, how the parts fit (connector polarization), and where you put the parts down. Putting equipment back together correctly can be complicated and confusing. "Which screw goes where?" is an interesting question.
6. Use the correct tool for each job.
7. Try to have the documentation for the equipment you are trying to repair.
8. If you are going to solder anything, use ROSIN CORE solder or water-soluble flux only (*not* acid core). Clean up leftover flux when you finish.
9. If you use a meter, be sure the power is off before you attempt to measure resistance.
10. Be careful of capacitors with voltage across them (charge stored in them) even with the power off.
11. Remember, some components are polarized (the + end is different from the – end) that is, batteries, capacitors, diodes, transistors, and so forth.
12. Is it clean inside the unit? A small vacuum cleaner might suck up some of the dust. Does the fan have a filter? Is the filter clean? Air may be blown at the unit to remove dust. Try not to blow the dust into the disks.
13. Check to see whether there are internal fuses in the unit.
14. Is there a thermal overload sensor that has tripped? Has it failed?
15. Try disconnecting and reconnecting each connector, one at a time. Sometimes this works. Look for discolored or corroded contacts.
16. Look for discolored or burned parts. Look for crimped wires due to improper assembly.
17. Does anything smell like it has been burned?
18. Can you isolate the problem to a specific unit? Do you have a spare available for a parts swap? If you have a keyboard problem, it might be the cable. A keyboard spare is not expensive (about $40). On the other hand, a loaner or a parts swap might give you a clue to the solution of the problem.
19. Some computers have a battery (or more than one in the case of portables). Are they supplying the correct voltage?
20. Once you turn the power on keep your eyes open for smoke. Does any part or group of parts get very hot?
21. If you have a voltmeter, check the power supply voltages. Are they within tolerance?
22. If there is a fan, is it spinning when the power is turned on?

23. If you have an oscilloscope, check to see that all the oscillators (computer clocks) are running. Are they within tolerance?

24. Does the floppy disk drive spin when addressed during the boot process?

25. Can you hear or feel the hard disk spinning (if there is one)?

By now you have done most of the first-echelon tasks, and it is time for expert help. Don't fool with things you don't understand; it is possible to make a problem worse.

Chapters 13, 14, and 15 contain details of the power on self test (POST), the diagnostic beep codes, and the diagnostic error codes available with the computer.

For the user who is more technically inclined and who wishes to pursue the diagnostic process at a more sophisticated level, there are three accessories available. The first is a product called "LOGIMER" which is offered for sale by Total Power International, Inc., Test Instruments Group, 418 Bridge Street, Lowell, MA 01850. Their telephone number is (508) 453-7272 and their FAX number is (508) 453-7395. The price is $425.

The "LOGIMER" consists of a plug-in PC card and three ROM integrated circuits. The card is used to diagnose failures in 8088, 80286, and 80386 computers and works with XT or AT computers. The "LOGIMER" performs a systematic approach to failure diagnosis. In the case when the video monitor is not operational, the card contains a two-character display that will indicate the source of most failures. The "LOGIMER" performs over one thousand individual tests in about a minute. Some of the devices tested are as follows:

1. CPU
2. Registers
3. BIOS Checksum
4. Timer 8253 / 8254
5. DMA 8237
6. RAM refresh
7. Keyboard controller 8042/8742
8. RAM address, data, parity, chip select, and logic
9. RAM extension card up to 16 megabytes
10. Protected mode for 80286 and 80386
11. Interrupt controllers—master and slave 8259
12. Display adapters' memory, initialization, monochrome, and color
13. CMOS battery
14. NEAT chip set

The "LOGIMER" may be used for equipment burn-in, may be set up to loop on tests, has the capability to log data, and supports "print screen."

The second product is called the "POSTcard" (for power-on self test) and is manufactured by Award Software, Inc., 130 Knowles Drive, Los Gatos, CA 95030. Their telephone number is (408) 370-7979 and the price is $399.

The "POSTcard" appears to be very similar to the "LOGIMER." It plugs into an 8-bit expansion slot. The "POSTcard" can be used to test systems in virtually any stage of development, from bare-bones configurations consisting of only a system board and power supply to completely assembled computers. The "POSTcard" has a comprehensive diagnostic mode, which has tests for floppy disks, fixed disks, serial and parallel ports, math coprocessors, and extended memory.

The third product is called the "Check-It Toolkit II" manufactured by Performance Computer and offered for sale by the Programmer's Shop, 5 Pond Park Road, Hingham, MA 02043. Their telephone numbers are (617) 740-2510 and (800) 421-8006 and their FAX number is (617) 749-2018. The price is $699.

"Check-It Toolkit II" consists of 3 items: "Align-It," "Check-It Deluxe," and "KickStart II."

"Align-It" is a floppy drive alignment kit. It includes floppy drive diagnostic and alignment software and spiral test diskettes for both 3.5-inch and 5.25-inch drives of all densities.

"Check-It Deluxe" is a PC status and diagnostic utility. It displays hardware and software configuration and status. It includes diagnostics for motherboard, memory, hard and floppy drives, video, communication ports, printer, keyboard, mouse, and joystick. Performance panels measure speed of CPU, video, and coprocessor throughput. Parallel and serial port loopback plugs are supplied as a part of this utility.

"KickStart II" is a POST diagnostic card. The card assists in diagnosing system failures and is especially helpful when the monitor doesn't work. The card contains LED's to show power status, and both PC and AT address and data buses; self-test numbers are output to I/O port 80 by BIOS during boot. The card also contains a dual serial port, a parallel port, a real-time clock for logging results, remote access, and ROM diagnostics.

3

Microprocessor Types

CPU	Manufacturer	Second Source	Process	Speed (MHZ)	BUS Width	Mode	Maximum Memory
8086	Intel	Yes	HMOS	5–10	16	Real	1 MByte
8088	Intel	Yes	HMOS	5–8	8	Real	1 MByte
80C86	Intel	Yes	CMOS	5–8	16	Real	1 MByte
80C88	Intel	Yes	CMOS	5–8	8	Real	1 MByte
80186	Intel	Yes	NMOS	8–10	16	Real	1 MByte
80188	Intel	Yes	NMOS	8	8	Real	1 MByte
80C186	Intel	No	CHMOS	10–16	16	Real	1 MByte
80C188	Intel	No	CHMOS	8	8	Real	1 MByte
V20	NEC	No	CMOS	5–10	8	Real	1 MByte
V30	NEC	No	CMOS	5–10	16	Real	1 MByte
80286	Intel	Yes	HMOS	6–12.5	16	Real Virtual Protect	16 MByte 1 GByte
80C286	Harris	Yes	CMOS	10–16	16	Real Virtual Protect	16 MByte 1 GByte
80386DX	Intel	No	CHMOS	16–25	32	Real Virtual Protect	4 GByte 16 TByte
80386SX	Intel	No	CHMOS	16	16	Real Virtual Protect	16 MByte 1 GByte
80386	Intel	No	CHMOS	16	16	Protect	16 MByte

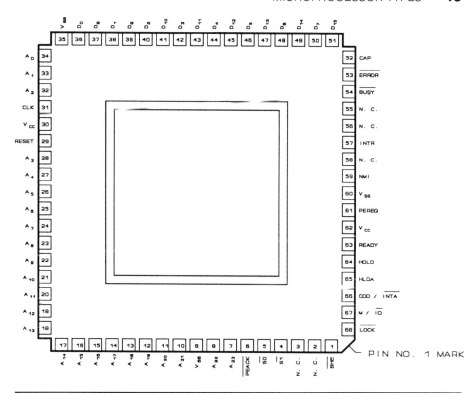

80286 Pin configuration—view looking at lid of chip. Package is a
68-lead JEDEC Type A Leadless Chip Carrier (LCC)
(LCC is mounted lid down into socket)

This is, therefore, a COMPONENT PAD VIEW, as viewed from underside of component when it is mounted on the printed circuit board. Note that pads marked "N. C." must not be connected.

MEMORY SPEEDS AND COPROCESSORS FOR SOME MICROPROCESSOR TYPES

If you purchase memory that has an access time that is less than your processor requires (faster chips), you will not improve the performance of your system nor will you process data any faster than if you bought the slower memory. Similarly, purchasing a faster mathematics coprocessor than is required will not make the execution of the arithmetic functions any faster.

Following the recommendations of the processor board manufacturer is always a good guide. Some computer users purchase the next higher speed memory or coprocessor to allow an extra margin against failure and to provide a "user comfort factor" by using a better part than is required.

Complying with the following chart on page 15 seems to provide satisfactory results.

EXPANSION MEMORY FOR THE NEWEST MACHINES

Intel has announced a line of 72-pin single in-line memory modules (SIMMs) for select IBM, Compaq, Hewlett-Packard, and Zenith systems. These SIMMs plug directly into a socket on the PC's motherboard and provide the user with the additional memory required to run Windows 3.0, OS/2, and other applications.

1 Megabyte—$225

For IBM Models 55SX, 65SX and 70 (16 Mhz and 20 Mhz)
For Compaq Models 386N and 386s/20
For HP Vectra 486
For Zenith Models 386/20, 386/25, and 386/33

2 Megabyte—$445

For IBM Models 50Z, 55SX, 65SX, 70 (16 Mhz and 20 Mhz) and P70. Also available for 70 (25 Mhz)
For Compaq Models 386N and 386s/20
For HP Vectra 386/25

4 Megabyte—$945

For IBM Models 55SX and 65SX
For Compaq Models 386N and 386s/20
For HP Vectra 486
For Zenith Models 386/20, 386/25, and 386/33

CPU	CPU Speed	Standard Part	0 Wait State	1 Wait State	Interleaved	Coprocessor	Coprocessor Speed
8088	5 MHz	200 NSEC	-	-	-	8087	5 MHz
V20	5 MHz	200 NSEC	-	-	-	8087	5 MHz
8088	8 MHz	150 NSEC	-	-	-	8087-2	8 MHz
V20-8	8 MHz	150 NSEC	-	-	-	8087-2	8 MHz
8088	10 MHz	120 NSEC	-	-	-	8087-1	10 MHz
V20-10	10 MHz	120 NSEC	-	-	-	8087-1	10 MHz
8086	8 MHz	150 NSEC	-	-	-	8087-2	8 MHz
V30	8 MHz	150 NSEC	-	-	-	8087-2	8 MHz
80286	6 MHz	-	200 NSEC	200 NSEC	-	80287	6 MHz
80286	8 MHz	-	120 NSEC	200 NSEC	-	80287-8	8 MHz
80286	10 MHz	-	100 NSEC	150 NSEC	-	80287-8	8 MHz
80286	12 MHz	-	80 NSEC	120 NSEC	-	80287-10	10 MHz
80286	16 MHz	-	60 NSEC	100 NSEC	120 NSEC	80C287	12 MHz
80286	20 MHz	-	<50 NSEC	80 NSEC	80 NSEC	80C287	12 MHz
80386	16 MHz	-	60 NSEC	100 NSEC	120 NSEC	80387-16	16 MHz
80386	20 MHz	-	<50 NSEC	80 NSEC	100 NSEC	80387-20	20 MHz
80386	25 MHz	-	<40 NSEC	80 NSEC	80 NSEC	80387-25	25 MHz
80386	33 MHz	-	<30 NSEC	50 NSEC	50 NSEC	80387-33	33 MHz

4

CPU Registers

The iAPX (Intel Advanced Processor Architecture) 86, 88, 186, and 286 families all contain the same basic set of registers, instructions, and addressing modes. The registers are grouped in the following categories:

General Registers

Eight 16-bit general-purpose registers may be used to contain arithmetic and logical operands. Four of these (AX, BX, CX, and DX) can be used as 16-bit registers or split into pairs of 8-bit registers.

Segment Registers

Four 16-bit special-purpose registers select, at any given time, the segments of memory that are immediately addressable for code, stack, and data.

Base and Index Registers

Four of the general-purpose registers may also be used to determine offset addresses of operands in memory. These registers may contain base addresses or indexes to particular locations within a segment. The addressing mode selects the specific registers for operand and address calculations.

Status and Control Registers

Two 16-bit special-purpose registers record or alter certain aspects of the processor state. These are the instruction pointer register, which contains the offset address of the next sequential instruction to be executed, and the status word register, which contains status and control flag bits.

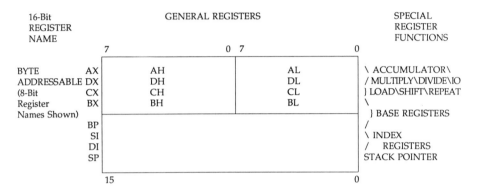

iAPX 86/10 and 80186 register set.

Segment Registers

Status and Control Registers

Status Word Discription

The status word records specific characteristics of the result of logical and arithmetic instructions (bits 0, 2, 4, 6, 7, and 11) and controls the operation of the processor within a given mode (bits 8, 9, and 10). The status word is 16 bits wide.

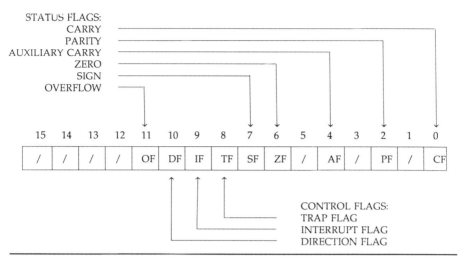

Status word format.

Bit Position	Symbol	Description
0	CF	CARRY FLAG—Set on high-order bit carry or borrow; cleared otherwise.
2	PF	PARITY FLAG—Set if low-order 8 bits of result contain an even number of 1 bits; cleared otherwise.
4	AF	AUXILIARY CARRY FLAG—Set on carry from or borrow to the low-order 4 bits of AL; cleared otherwise.
6	ZF	ZERO FLAG—Set if result is zero; cleared otherwise.
7	SF	SIGN FLAG—Set equal to high-order bit of result (0 if positive, 1 if negative).
8	TF	SINGLE STEP FLAG—Once set, a single-step interrupt occurs after the next instruction executes. TF is cleared by the single-step interrupt.
9	IF	INTERRUPT-ENABLE FLAG—When set, maskable interrupts will cause the CPU to transfer control to an interrupt vector specified location.
10	DF	DIRECTION FLAG—Causes string instructions to auto-decrement the appropriate index register when set. Clearing DF causes auto-increment.
11	OF	OVERFLOW FLAG—Set if the signed result cannot be expressed within the number of bits in the destination operand; cleared otherwise.

5

Floppy Disk Data

Diskette Care and Handling

1. Protect the diskette by keeping it in its storage envelope when not in use.
2. When using a diskette label, write on the label before adhering it to the diskette.
3. Do not bend or fold the diskette.
4. When inserting or removing the diskette from the drive, be gentle.
5. Check the write-protect tab when in use to see that it is fully adhered to the diskette and that it does not snag upon insertion or removal from the drive.
6. Never touch the magnetic oxide surface of the diskette. Handle the diskette by the edges.
7. Avoid storing the diskette in areas where the temperature variation is extreme. The normal range is 10°C–52°C (50°F–125°F).
8. Never place the diskette near magnets, paper clips, on top of the CPU, or near the monitor.
9. Use diskettes with center-reinforcing rings for long life.
10. Periodically clean the drive heads with an approved cleaning kit.

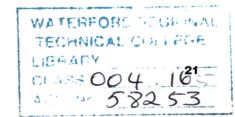

Formatted Capacity	Size	Tracks	Sides	Sectors	Media	ID Byte	Total Sectors
160 KBytes	5.25"	40	1	8	2SD	FE	320
180 KBytes	5.25"	40	1	9	2SD	FC	360
320 KBytes	5.25"	40	2	8	2DD	FF	640
360 KBytes	5.25"	40	2	9	2DD	FD	720
720 KBytes	3.5"	80	2	9	2DD	F9	1,440
1.2 MBytes	5.25"	80	2	15	2HD	F9	2,400
1.44 MBytes	3.5"	80	2	18	2HD	F0	2,880

Maximum Number Of Files In The Root Directory

Formatted Disk Capacity	Number Of Entries In Root Directory
160K	64
180K	64
320K	112
360K	112
720K	112
1.2MB	224
1.44MB	224
Fixed Disk	512

$$\text{Directory Entries} = \text{Number of Sectors for Root Directory} \times \frac{\text{Bytes/Sector}}{32 \text{ Bytes/Entry}}$$

$$= 7 \times \frac{512}{32} = 112 \text{ (for 360K)}$$

To avoid this limitation use sub-directories.

Number of Diskettes Required for a Full Backup

Bytes To Backup	Floppy Size			
	360K	720K	1.2M	1.44M
10 Mbytes	29	15	9	8
20 Mbytes	59	29	18	15
30 Mbytes	83	44	27	22
40 Mbytes	116	58	35	29
70 Mbytes	200	100	60	50

The figure above shows the layout of tracks and sectors on a floppy diskette. The number of tracks and sectors varies between types of diskettes. The single index hole on a soft-sectored floppy diskette indicates to the controller when sector 0 passes under the recording head. As the other sectors are located by the controller timing and software the diskette is called *soft*-sectored. Each track is a concentric circle on the diskette. For double sided diskettes there are tracks on both sides of the media. The

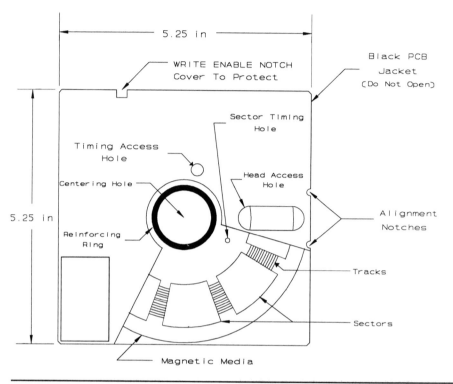

Floppy diskette.

tracks are spaced 48 tracks per inch (tpi) on the single density (SD) and double density (DD) diskettes. The tracks are spaced 96 tracks per inch (tpi) on the high density (HD or HC for high capacity) diskettes. Tracks are located only in a circular band in the middle of the diskette and are available to the recording heads thru the access hole. The band of tracks is five sixths (5 / 6) of an inch wide. For the 48-tpi drives you have only 40 tracks on a side. For the 96-tpi drives you have 80 tracks on a side. There are 512 data bytes on each section of a track in each sector. To calculate the capacity of a diskette multiply the number of sectors by the number of tracks and then multiply the product by the number of bytes per sector (512 for all IBM type diskettes). To obtain the capacity in kilobytes, divide the capacity by 1,024 (a K = 1024). The standard 5.25 inch, 2 sided DD diskettes hold 360 Kbytes while the standard 5.25 inch, HD (or HC) diskettes hold 1.2 Mbytes.

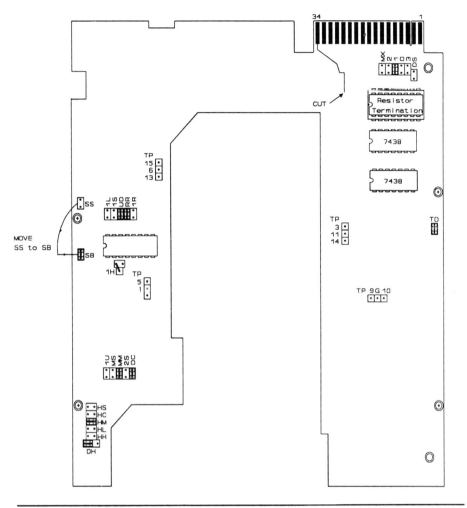

360K floppy disk configuration setting—Type A. Typical unit—
Mitsubishi Electric model M4853-342U REV. D.

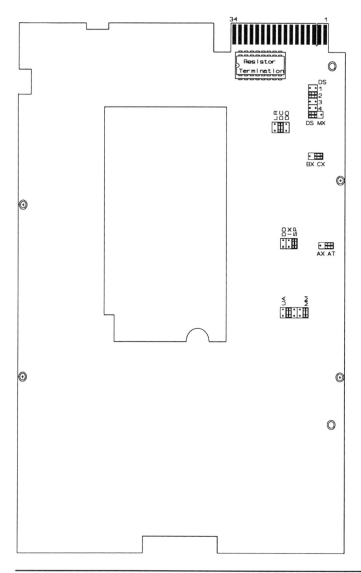

360K floppy disk configuration setting—Type B

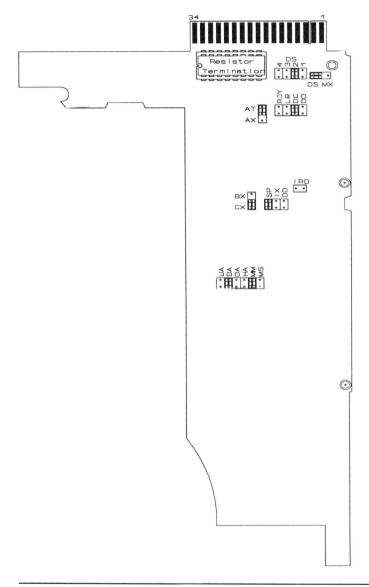

360K floppy disk configuration setting—Type C

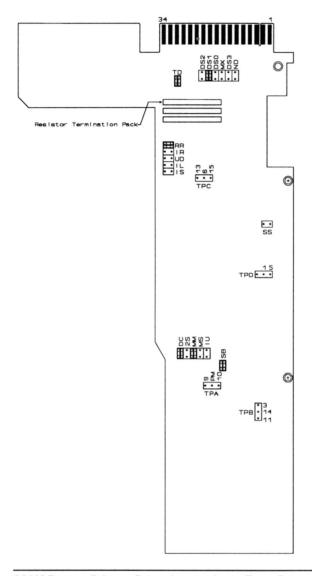

360K floppy disk configuration setting—Type D

GENERAL INFORMATION

The first floppy disk was invented at IBM during the early 1960s. The diskette was 15 inches in diameter and on it was stored the information for "booting" a large mainframe CPU.

As years went by the technology improved and IBM discovered how to store more bits in the same area on the surface of the diskette (increased storage capacity). Advances in head design, improvements in writing electronics and data recovery circuitry, and mechanical design to closer tolerances all contributed to increased storage capacity, lower costs, and higher reliability.

The first step in reducing the physical size of the disk drive and diskette was to reduce the diameter to approximately one-half the previous size, to 7.5 inches (nominally, the 8-inch floppy). The 8-inch floppy was embraced by the minicomputer industry, and computers such as the Digital Equipment Corporation PDP-11 ran systems that utilized a CPU and a pair of drives.

The next size reduction occurred in the late 1970s when the diskette diameter was reduced to 5.25 inches. This was followed in 1984 by the 3.5-inch diskette introduced by the Sony Corporation.

A 5.25-inch floppy diskette consists of the magnetic medium, which is permanently encased in a square, sealed envelope with an access hole for the drive heads. A disk storage sleeve is provided for use when the diskette is not installed in the drive. The magnetic medium is a thin, circular, Mylar disk that has been coated with the actual recording material. The recording material is ferric oxide metal (common rust) that has been polished to provide a smooth surface on which the heads glide. Now you know what happens to all those chopped-up automobiles! The sealed envelope into which the coated Mylar disk is placed is made of lintless paper or plastic with some very fine combing material bonded to the inside of the envelope. The combing material serves as a dust cleanser and lubricant as the Mylar disk spins clockwise inside the sealed envelope.

The sealed envelope may be notched to allow writing on the disk, but if the notch is missing or covered the disk may only be read. If the disk is not notched, or if the notch is covered, the contents of the disk are protected from being modified. If the write-protect covering is removed or a disk with no notch has one added, the write-protection feature is removed.

A hole in the center of the Mylar disk, surrounded by a larger hole in the envelope, is for use by the spindle in rotating the disk inside its sealed envelope. Often the Mylar disk has a reinforcing ring attached around the spindle drive hole. Generally, disks with reinforcing rings are 360 Kilobyte capacity as opposed to 1.2 Megabyte capacity, but this is not always the case.

About 1 inch out from the center of the diskette is a small hole called the sector notch. This index hole in both the envelope and the medium is used to provide timing information to synchronize operation of the disk drive. The sector hole is electronically sensed and thus any location on the diskette surface may be determined by its rotational distance from the hole and its radial position relative to the center of the diskette.

The read/write head is moved radially along a line from the center of the diskette and is able to contact the surface of the diskette through a slot in the envelope. When both sides of the diskette are used, there is a read/write head on each side. When only one side of the diskette is used, a pad rides on the other side to ensure uniform contact pressure. The diskette spins at 360 RPM.

The 3.5-inch floppy (called a "micro-floppy" or micro disk) is similar in many respects to the 5.25-inch floppy diskette. The 3.5-inch floppy is obviously smaller, and is encased in a hardened plastic shell as opposed to a paper or plastic envelope. The 3.5-inch floppy diskette is considered to be shirt-pocket size. Recording is still performed magnetically.

The read/write window on the 3.5-inch floppy disk is always closed by a metal slide called a shutter when the floppy disk is not installed in its disk drive. The closed container provides improved protection for the medium from environmental damage such as dust and improper handling. However, the 3.5-inch diskette is more expensive.

A sector notch is again used for timing synchronization, and the read/write head assembly moves radially as the magnetic medium spins inside its hard shell.

Write protection is provided by a small tab. When you can see through the window covered by the tab, the contents of the floppy disk are write-protected. When the plastic tab blocks your view, the diskette may be written as well as read.

The 3.5-inch floppy diskettes are available in two capacities, 720 Kilobytes (HD) and 1.44 Megabytes (DD). Interestingly, the same magnetic medium is used in both. The only difference is the extra sense hole in the HD case. Without this hole, if you try to format a HD diskette as DD the computer gives you an "invalid media error" message.

LMT Marketing, Inc., 4411 Dupont Court, Ventura, CA 93003, telephone 1-(800) 255-1279 or (805) 644-1797, FAX (805) 644-1814 offers the Double Disk Converter for $39.95. The Double Disk Converter is used to punch a precision rectangular hole in 3.5-inch floppy diskettes, which converts HD diskettes into DD diskettes.

Not only does LMT Marketing guarantee the Double Disk Converter for one year, but they even offer a replacement for any disk that does not convert error-free.

Depending on the computer you own, the typical BIOS Diskette Service performs BIOS-level read, write, format, initialization, and diagnostic support for up to two internal diskette drives. Knowing what kind of drives you have can be very important in some applications. Telling one kind of drive from another can sometimes be difficult, particularly when the drive is not installed in a system. Often you can't tell by looking and sometimes the model number is not translatable into any reasonable data.

From our previous discussion we have seen that there are seven varieties of formatted capacity (160 Kbytes, 180 Kbytes, 320 Kbytes, 360

Kbytes, 720 Kbytes, 1.2 Mbytes, and 1.44 Mbytes). There are also two sizes (3.5-inch and 5.25-inch).

Obviously, the 3.5-inch drives are easy to distinguish from the 5.25-inch drives, so let us deal with the 3.5-inch drives first. As pointed out above, the 1.44 Mbyte drives need a sense hole in a particular location. If there is no sensor in that location, the drive is for 720 Kbyte diskettes.

The 5.25-inch drives come in two physical sizes—half-height and full-height. The front panel on the half-height drives is 1.75 inches, and the front panel on the full-height drives is 3.5 inches.

Unless you are working with a very old PC, if the drive is full-height and has 2 heads it is a 360 Kbyte drive. If it has one head it is a 180 Kbyte drive. Remember, the single head is opposed by a pressure pad.

Starting with the PCjr and the AT, half-height drives were introduced. The PCjr's disk drives have a black faceplate, and the AT uses drives with a tan faceplate. All the PCjr's floppy disk drives (black faceplate) are 360 Kbyte capacity.

If the drive has a tan faceplate and a sunburst symbol (often below the disk in-use light), it is also a 360 Kbyte capacity drive. If you do not see the sunburst symbol, in all probability the disk drive has a 1.2 Mbyte capacity and is a high-capacity (HC or HD) drive.

Half-height drives use a handle instead of a latch to secure the diskette in the drive once it has been inserted. Once the handle is in the closed position the computer can recognize that the floppy is in place, but not before. When the handle is turned to the open position there is usually a spring mechanism that ejects the floppy a sufficient distance so that it may be grasped between two fingers and removed. If the floppy diskette does not eject, simply activate the handle mechanism again. The half-height floppy drives for the PCjr do not have a spring mechanism, but the panel is designed with sufficient finger room to grasp the diskette with two fingers and pull it out.

THE SECOND FLOPPY DRIVE

Often a computer system is delivered with only one floppy disk drive (and today usually with a hard disk drive). The floppy disk drive is designated as drive "A:". If you wanted to copy a file from one floppy diskette to another you placed the source diskette in the drive, issued the command "COPY A:(filename) B:" or "COPY A:*.* B:" (for many files). "COPY A:*.* A:" also worked.

DOS was very friendly and prompted you when to change from the source diskette to the destination (or target) diskette, and eventually the copy operation was completed. If there were many files to copy, the switching back and forth of the diskettes became a tedious and tiresome procedure, but it worked. In the case described, the source floppy was interpreted to be A: and the destination floppy was interpreted to be B:. Naturally, you always write-protected the source diskette before starting, to avoid disasters.

If the first floppy drive was 1.2 Megabytes you could even have the source floppy diskette formatted to be a 1.2 Megabyte type and the destination floppy diskette formatted to be a 360 Kilobyte type; so long as the data fit, the process worked.

A problem arises when you add a second drive, and drive A: is a 1.2 Megabytes type and drive B: is a 360 Kilobyte type. If you now want to copy files from one 1.2 Megabyte floppy disk to a second 1.2 Megabyte floppy disk, the command "COPY A:*.* A:" now yields the message "file cannot be copied onto itself." Clearly, now "COPY A:*.* B:" just copies files from the 1.2 Megabyte diskette to the 360 Kilobyte diskette.

The obvious first solution is to copy the files from the first floppy diskette to the hard disk and then back to the second floppy. When copying many files, this again becomes a tedious process.

The proper solution to this problem is obscure but the solution has been provided by DOS. The first thing to do is to install "DRIVER.SYS" supplied with your version of DOS into "CONFIG.SYS." You then assign a second logical drive letter to the 1.2 Megabyte floppy drive. If the original letter assigned to the 1.2 Megabyte floppy drive was A: and you have one hard disk drive, the second logical floppy disk drive letter becomes D:. You may now execute the command "COPY A:*.* D:", and all will be well.

The format of the command added to "CONFIG.SYS" is:

```
DEVICE=DRIVER.SYS/D:ddd[/T:ttt][/S:ss][/H:hh]
[/C][/N][/F:f]
```

Assuming that you have a 1.2 Megabyte floppy disk drive as the first physical diskette drive and a 360 Kilobyte floppy disk drive as the second physical diskette drive plus a single fixed disk, the command added to "CONFIG.SYS" is:

```
device=driver.sys/d:0/T:80/S:15/H:2/C/F:1
```

This assigns the logical drive letter D to the first diskette drive. It can now be referenced as both A: and D: and the command "COPY A:file1 D:" copies file 1 from one diskette to a second diskette using the 1.2 Megabyte diskette drive only. DOS prompts you to insert the diskette for the appropriate logical drive.

As to the assignment of logical drive letters, the first internal diskette drive is assigned the letter A:. The second internal diskette drive is assigned the letter B:. The drive letter B: is used automatically, even if there is only one physical diskette drive. This means that on machines with only one diskette drive there are two logical diskette drives, A: and B:.

The letters from C: upward are assigned in the order in which devices (or device drivers) are encountered. The first fixed disk, or the first block device driver, cannot have a drive letter assigned lower than C:. The existence of internal physical devices (diskettes and fixed disks) is checked first. Then "CONFIG.SYS" is checked for the device drivers. For DOS to recognize an external physical device, the "CONFIG.SYS" file must have the correct driver information.

For machines with an external drive, if the external device driver is loaded twice where /D:dd is the same, it generates two logical drives for the one physical drive.

The existence of any VDISKs will not affect the drive letter assign ments if the "DEVICE=VDISK.SYS" commands are placed after the "DEVICE=DRIVER.SYS" commands in the "CONFIG.SYS" file.

FLOPPY DISKETTE DRIVE MODEL NUMBERS

Manufacturer	Model Number	Type
CDC	9409	360Kb
Cumulus	123502	1.2Mb
Epson	SD-680L	1.2Mb
Fujitsu	M2553K	1.2Mb
Mitsubishi Electric	M4853-342U	360Kb
Mitsubishi Electric	504B	1.2Mb
Mitsubishi Electric	MF355	1.44Mb
NEC	1035	720Kb
Shugart	SA455	360Kb
Sony	MPF17W52D	1.44Mb
Tandon	TM100-1A	180Kb
Tandon	TM100-2A	360Kb
Teac	FD-55B	360Kb
Teac	FD-55BR	360Kb
Teac	FD-235F	720Kb
Teac	FD-55GFR	1.2Mb
Teac	FD-55GFV	1.2Mb
Teac	FD-235HF	1.44Mb
TEC	FB501	180Kb
Toshiba	ND352S	720Kb
Toshiba	ND3565	1.44Mb

Sometimes a B in the model number indicates a 360Kb drive and an F indicates a 1.2Mb drive.

TYPICAL JUMPERING FOR A 360 KILOBYTE FLOPPY DISKETTE DRIVE

Designation	Jumpered	Function
DS0	no	Drive Select Zero
DS1	YES	Drive Select One
DS2	no	Drive Select Two
DS3	no	Drive Select Three
MX	no	If Jumpered, Drive Will Respond To All Drive Selects
MM	YES	Motor Started By Drive Select
MS	no	If Jumpered, Motor Started By Motor On
SR(XT)	YES	If Jumpered, Drive Responds To Pin 34 For Disk Change
HR(XT)	no	If Jumpered, Drive Responds To Ready
SR(AT)	no	If Jumpered, Drive Responds To Pin 34 For Disk Change
HR(AT)	YES	If Jumpered, Drive Responds To Ready

TYPICAL JUMPERING FOR A 1.2 MEGABYTE FLOPPY DISKETTE DRIVE

Designation	Jumpered	Function
DS0	no	Drive Select Zero
DS1	YES	Drive Select One
DS2	no	Drive Select Two
DS3	no	Drive Select Three
MX	no	If Jumpered, Drive Will Respond To All Drive Selects
ND	no	Not Used
RR	YES	Ready Gated By Drive Select
IR	no	Controls LED Lighting (On = Power, Off = Access)
UD	YES	Not Used
IL	YES	Controls LED Lighting
IS	no	Controls LED Lighting
DC	YES	Disk Change On Pin 34
2S	no	If Jumpered, Hold Ready Is Sent On Pin 34
MM	YES	Motor Started By Drive Select
MS	no	If Jumpered, Motor Started By Motor On
IU	YES	In-use Controlled By Input
SB	YES	If Jumpered, Single Speed (360 RPM)
SS	no	Dual Speed (300 RPM and 360 RPM)

6

Hard Disk Drive Types

If you don't have a hard (Winchester) drive, it is probably at the top of your want list. If you do, you probably want a bigger one.

If you feel your hard drive is too slow, the solution to your problem may require nothing more than the time it takes to low-level REFORMAT your drive at the optimum INTERLEAVE. A program called "SpinRite II" by Gibson Research, sold at $89 by the Programmer's Shop, 5 Pond Park Road, Hingham, MA 02043, telephone (617) 740-2510 and (800) 421-8006, will optimize hard disk performance and protect your data. "SpinRite II" will perform low level hard drive tests, non-destructive reformatting, detection and elimination of correctable hard disk errors, and will keep a technical log, partition the hard drive, find the optimum interleave, and lock out bad sectors.

Interleaving is beneficial whenever the hard drive can transfer data faster than the CPU can accept it. During the 16.6 milliseconds it takes for one revolution of the disk, approximately 8,704 characters of data can be read from one track. (Usually each track is divided into 17 sectors of 512 bytes [characters] per sector.) If the processor cannot keep up, the proper interleave will help. The optimum interleave will be determined by the number of characters the processor can accept in one revolution.

For example, let us say the processor can accept 3,702 characters in 16.6 milliseconds. Instead of numbering the sectors sequentially from 1 to 17, we will reformat the sector numbering. With an interleave factor of 3, the sectors will be numbered 1-7-13-2-8-14-3-9-15-4-10-16-5-11-17-6-12. This allows the CPU to store the data for sector #1 while sectors #7 and #13 are passing under the read/write head and then continue with sector #2

The following table relates drive models to their capacity, form factor, format, and access time.

Manufacturer	Model Number	Form Factor	Interface	Cylinders	Heads	Sectors	Capacity Formatted	Access Time	Price
Alps Electric	DRND-10A	3-1/2	MFM	615	2	17	10 Mbyte	60 ms	
Alps Electric	DRND-20A	3-1/2	MFM	615	4	17	20 Mbyte	60 ms	
Alps Electric	RPO-20A	3-1/2	RLL	615	2	26	20 Mbyte	60 ms	
Alps Electric	DRPO-20D	3-1/2	RLL	615	2	26	20 Mbyte	60 ms	
Ampex	PYXIS-7	5-1/4	MFM	320	2	17	5 Mbyte	90 ms	
Ampex	PYXIS-13	5-1/4	MFM	320	4	17	10 Mbyte	90 ms	
Ampex	PYXIS-20	5-1/4	MFM	320	6	17	15 Mbyte	90 ms	
Ampex	PYXIS-27	5-1/4	MFM	320	8	17	20 Mbyte	90 ms	
Atasi	3020		MFM	645	3	17	17 Mbyte		
Atasi	3033		MFM	645	5	17	28 Mbyte		
Atasi	3046		MFM	645	7	17	39 Mbyte		
Atasi	3051		MFM	704	7	17	43 Mbyte		
Atasi	3053		MFM	733	7	17	44 Mbyte		
Atasi	3075		MFM	1024	8	17	67 Mbyte		
Atasi	3085		MFM	1024	8	17	67 Mbyte		
BASF	6185		MFM	440	6	17	23 Mbyte		
BASF	6186		MFM	440	4	17	15 Mbyte		
BASF	6187		MFM	440	2	17	8 Mbyte		
Bull	D-530		MFM	987	3	17	25 Mbyte		
Bull	D-550		MFM	987	5	17	43 Mbyte		
Bull	D-570		MFM	987	7	17	59 Mbyte		
C. Itoh	YD-3530	5-1/4	MFM	731	5	17	32 Mbyte		
C. Itoh	YD-3540	5-1/4	MFM	731	7	17	45 Mbyte	26 ms	
C. Itoh	YD-3042	5-1/4	SCSI	788	4		43 Mbyte	26 ms	
C. Itoh	YD-3082	5-1/4	SCSI	788	8		87 Mbyte	26 ms	
Cardiff	F-3053	3-1/2	MFM	1024	5	17	44 Mbyte	20 ms	

Manufacturer	Model Number	Form Factor	Interface	Cylinders	Heads	Sectors	Capacity Formatted	Access Time	Price
Cardiff	F-3080	3-1/2	ESDI/SCSI	1024	5	26	68 Mbyte	26 ms	
Cardiff	F-3127	3-1/2	ESDI/SCSI	1024	5	35	109 Mbyte	35 ms	
CDC	94244-219	5-1/4	AT	1747	4		219 Mbyte	16 ms	
CDC	94244-383	5-1/4	AT	1747	7		383 Mbyte	16 ms	
CDC	94354-126		AT	1072	7	29	111 Mbyte		
CDC	94354-160		AT	1072	9	29	143 Mbyte		
CDC	94354-200		AT	1072	9	36	177 Mbyte		
CDC	94354-230		AT	1272	9	36	211 Mbyte		
CDC	77731614	5-1/4	MFM	670	4	17	23 Mbyte		
CDC	77731608	5-1/4	MFM	670	5	17	29 Mbyte		
CDC	77731613		MFM	733	5	17			
CDC Wren-1	94155-21	5-1/4	MFM	697	3	17	21 Mbyte	28 ms	
CDC	94155-25		MFM	697	4	17	24 Mbyte		
CDC	94155-28		MFM	697	4	17	24 Mbyte		
CDC Wren-1	94155-36	5-1/4	MFM	697	5	17	36 Mbyte	28 ms	
CDC	94155-38	5-1/4	MFM	733	5	17	31 Mbyte		
CDC Wren-2	94155-48	5-1/4	MFM	925	5	17	40 Mbyte	28 ms	
CDC Wren-2	94295-51	5-1/4	MFM	989	5	17	43 Mbyte	28 ms	
CDC Wren-2	94155-57	5-1/4	MFM	925	5	17	48 Mbyte	28 ms	
CDC Wren-2	94155-67	5-1/4	MFM	925	6	17	56 Mbyte	28 ms	
CDC Wren-2	94155-77	5-1/4	MFM	925	7	17	64 Mbyte	28 ms	
CDC Wren-2	94155-85	5-1/4	MFM	1024	8	17	71 Mbyte	28 ms	
CDC Wren-2	94155-86	5-1/4	MFM	925	8	17	72 Mbyte	28 ms	
CDC	94205-51	5-1/4	MFM	989	9	17	43 Mbyte	32 ms	
CDC	94335-55	3-1/2	MFM		5	17	46 Mbyte	25 ms	
CDC	94335-100	3-1/2	MFM		9	17	83 Mbyte	25 ms	
CDC Swift-2	94355-55	3-1/2	MFM		5	17	46 Mbyte	16.5 ms	
CDC Swift	94355-100	3-1/2	MFM	1072	9	17	88 Mbyte	15 ms	

Manufacturer	Model Number	Form Factor	Interface	Cylinders	Heads	Sectors	Capacity Formatted	Access Time	Price
CDC Wren-2	94155-135	5-1/4	RLL	960	9	26	115 Mbyte	28 ms	
CDC Wren-2	94205-77	5-1/4	RLL	989	5	26	63 Mbyte	28 ms	
CDC	94335-150	3-1/2	RLL		9	26	128 Mbyte	25 ms	
CDC	94355-150	3-1/2	RLL	1072	9	28	133 Mbyte	15 ms	
CDC Wren-2	94156-48		ESDI	925	5		40 Mbyte	28 ms	
CDC Wren-2	94156-67		ESDI	925	7		56 Mbyte		
CDC Wren-2	94156-86		ESDI	925	9		72 Mbyte		
CDC Wren-3	94166-101	5-1/4	ESDI	969	5		86 Mbyte	16.5 ms	
CDC Wren-3	94166-141	5-1/4	ESDI	969	7		121 Mbyte	16.5 ms	
CDC Wren-3	94166-182	5-1/4	ESDI	969	9		155 Mbyte	16.5 ms	
CDC Wren V	94181-702	5-1/4	ESDI	1549	15		702 Mbyte	16 ms	
CDC Wren V	94186-265	5-1/4	ESDI	1412	9		265 Mbyte		
CDC Wren V	94186-324	5-1/4	ESDI	1412	11		324 Mbyte		
CDC Wren V	94186-383	5-1/4	EDSI	1412	13		383 Mbyte	19.5 ms	
CDC Wren V	94186-383H	5-1/4	EDSI	1224	15		383 Mbyte	14.5 ms	
CDC Wren V	94186-442	5-1/4	EDSI	1412	15		442 Mbyte	16 ms	
CDC Wren VI	94196-766	5-1/4	EDSI	1632	15		766 Mbytes	16.5 ms	
CDC Wren-3	94216-106	5-1/4	EDSI	1024	5		91 Mbyte	16.5 ms	
CDC Wren VI	94246-182	5-1/4	EDSI	1453	4		182 Mbyte	16.0 ms	
CDC Wren VI	94246-383	5-1/4	EDSI	1747	7		383 Mbyte	16.0 ms	
CDC Swift	94356-111	3-1/2	EDSI	1072	5	36	98 Mbyte		
CDC Swift	94356-155	3-1/2	EDSI	1072	7	36	138 Mbyte	15 ms	
CDC Swift	94356-200	3-1/2	EDSI	1072	9	36	177 Mbyte	15 ms	
CDC	WREN III	5-1/4	EDSI	969	5		106 Mbyte	18 ms	
CDC Wren-3	9-161-86	5-1/4	SCSI	969			86 Mbyte	16.5 ms	
CDC Wren-3	94161-121	5-1/4	SCSI	969			121 Mbyte	16.5 ms	
CDC Wren-4	94171-300	5-1/4	SCSI	1365	9		300 Mbyte	16.5 ms	
CDC Wren V	94171-344	5-1/4	SCSI	1549	9		344 Mbyte	17.5 ms	

Manufacturer	Model Number	Form Factor	Interface	Cylinders	Heads	Sectors	Capacity Formatted	Access Time	Price
CDC Wren IV	94171-350	5-1/4	SCSI	1412	9		350 Mbyte	16.5 ms	
CDC Wren IV	94171-376	5-1/4	SCSI	1549	9		376 Mbyte	17.5 ms	
CDC Runner	94181-385H	5-1/4	SCSI		15			10.7 ms	
CDC Wren V	94181-574	5-1/4	SCSI	1549	15		574 Mbyte	16 ms	
CDC Wren V	94181-702	5-1/4	SCSI	1549	15		702 Mbyte	16 ms	
CDC Wren V	94186-383	5-1/4	SCSI	1412	13		383 Mbyte	19.5 ms	
CDC Wren V	94186-383H	5-1/4	SCSI	1224	15		383 Mbyte	14.5 ms	
CDC Wren V	94186-442	5-1/4	SCSI	1412	15		442 Mbyte	16 ms	
CDC Wren VI	94191-766	5-1/4	SCSI	1632	15		766 Mbyte	16.5 ms	
CDC Wren-3	94211-91	5-1/4	SCSI	969			91 Mbyte	16.5 ms	
CDC Wren-3	94211-106	5-1/4	SCSI	1024	5			18 ms	
CDC Wren V	94221-190	5-1/4	SCSI	1547	5		190 Mbyte	8.3 ms	
CDC Wren V	94211-209	5-1/4	SCSI	1547	5			18 ms	
CDC Swift	94351-128	3-1/2	SCSI	1068	7	36			
CDC Swift	94351-134	3-1/2	SCSI		7		134 Mbyte	15 ms	
CDC Swift	94351-172	3-1/2	SCSI		9		172 Mbyte	15 ms	
CDC Swift	94351-160	3-1/2	SCSI	1068	9	36	142 Mbyte		
CDC Swift	94351-200	3-1/2	SCSI	1068	9	36	177 Mbyte		
CDC Swift	94351-200S	3-1/2	SCSI	1068	9	36	177 Mbyte		
CDC Swift	94351-230S	3-1/2	SCSI	1272	9	36	211 Mbyte		
CDC Sabre	9720-368	8.0	SCSI	1217	10		316 Mbyte	18 ms	
CDC Sabre	9720-500	8.0	SCSI	1217	10		427 Mbyte	18 ms	
CDC Sabre	9720-736	8.0	SCSI	1635	15		637 Mbyte	16 ms	
CDC Sabre	9720-850	8.0	SCSI	1381	15		727 Mbyte	16 ms	
CDC Sabre	9720-1230	8.0	SCSI	1635	15		1056 Mbyte	16 ms	
CDC	WREN III	5-1/4	SCSI	969	5		106 Mbyte	18 ms	
CDC Sabre	368	8.0	SMD		10		368 Mbyte	18 ms	
CDC Sabre	500	8.0	SMD		10		500 Mbyte	18 ms	

Manufacturer	Model Number	Form Factor	Interface	Cylinders	Heads	Sectors	Capacity Formatted	Access Time	Price
CDC Sabre	736	8.0	SMD		15		741 Mbyte	16 ms	
CDC Sabre	850	8.0	SMD		15		851 Mbyte	16 ms	
CDC Sabre	1230	8.0	SMD	1635	15		1236 Mbyte		
Century Data	CAST-10203E	5-1/4	ESDI	1050	3	35	55 Mbyte	28 ms	
Century Data	CAST-10304	5-1/4	ESDI	1050	4	35	75 Mbyte	28 ms	
Century Data	CAST-10305	5-1/4	ESDI	1050	5	35	94 Mbyte	28 ms	
Century Data	CAST-14404	5-1/4	ESDI	1590	4	35	114 Mbyte	25 ms	
Century Data	CAST-14405	5-1/4	ESDI	1590	5	35	140 Mbyte	25 ms	
Century Data	CAST-14406	5-1/4	ESDI	1590	6	35	170 Mbyte	25 ms	
Century Data	CAST-24509	5-1/4	ESDI	1599	9	35	258 Mbyte	18 ms	
Century Data	CAST-24611	5-1/4	ESDI	1599	11	35	315 Mbyte	18 ms	
Century Data	CAST-24713	5-1/4	ESDI	1599	13	35	372 Mbyte	18 ms	
Century Data	CAST-10203S	5-1/4	SCSI	1050	3	35	55 Mbyte	28 ms	
Century Data	CAST-10304S	5-1/4	SCSI	1050	4	35	75 Mbyte	28 ms	
Century Data	CAST-10305S	5-1/4	SCSI	1050	5	35	94 Mbyte	28 ms	
Century Data	CAST-14404S	5-1/4	SCSI	1590	4	35	114 Mbyte	25 ms	
Century Data	CAST-14405S	5-1/4	SCSI	1590	5	35	140 Mbyte	25 ms	
Century Data	CAST-14406S	5-1/4	SCSI	1590	6	35	170 Mbyte	25 ms	
Century Data	CAST-24509S	5-1/4	SCSI	1599	9	35	258 Mbyte	18 ms	
Century Data	CAST-24611S	5-1/4	SCSI	1599	11	35	315 Mbyte	18 ms	
Century Data	CAST-24713S	5-1/4	SCSI	1599	13	35	372 Mbyte	18 ms	
CMI	3426		MFM	615	4	17	20 Mbyte		
CMI	5206		MFM	306	2	17	5 Mbyte		
CMI	5205		MFM	256	2	17	4 Mbyte		
CMI	5410		MFM	256	4	17	8 Mbyte		
CMI	5412		MFM	306	4	17	10 Mbyte		
CMI	5616		MFM	256	6	17	13 Mbyte		
CMI	5619		MFM	306	6	17	15 Mbyte		

Manufacturer	Model Number	Form Factor	Interface	Cylinders	Heads	Sectors	Capacity Formatted	Access Time	Price
CMI	6213		MFM	640	2	17	11 Mbyte		
CMI	6426		MFM	640	4	17	21 Mbyte		
CMI	6640		MFM	615	6	17	33 Mbyte		
CMI	7660		MFM	960	6	17	50 Mbyte		
CMI	7880		MFM	960	8	17	67 Mbyte		
Cogito	CG-906		MFM	306	2		5 Mbyte		
Cogito	CG-912		MFM	306	4		11 Mbyte		
Cogito	PT-912		MFM	612	2		11 Mbyte		
Cogito	PT-925		MFM	612	4		21 Mbyte		
Conner Peripherals	CP-342	3-1/2	RLL	805	4		40 Mbyte	29 ms	
Conner Peripherals	CP-344	3-1/2	RLL	805	4	27	42 Mbyte	29 ms	
Conner Peripherals	CP-3022	3-1/2	RLL	636	2		21 Mbyte	27 ms	
Conner Peripherals	CP-3024	3-1/2	RLL	636	2	34	21 Mbyte	27 ms	
Conner Peripherals	CP-3044	3-1/2	RLL	1047	2	41	42 Mbyte	25 ms	$325
Conner Peripherals	CP-3102	3-1/2	RLL	776	8		104 Mbyte	25 ms	
Conner Peripherals	CP-3104	3-1/2	RLL	776	8	34	104 Mbyte	25 ms	$519
Conner Peripherals	CP-2304	3-1/2	RLL	1348	8	39	209 Mbyte	19 ms	
Conner Peripherals	CP-340	3-1/2	SCSI	788	4	27	42 Mbyte	29 ms	$289
Conner Peripherals	CP-3020	3-1/2	SCSI	636	2	34	21 Mbyte	27 ms	
Conner Peripherals	CP-3040	3-1/2	SCSI	1047	2	41	42 Mbyte	25 ms	$279
Conner Peripherals	CP-3100	3-1/2	SCSI	776	8	34	104 Mbyte	25 ms	$469
Conner Peripherals	CP-3200	3-1/2	SCSI	1348	8	39	209 Mbyte	19 ms	$779
Core International	AT 32	5-1/4	MFM	733	5	17	31 Mbyte	21 ms	
Core International	AT 30	5-1/4	MFM	733	5	17	31 Mbyte	26 ms	
Core International	AT 40	5-1/4	MFM	924	5	17	40 Mbyte	26 ms	
Core International	AT 63	5-1/4	MFM	988	5	17	42 Mbyte	26 ms	
Core International	AT 72	5-1/4	MFM	924	9	17	72 Mbyte	26 ms	
Core International	Optima 30	5-1/4	MFM	733	5	17	31 Mbyte	21 ms	

Manufacturer	Model Number	Form Factor	Interface	Cylinders	Heads	Sectors	Capacity Formatted	Access Time	Price
Core International	Optima 30	5-1/4	MFM	963	5	17	41 Mbyte	26 ms	
Core International	Optima 70	5-1/4	MFM	918	5	17	71 Mbyte	26 ms	
Core International	AT 32	5-1/4	RLL	733	5	26	48 Mbyte	21 ms	
Core International	AT 30	5-1/4	RLL	733	5	26	48 Mbyte	26 ms	
Core International	AT 40	5-1/4	RLL	924	5	26	61 Mbyte	26 ms	
Core International	AT 63	5-1/4	RLL	988	5	26	65 Mbyte	26 ms	
Core International	AT 72	5-1/4	RLL	924	9	26	107 Mbyte	26 ms	
Core International	Optima 30	5-1/4	RLL	733	5	26	48 Mbyte	21 ms	
Core International	Optima 40	5-1/4	RLL	963	5	26	64 Mbyte	26 ms	
Core International	Optima 70	5-1/4	RLL	918	9	26	109 Mbyte	26 ms	
Core International	HC 40	5-1/4	ESDI	564	4	35	40 Mbyte	10 ms	
Core International	HC 90	5-1/4	ESDI	969	5	35	91 Mbyte	16 ms	
Core International	HC 150	5-1/4	ESDI	969	9	35	156 Mbyte	16 ms	
Core International	HC 260	5-1/4	ESDI	1212	12	35	260 Mbyte	25 ms	
Core International	HC 310	5-1/4	ESDI	1582	12	35	311 Mbyte	16 ms	
Disctron	D-503		MFM	153	2	17	3 Mbyte		
Disctron	D-504		MFM	215	2	17	4 Mbyte		
Disctron	D-506		MFM	153	4	17	5 Mbyte		
Disctron	D-507		MFM	306	2	17	5 Mbyte		
Disctron	D-509		MFM	215	4	17	8 Mbyte		
Disctron	D-512		MFM	153	8	17	11 Mbyte		
Disctron	D-513		MFM	215	6	17	11 Mbyte		
Disctron	D-514		MFM	306	4	17	11 Mbyte		
Disctron	D-518		MFM	215	8	17	15 Mbyte		
Disctron	D-519		MFM	306	6	17	16 Mbyte		
Disctron	D-526		MFM	306	8	17	21 Mbyte		
DMA	306		MFM	612	2	17	11 Mbyte		
Elcoh	DISCACHE10		MFM	320	4	17	10 Mbyte		

Manufacturer	Model Number	Form Factor	Interface	Cylinders	Heads	Sectors	Capacity Formatted	Access Time	Price
Elcoh	DISCACHE20		MFM	320	8	17	20 Mbyte		
Fuji	FK305-26	3-1/2	MFM	615	4	17	21 Mbyte	80 ms	
Fuji	FK305-39	3-1/2	MFM	615	6	17	32 Mbyte	80 ms	
Fuji	FK309-26	3-1/2	MFM	615	4	17	21 Mbyte	80 ms	
Fuji	FK301		MFM	306	4	17	10 Mbyte		
Fuji	FK302-13		MFM	612	2	17	10 Mbyte		
Fuji	FK302-26		MFM	612	4	17	21 Mbyte		
Fuji	FK302-39		MFM	612	6	17	32 Mbyte		
Fuji	FK303-52	3-1/2	MFM	615	8	17	40 Mbyte	80 ms	
Fuji	FK305-39R	3-1/2	RLL	615	4	26	32 Mbyte	80 ms	
Fuji	FK305-58R	3-1/2	RLL	615	6	26	49 Mbyte	80 ms	
Fuji	FK309-39R	3-1/2	RLL	615	4	26	32 Mbyte	80 ms	
Fuji	FK308S-58R	3-1/2	SCSI	615	6		45 Mbyte	80 ms	
Fuji	FK308S-39R	3-1/2	SCSI	615	4		32 Mbyte	80 ms	
Fuji	FK309S-50R	3-1/2	SCSI	615	4		41 Mbyte	80 ms	
Fujitsu	M2611T	3-1/2	AT	1334	2		45 Mbyte	25 ms	$279
Fujitsu	M2612T	3-1/2	AT	1334	4		90 Mbyte	25 ms	$459
Fujitsu	M2613T	3-1/2	AT	1334	6		135 Mbyte	25 ms	$555
Fujitsu	M2614T	3-1/2	AT	1334	8		180 Mbyte	25 ms	$689
Fujitsu	2230 AS		MFM	320	2	17	5 Mbyte		
Fujitsu	2233 AS		MFM	320	4	17	10 Mbyte		
Fujitsu	2234 AS		MFM	320	6	17	15 Mbyte		
Fujitsu	2235 AS		MFM	320	8	17	20 Mbyte		
Fujitsu	2241 AS		MFM	754	4	17	26 Mbyte		
Fujitsu	M2226D2	3-1/2	MFM	615	6	17	30 Mbyte	35 ms	
Fujitsu	M2227D2	3-1/2	MFM	615	8	17	42 Mbyte	35 ms	
Fujitsu	M2242AS2	5-1/4	MFM	754	7	17	43 Mbyte	30 ms	
Fujitsu	M2243AS2	5-1/4	MFM	754	11	17	67 Mbyte	30 ms	

Manufacturer	Model Number	Form Factor	Interface	Cylinders	Heads	Sectors	Capacity Formatted	Access Time	Price
Fujitsu	M2243T	5-1/4	MFM	1186	7	17	68 Mbyte	25 ms	
Fujitsu	M2225DR	3-1/2	RLL	615	4	26	32 Mbyte	35 ms	
Fujitsu	M2226DR	3-1/2	RLL	615	6	26	49 Mbyte	35 ms	
Fujitsu	M2227DR	3-1/2	RLL	615	8	26	65 Mbyte	35 ms	
Fujitsu	M2243R	5-1/4	RLL	1186	7	26	110 Mbyte	25 ms	
Fujitsu	2244E	5-1/4	ESDI	823	5	35	73 Mbyte	25 ms	
Fujitsu	2245E	5-1/4	ESDI	823	7	35	120 Mbyte	25 ms	
Fujitsu	M2246E	5-1/4	ESDI	823	10	35	172 Mbyte	25 ms	
Fujitsu	M2249	5-1/4	ESDI	1243	15		389 Mbyte	18 ms	
Fujitsu	M2263	5-1/4	ESDI	1658	15		778 Mbyte	16 ms	$1699
Fujitsu	2244SA		SCSI	823	5	35	73 Mbyte	25 ms	
Fujitsu	M2245SA		SCSI	823	7	35	120 Mbyte	25 ms	
Fujitsu	M2246SA	5-1/4	SCSI	823	10	35	171 Mbyte	25 ms	
Fujitsu	M2249	5-1/4	SCSI	1243	15		389 Mbyte	18 ms	
Fujitsu	M2263	5-1/4	SCSI	1658	15		778 Mbyte	16 ms	
Fujitsu	M2344KS	5-1/4	SCSI	624	27		690 Mbyte	16 ms	
Fujitsu	M2611S	3-1/2	SCSI	1334	2		45 Mbyte	25 ms	
Fujitsu	M2612S	3-1/2	SCSI	1334	4		90 Mbyte	25 ms	
Fujitsu	M2613S	3-1/2	SCSI	1334	6		136 Mbyte	25 ms	
Fujitsu	M2614S	3-1/2	SCSI	1334	8		182 Mbyte	25 ms	
Hitachi	DK301-1	3-1/2	MFM	306	4	17	10 Mbyte	85 ms	
Hitachi	DK301-2	3-1/2	MFM	306	6	17	15 Mbyte	85 ms	
Hitachi	DK511-3	5-1/4	MFM	699	5	17	28 Mbyte	30 ms	
Hitachi	DK511-5	5-1/4	MFM	699	7	17	40 Mbyte	30 ms	
Hitachi	DK511-8	5-1/4	MFM	823	10	17	67 Mbyte	23 ms	
Hitachi	DK521-5	5-1/4	MFM	823	6	17	51 Mbyte	25 ms	
Hitachi	DK512-8	5-1/4	ESDI	823	5		67 Mbyte	23 ms	
Hitachi	DK512-12	5-1/4	ESDI	823	7		94 Mbyte	23 ms	

Manufacturer	Model Number	Form Factor	Interface	Cylinders	Heads	Sectors	Capacity Formatted	Access Time	Price
Hitachi	DK512-17	5-1/4	ESDI	823	10		134 Mbyte	23 ms	
Hitachi	DK514-38	5-1/4	ESDI	903	14	51	330 Mbyte	16 ms	
Hitachi	DK522-10	5-1/4	ESDI	823	6	36	103 Mbyte	25 ms	
Hitachi	DK512C-8	5-1/4	SCSI	823	5		67 Mbyte	23 ms	
Hitachi	DK512C-12	5-1/4	SCSI	823	7		94 Mbyte	23 ms	
Hitachi	DK512C-17	5-1/4	SCSI	819	10	35	134 Mbyte	23 ms	
Hitachi	DK522C-10	5-1/4	SCSI	819	6	35	88 Mbyte	25 ms	
IMI	5006		MFM	306	2	17	5 Mbyte		
IMI	5012		MFM	306	4	17	10 Mbyte		
IMI	5018		MFM	306	6	17	15 Mbyte		
Imprimis	94205-51		MFM	989	5	17	43 Mbyte		
Imprimis	94204-74		AT	948	5	27	65.5 Mbyte		
Imprimis	94205-77		RLL	989	5	26	65.8 Mbyte		
Imprimis	94204-71		AT	1032	5	27	71.3 Mbyte		
Imprimis	94204-81		AT	1032	5	27	71.3 Mbyte		
Imprimis	94353-90		AT	1072	5	29	79.6 Mbyte		
Imprimis	94355-100		MFM	1072	9	17	84 Mbyte		
Imprimis	94356-111		ESDI	1072	5	36	98.8 Mbyte		
Imprimis	94354-111		AT	1072	5	36	98.8 Mbyte		
Imprimis	94351-111		SCSI	1068	5	36	98.4 Mbyte		
Imprimis	94354-126		AT	1072	7	29	111.4 Mbyte		
Imprimis	94351-125		SCSI	1068	7	29	111 Mbyte		
Imprimis	94353-133		AT	1272	5	36	117.2 Mbyte		
Imprimis	94351-133s		SCSI	1268	5	36	116.9 Mbyte		
Imprimis	94355-150		RLL	1072	9	26	128.4 Mbyte		
Imprimis	94355-156		RLL	1072	7	36	138.3 Mbyte		
Imprimis	94354-156		AT	1072	7	36	138.3 Mbyte		
Imprimis	94356-156		ESDI	1072	7	36	138.3 Mbyte		

Manufacturer	Model Number	Form Factor	Interface	Cylinders	Heads	Sectors	Capacity Formatted	Access Time	Price
Imprimis	94351-155		SCSI	1068	7	36	137.8 Mbyte		
Imprimis	94351-155s		ESDI / SCSI	1068	7	36	137.8 Mbyte		
Imprimis	94354-162		AT	1072	9	29	143.3 Mbyte		
Imprimis	94351-160		SCSI	1068	9	29	142.7 Mbyte		
Imprimis	94354-186		AT	1272	7	36	164.1 Mbyte		
Imprimis	94351-186		SCSI	1268	7	36	163.6 Mbyte		
Imprimis	94351-186s		ESDI / SCSI	1268	7	36	163.6 Mbyte		
Imprimis	94356-201		ESDI	1072	9	36	177.8 Mbyte		
Imprimis	94354-201		AT	1072	9	36	177.8 Mbyte		
Imprimis	94351-200		SCSI	1068	9	36	177.2 Mbyte		
Imprimis	94351-200s		ESDI / SCSI	1068	9	36	177.2 Mbyte		
Imprimis	94354-239		AT	1272	9	36	211 Mbyte		
Imprimis	94351-230		SCSI	1268	9	36	210.3 Mbyte		
Imprimis	94351-230s		ESDI / SCSI	1268	9	36	210.3 Mbyte		
Imprimis	94216-106		ESDI	1024	5	36	94.4 Mbyte		
Imprimis	94211-106		SCSI	1024	5	36	94.4 Mbyte		
Imprimis	94211-091		SCSI	1024	5	36	94.4 Mbyte		
Imprimis	94221-125		SCSI	1544	3	45	106.7 Mbyte		
Imprimis	94246-182		ESDI	1453	4	54	160.7 Mbyte		
Imprimis	94221-209		SCSI	1544	5	45	177.9 Mbyte		
Imprimis	94221-209m		SCSI	1544	5	45	177.9 Mbyte		
Imprimis	94244-274		AT	1747	5	54	241.5 Mbyte		
Imprimis	94246-383		ESDI	1747	7	54	338.1 Mbyte		
Imprimis	94244-383		AT	1747	7	54	338.1 Mbyte		
Imprimis	94241-383		SCSI	1747	7	54	338.1 Mbyte		
Imprimis	94241-502		SCSI	1755	7	70	440.3 Mbyte		
Imprimis	94155-86		MFM	925	9	17	72.5 Mbyte		
Imprimis	94155-86p		MFM	925	9	17	72.5 Mbyte		

Manufacturer	Model Number	Form Factor	Interface	Cylinders	Heads	Sectors	Capacity Formatted	Access Time	Price
Imprimis	94155-96		MFM	1024	9	17	80.2 Mbyte		
Imprimis	94155-96p		MFM	1024	9	17	80.2 Mbyte		
Imprimis	94155-135		MFM	960	9	26	115 Mbyte		
Imprimis	94166-182		ESDI	969	9	36	160.7 Mbyte		
Imprimis	94166-155		ESDI	969	9	36	160.7 Mbyte		
Imprimis	94161-182		SCSI	967	9	36	160.4 Mbyte		
Imprimis	94171-300		SCSI	1412	9	46	299.3 Mbyte		
Imprimis	94171-307		SCSI	1412	9	46	299.3 Mbyte		
Imprimis	94171-327		SCSI	1412	9	46	299.3 Mbyte		
Imprimis	94171-350		SCSI	1412	9	46	299.3 Mbyte		
Imprimis	94171-344		SCSI	1549	9	45	321.2 Mbyte		
Imprimis	94171-376		SCSI	1549	9	45	321.2 Mbyte		
Imprimis	94186-383		ESDI	1412	13	36	338.3 Mbyte		
Imprimis	94181-385h		SCSI	791	15	56	334.1 Mbyte		
Imprimis	94186-383h		ESDI	1224	15	36	338.4 Mbyte		
Imprimis	94186-442		ESDI	1412	15	36	390.4 Mbyte		
Imprimis	94181-702		SCSI	1546	15	50	593.7 Mbyte		
Imprimis	94196-766		ESDI	1632	15	54	676.8 Mbyte		
Imprimis	94191-766		SCSI	1632	15	54	676.8 Mbyte		
Imprimis	94601-767h		SCSI	1356	15	64	666.5 Mbyte		
Imprimis	94601-12g		SCSI	1931	15	71	1052.9 Mbyte		
Imprimis	94155-21		MFM	697	3	17	18.2 Mbyte		
Imprimis	94155-25		MFM	697	4	17	24.3 Mbyte		
Imprimis	94155-36		MFM	697	5	17	30.3 Mbyte		
Imprimis	94155-38		MFM	733	5	17	31.9 Mbyte		
Imprimis	94151-42		SASI	921	5	17	40.1 Mbyte		
Imprimis	94151-62		SASI	921	7	17	56.1 Mbyte		
Imprimis	94151-80		SASI	921	9	17	72.1 Mbyte		

Manufacturer	Model Number	Form Factor	Interface	Cylinders	Heads	Sectors	Capacity Formatted	Access Time	Price
Imprimis	94155-48		MFM	925	5	17	40.3 Mbyte		
Imprimis	94155-48p		MFM	925	5	17	40.3 Mbyte		
Imprimis	94155-57		MFM	925	6	17	48.3 Mbyte		
Imprimis	94155-57p		MFM	925	6	17	48.3 Mbyte		
Imprimis	94155-67		MFM	925	7	17	56.4 Mbyte		
Imprimis	94155-67p		MFM	925	7	17	56.4 Mbyte		
Imprimis	94155-92		MFM	925	9	17	77.5 Mbyte		
Imprimis	94155-92p		MFM	989	9	17	77.5 Mbyte		
Imprimis	94155-130		RLL	1024	9	26	122.7 Mbyte		
Imprimis	94156-48		ESDI	925	9	17	72.5 Mbyte		
Imprimis	94156-67		ESDI	925	7	17	56.4 Mbyte		
Imprimis	94156-86		ESDI	925	7	17	56.4 Mbyte		
Imprimis	94161-86		SCSI	969	5	35	86.8 Mbyte		
Imprimis	94161-103		SCSI	969	6	35	104.2 Mbyte		
Imprimis	94161-121		SCSI	969	7	35	121.6 Mbyte		
Imprimis	94161-138		SCSI	969	8	35	138.9 Mbyte		
Imprimis	94166-86		ESDI	969	5	35	86.8 Mbyte		
Imprimis	94166-103		ESDI	969	6	35	104.2 Mbyte		
Imprimis	94166-121		ESDI	969	7	35	121.6 Mbyte		
Imprimis	94166-138		ESDI	969	8	35	138.9 Mbyte		
Imprimis	94246-182		ESDI	1453	4	54	160.7 Mbyte		
Imprimis	92244-219		AT	1747	4	54	193.2 Mbyte		
JCT	100	5-1/4	MFM			17	5 Mbyte	110 ms	
JCT	105	5-1/4	MFM			17	7 Mbyte	110 ms	
JCT	110	5-1/4	MFM			17	14 Mbyte	110 ms	
JCT	120	5-1/4	MFM			17	20 Mbyte	110 ms	
JCT (Commodore)	1000		MFM				5 Mbyte		
JCT (Commodore)	1005		MFM				7 Mbyte		

Manufacturer	Model Number	Form Factor	Interface	Cylinders	Heads	Sectors	Capacity Formatted	Access Time	Price
JCT (Commodore)	1010		MFM				14 Mbyte		
Kalok	KL320	3-1/2	MFM	615	4	17	20 Mbyte	48 ms	$219
Kalok	KL330	3-1/2	RLL	616	4	26	32 Mbyte	48 ms	$239
Kalok	KL332		RLL	615	4	30	40 Mbyte	48 ms	
Kalok	KL341		SCSI	644	4	30	42.5 Mbyte	30 ms	
Kalok	KL343		AT	644	4	30	42.5 Mbyte	33 ms	$229
Kyocera	KC20A	3-1/2	MFM	616	4	17	20 Mbyte	65 ms	
Kyocera	KC20B	3-1/2	MFM	616	4	17	20 Mbyte	65 ms	
Kyocera	KC30A	3-1/2	RLL	615	4	26	30 Mbyte	65 ms	
La Pine	3522		MFM	306	4	17	10 Mbyte		
La Pine	LT 10		MFM	615	2	17	10 Mbyte		
La Pine	LT 20		MFM	615	4	17	20 Mbyte		
La Pine	LT 200		MFM	614	4	17	20 Mbyte		
La Pine	LT 2000		MFM	614	4	17	20 Mbyte		
La Pine	LT 300		RLL	614	4	26	32 Mbyte		
Maxtor	XT-1065	5-1/4	MFM	918	7	17	56 Mbyte	28 ms	
Maxtor	XT-1085	5-1/4	MFM	1024	8	17	71 Mbyte	28 ms	$799
Maxtor	XT-1105	5-1/4	MFM	918	11	17	87 Mbyte	27 ms	
Maxtor	XT-1140	5-1/4	MFM	918	15	17	119 Mbyte	27 ms	$1495
Maxtor	XT-2085	5-1/4	MFM	1224	7	17	74 Mbyte	30 ms	
Maxtor	XT-2140	5-1/4	MFM	1224	11	17	117 Mbyte	30 ms	
Maxtor	XT-2190	5-1/4	MFM	1224	15	17	159 Mbyte	29 ms	$1549
Maxtor	XT-1120R	5-1/4	RLL	1024	8	25	104 Mbyte	27 ms	
Maxtor	XT-1240R	5-1/4	RLL	1024	15	25	196 Mbyte	27 ms	
Maxtor	XT-4170E	5-1/4	ESDI	1224	7	36	157 Mbyte	14 ms	$1249
Maxtor	XT-4175	5-1/4	ESDI	1224	7	35	150 Mbyte	27 ms	
Maxtor	XT-4380E	5-1/4	ESDI	1224	15	36	338 Mbyte	16 ms	$1995
Maxtor	XT-8380E	5-1/4	ESDI	1632	8	54	360 Mbyte	14.5 ms	$2295

Manufacturer	Model Number	Form Factor	Interface	Cylinders	Heads	Sectors	Capacity Formatted	Access Time	Price
Maxtor	XT-8760E	5-1/4	ESDI	1632	15	54	676 Mbyte	16.5 ms	$3095
Maxtor	XT-3170	5-1/4	SCSI	1224	9	48	146 Mbyte	30 ms	
Maxtor	XT-3280	5-1/4	SCSI	1224	15			30 ms	
Maxtor	XT-3380	5-1/4	SCSI		15			27 ms	
Maxtor	XT-4170S	5-1/4	SCSI	1224	7	36	157 Mbyte	14 ms	$1299
Maxtor	XT-4280S	5-1/4	SCSI	1224	11	36	338 Mbyte	27 ms	
Maxtor	XT-4380S	5-1/4	SCSI	1224	15	36	337 Mbyte	16 ms	$1995
Maxtor	XT-8380S	5-1/4	SCSI	1632	8	54	360 Mbyte	14.5 ms	$2295
Maxtor	XT-8760S	5-1/4	SCSI	1632	15	54	676 Mbyte	16.5 ms	$3395
Maxtor	LXT-200	3-1/4	SCSI		7		201 Mbyte	15 ms	$779
Maxtor	LXT-100	3-1/4	SCSI		8		96 Mbyte	27 ms	
Maxtor	RXT-800S	5-1/4	SCSI		2		786 Mbyte		
(WORM Optical)									
Maxtor	Tahiti	5-1/4	SCSI		2		650 Mbyte	35ms	$3899
(R/W Optical)									
Memorex	321		MFM	320	2	17	5 Mbyte		
Memorex	322		MFM	320	4	17	10 Mbyte		
Memorex	323		MFM	320	6	17	15 Mbyte		
Memorex	324		MFM	320	8	17	20 Mbyte		
Memorex	450		MFM	612	2	17	10 Mbyte		
Memorex	512		MFM	961	3	17	25 Mbyte		
Memorex	513		MFM	961	5	17	41 Mbyte		
Memorex	514		MFM	961	7	17	58 Mbyte		
Micropolis	1743-5	3-1/2	AT	1140	5	28	112 Mbyte	15 ms	
Micropolis	1744-6	3-1/2	AT	1140	6	28	135 Mbyte	15 ms	
Micropolis	1744-7	3-1/2	AT	1140	7	28	157 Mbyte	15 ms	
Micropolis	1745-8	3-1/2	AT	1140	8	28	180 Mbyte	15 ms	
Micropolis	1745-9	3-1/2	AT	1140	9	28	202 Mbyte	15 ms	

Manufacturer	Model Number	Form Factor	Interface	Cylinders	Heads	Sectors	Capacity Formatted	Access Time	Price
Micropolis	1302	5-1/4	MFM	830	3	17	21 Mbyte		
Micropolis	1303	5-1/4	MFM	830	5	17	36 Mbyte		
Micropolis	1304	5-1/4	MFM	830	6	17	43 Mbyte		
Micropolis	1323	5-1/4	MFM	1024	4	17	35 Mbyte	28 ms	
Micropolis	1323A	5-1/4	MFM	1024	5	17	44 Mbyte	28 ms	
Micropolis	1324	5-1/4	MFM	1024	6	17	53 Mbyte	28 ms	
Micropolis	1324A	5-1/4	MFM	1024	7	17	62 Mbyte	28 ms	
Micropolis	1325	5-1/4	MFM	1024	8	17	71 Mbyte	28 ms	
Micropolis	1333A	5-1/4	MFM	1024	5	17	44 Mbyte	28 ms	
Micropolis	1334	5-1/4	MFM	1024	6	17	53 Mbyte	28 ms	
Micropolis	1335	5-1/4	MFM	1024	8	17	71 Mbyte	28 ms	$575
Micropolis	1352		EDSI	1024	2	36		23 ms	
Micropolis	1352A		EDSI	1024	3	36	41 Mbyte	23 ms	
Micropolis	1353	5-1/4	EDSI	1024	4	36	75 Mbyte	23 ms	
Micropolis	1353A	5-1/4	EDSI	1024	5	36	94 Mbyte	23 ms	
Micropolis	1354	5-1/4	EDSI	1024	6	36	113 Mbyte	23 ms	
Micropolis	1354A	5-1/4	EDSI	1024	7	36	132 Mbyte	23 ms	
Micropolis	1355	5-1/4	ESDI	1024	8	36	150 Mbyte	23 ms	$949
Micropolis	1516-10S	5-1/4	EDSI	1840	10	72	678 Mbyte	13.5 ms	
Micropolis	1517-13	5-1/4	EDSI	1925	13	72	922 Mbyte	14 ms	
Micropolis	1518-14	5-1/4	EDSI	1925	14	72	993 Mbyte	14 ms	
Micropolis	1518-15	5-1/4	EDSI	1925	15	72	1064 Mbyte	14 ms	
Micropolis	1556-11	5-1/4	EDSI	1224	11	36	248 Mbyte	18 ms	
Micropolis	1557-12	5-1/4	EDSI	1224	12	36	270 Mbyte	18 ms	
Micropolis	1557-13	5-1/4	EDSI	1224	13	36	293 Mbyte	18 ms	
Micropolis	1557-14	5-1/4	EDSI	1224	14	36	315 Mbyte	18 ms	
Micropolis	1557-15	5-1/4	EDSI	1224	15	36	338 Mbyte	18 ms	
Micropolis	1558	5-1/4	ESDI	1224			338.1 Mbyte	18 ms	$1619

Manufacturer	Model Number	Form Factor	Interface	Cylinders	Heads	Sectors	Capacity Formatted	Access Time	Price
Micropolis	1566-11	5-1/4	EDSI	1632	11	54	496 Mbyte	16 ms	
Micropolis	1567-12	5-1/4	EDSI	1632	12	54	541 Mbyte	16 ms	
Micropolis	1567-13	5-1/4	EDSI	1632	13	54	586 Mbyte	16 ms	
Micropolis	1568-14	5-1/4	EDSI	1632	14	54	631 Mbyte	16 ms	$1895
Micropolis	1568-15	5-1/4	ESDI	1632	15	54	676.8 Mbyte	16 ms	$2499
Micropolis	1653-4	5-1/4	EDSI	1249	4	36	92 Mbyte	16 ms	
Micropolis	1653-5	5-1/4	EDSI	1249	5	36	115 Mbyte	16 ms	
Micropolis	1654-6	5-1/4	EDSI	1249	6	36	138 Mbyte	16 ms	
Micropolis	1654-7	5-1/4	EDSI	1249	7	36	161 Mbyte	16 ms	$795
Micropolis	1663-4	5-1/4	EDSI	1780	4		197 Mbyte	14 ms	
Micropolis	1663-5	5-1/4	EDSI	1780	5		246 Mbyte	14 ms	
Micropolis	1664-6	5-1/4	EDSI	1780	6		295 Mbyte	14 ms	
Micropolis	1664-7	5-1/4	EDSI	1780	7		345 Mbyte	14 ms	$1245
Micropolis	1373	5-1/4	SCSI	1016	4	36	72 Mbyte	23 ms	
Micropolis	1373A	5-1/4	SCSI	1016	5	36	91 Mbyte	23 ms	
Micropolis	1374	5-1/4	SCSI	1016	6	36	109 Mbyte	23 ms	
Micropolis	1374A	5-1/4	SCSI	1016	7	36	127 Mbyte	23 ms	
Micropolis	1375	5-1/4	SCSI	1016	8	36	145 Mbyte	23 ms	$999
Micropolis	1576-11	5-1/4	SCSI	1220	11	36	243 Mbyte	18 ms	
Micropolis	1577-12	5-1/4	SCSI	1220	12	36	266 Mbyte	18 ms	
Micropolis	1577-13	5-1/4	SCSI	1220	13	36	287 Mbyte	18 ms	
Micropolis	1578-14	5-1/4	SCSI	1220	14	36	310 Mbyte	18 ms	
Micropolis	1578-15	5-1/4	SCSI	1220	15	36	331.7 Mbyte	18 ms	$1619
Micropolis	1586-11	5-1/4	SCSI	1628	11	54	490 Mbyte	16 ms	
Micropolis	1587-12	5-1/4	SCSI	1628	12	54	535 Mbyte	16 ms	
Micropolis	1587-13	5-1/4	SCSI	1628	13	54	579 Mbyte	16 ms	
Micropolis	1588-14	5-1/4	SCSI	1628	14	54	624 Mbyte	16 ms	
Micropolis	1588-15	5-1/4	SCSI	1628	15	54	667.6 Mbyte	16 ms	$2499

Manufacturer	Model Number	Form Factor	Interface	Cylinders	Heads	Sectors	Capacity Formatted	Access Time	Price
Micropolis	1596-10S	5-1/4	SCSI	1834	10	72	668 Mbyte	13.5 ms	
Micropolis	1597-13	5-1/4	SCSI	1919	13	72	909 Mbyte	14 ms	
Micropolis	1598-14	5-1/4	SCSI	1919	14	72	979 Mbyte	14 ms	
Micropolis	1598-15	5-1/4	SCSI	1919	15	72	1049 Mbyte	14 ms	$2875
Micropolis	1673-4	5-1/4	SCSI	1249	4		90 Mbyte	16 ms	
Micropolis	1673-5	5-1/4	SCSI	1249	5		112 Mbyte	16 ms	
Micropolis	1674-6	5-1/4	SCSI	1249	6		135 Mbyte	16 ms	
Micropolis	1674-7	5-1/4	SCSI	1249	7		158 Mbyte	16 ms	
Micropolis	1683-4	5-1/4	SCSI	1776	4	54	193 Mbyte	14 ms	
Micropolis	1683-5	5-1/4	SCSI	1776	5	54	242 Mbyte	14 ms	
Micropolis	1684-6	5-1/4	SCSI	1776	6	54	291 Mbyte	14 ms	
Micropolis	1684-7	5-1/4	SCSI	1776	7	54	340 Mbyte	14 ms	$1325
Micropolis	1773-5	3-1/2	SCSI	1140	5	28	112 Mbyte	15 ms	
Micropolis	1774-6	3-1/2	SCSI	1140	6	28	135 Mbyte	15 ms	
Micropolis	1774-7	3-1/2	SCSI	1140	7	28	157 Mbyte	15 ms	
Micropolis	1775-8	3-1/2	SCSI	1140	8	28	180 Mbyte	15 ms	
Micropolis	1775-9	3-1/2	SCSI	1140	9	28	202 Mbyte	15 ms	
Microscience	7040	3-1/2	AT	855	3	36	47 Mbyte	18 ms	
Microscience	7100	3-1/2	AT	855	7	36	110 Mbyte	18 ms	
Microscience	HH 312		MFM	306	4	17	10 Mbyte		
Microscience	HH 315		MFM	306	4	17	10 Mbyte		
Microscience	HH 325		MFM	612	4	17	21 Mbyte	80 ms	
Microscience	HH 612		MFM	306	4	17	11 Mbyte		
Microscience	HH 625		MFM	612	4	17	21 Mbyte		
Microscience	HH 712	5-1/4	MFM	612	2	17	10 Mbyte	105 ms	
Microscience	HH 725	5-1/4	MFM	612	4	17	21 Mbyte	105 ms	
Microscience	HH 825	5-1/4	MFM	615	4	17	21 Mbyte	65 ms	
Microscience	HH 1050	5-1/4	MFM	1024	5	17	44 Mbyte	28 ms	

55

Manufacturer	Model Number	Form Factor	Interface	Cylinders	Heads	Sectors	Capacity Formatted	Access Time	Price
Microscience	HH 1075	5-1/4	MFM	1024	7	17	65 Mbyte	28 ms	
Microscience	HH 1090	5-1/4	MFM	1314	7	17	80 Mbyte	28 ms	
Microscience	4050	3-1/2	MFM	1025	5	17	44 Mbyte	18 ms	
Microscience	HH 330		RLL	612	4	26	32 Mbyte	105 ms	
Microscience	HH 738	5-1/4	RLL	612	4	26	32 Mbyte	65 ms	
Microscience	HH 830	5-1/4	RLL	615	4	26	38 Mbyte	28 ms	
Microscience	HH 1060	5-1/4	RLL	1024	5	26	66 Mbyte	28 ms	
Microscience	HH 1095	5-1/4	RLL	1024	7	26	95 Mbyte	28 ms	
Microscience	HH 1120	5-1/4	RLL	1314	7	26	122 Mbyte	28 ms	
Microscience	HH 2085		ESDI						
Microscience	HH 2120	5-1/4	ESDI	1024	7	33	121 Mbyte	33 ms	
Microscience	5100	3-1/2	ESDI	855	7	36	110 Mbyte	36 ms	
Microscience	HH 1080		SCSI						
Microscience	HH 3120	5-1/4	SCSI	1314	7	26	122 Mbyte	28 ms	
Microscience	6100	3-1/2	SCSI	855	7	36	110 Mbyte	18 ms	
Miniscribe	7040A	3-1/2	AT				40.7 Mbyte	19 ms	$499
Miniscribe	7080A	3-1/2	AT				81.4 Mbyte	19 ms	$749
Miniscribe	8225AT	3-1/2	AT	745	2	28	21 Mbyte	28 ms	
Miniscribe	8051AT	3-1/2	AT	745	4		42 Mbyte	28 ms	
Miniscribe	8450AT	3-1/2	AT	745	4	28	42 Mbyte	40 ms	
Miniscribe	8225XT	3-1/2		805	2	26	21 Mbyte	68 ms	
Miniscribe	8425XT	3-1/2		615	4		21 Mbyte		
Miniscribe	8438XT	3-1/2		615	4				
Miniscribe	8450XT	3-1/2		805	4	26	42 Mbyte	45 ms	
Miniscribe	1006		MFM	306	2	17	5 Mbyte		
Miniscribe	1012		MFM	306	4	17	10 Mbyte		
Miniscribe	2006		MFM	306	2	17	5 Mbyte		
Miniscribe	2012		MFM	306	4	17	11 Mbyte		

Manufacturer	Model Number	Form Factor	Interface	Cylinders	Heads	Sectors	Capacity Formatted	Access Time	Price
Miniscribe	3053	5-1/4	MFM	1024	5	17	44 Mbyte	25 ms	$595
Miniscribe	3085	5-1/4	MFM	1170	7	17	71 Mbyte	20 ms	
Miniscribe	3212	5-1/4	MFM	612	2	17	11 Mbyte	85 ms	
Miniscribe	3212 Plus	5-1/4	MFM	612	2	17	11 Mbyte	53 ms	
Miniscribe	3412		MFM	306	4	17	11 Mbyte		
Miniscribe	3425	5-1/4	MFM	612	4	17	21 Mbyte	85 ms	
Miniscribe	3425 Plus	5-1/4	MFM	612	4	17	21 Mbyte	53 ms	$399
Miniscribe	3650	5-1/4	MFM	809	6	17	42 Mbyte	61 ms	
Miniscribe	3650F	5-1/4	MFM	809	6	17	42 Mbyte	46 ms	
Miniscribe	4010		MFM	480	2	17	8 Mbyte		
Miniscribe	4020		MFM	480	4	17	17 Mbyte		
Miniscribe	5330		MFM	480	6	17	25 Mbyte		
Miniscribe	5338		MFM	612	6	17	32 Mbyte		
Miniscribe	5440		MFM	480	8	17	32 Mbyte		
Miniscribe	5451		MFM	612	8	17	43 Mbyte		
Miniscribe	6032	5-1/4	MFM	1024	3	17	26 Mbyte	28 ms	
Miniscribe	6053	5-1/4	MFM	1024	5	17	44 Mbyte	28 ms	
Miniscribe	6074	5-1/4	MFM	1024	7	17	62 Mbyte	28 ms	
Miniscribe	6085	5-1/4	MFM	1024	8	17	71 Mbyte	28 ms	
Miniscribe	6212		MFM	612	2	17	10 Mbyte		
Miniscribe	7426		MFM	612	4	17	21 Mbyte		
Miniscribe	8212		MFM	612	2	17	11 Mbyte		
Miniscribe	8412		MFM	306	4	17	10 Mbyte		
Miniscribe	8425	3-1/2	MFM	615	4	17	21 Mbyte	68 ms	$229
Miniscribe	8425F	3-1/2	MFM	615	4	17	21 Mbyte	40 ms	$249
Miniscribe	8438	3-1/2	MFM				38 Mbyte	68 ms	$249
Miniscribe	8450	3-1/2	MFM				48 Mbyte	45 ms	$289
Miniscribe	3438	5-1/4	RLL	612	4	26	32 Mbyte	85 ms	

Manufacturer	Model Number	Form Factor	Interface	Cylinders	Heads	Sectors	Capacity Formatted	Access Time	Price
Miniscribe	3438 Plus	5-1/4	RLL	612	4	26	32 Mbyte	53 ms	
Miniscribe	3675	5-1/4	RLL	809	6	26	63 Mbyte	61 ms	
Miniscribe	6079	5-1/4	RLL	1024	5	26	68 Mbyte	28 ms	
Miniscribe	6128	5-1/4	RLL	1024	8	26	110 Mbyte	28 ms	
Miniscribe	8255	3-1/2	RLL	771	2	26	20 Mbyte		
Miniscribe	8434F	3-1/2	RLL	615	4	26	32 Mbyte	40 ms	
Miniscribe	8438	3-1/2	RLL	615	4	26	32 Mbyte	68 ms	
Miniscribe	8438F	3-1/2	RLL	615	4	26	32 Mbyte	40 ms	
Miniscribe	8450	3-1/2	RLL	771	4	26	40 Mbyte		
Miniscribe	3085E	5-1/4	ESDI	1270	3		72 Mbyte	17 ms	
Miniscribe	3130E	5-1/4	ESDI	1250	5		112 Mbyte	17 ms	
Miniscribe	3180E	5-1/4	ESDI	1250	7		157 Mbyte	17 ms	$999
Miniscribe	9380E	5-1/4	ESDI	1224	14		338 Mbyte	17 ms	$1699
Miniscribe	9424E	5-1/4	ESDI	1661	8		360 Mbyte	17 ms	
Miniscribe	9780E	5-1/4	ESDI	1661	15		676 Mbyte	17 ms	
Miniscribe	9230	5-1/4	ESDI/SCSI	1224	9		203 Mbyte	16 ms	
Miniscribe	9380	5-1/4	ESDI/SCSI	1224	15		338 Mbyte	16 ms	
Miniscribe	3085S	5-1/4	SCSI	1255	3		72 Mbyte	17 ms	
Miniscribe	3130S	5-1/4	SCSI	1255	5		115 Mbyte	17 ms	$849
Miniscribe	3180S	5-1/4	SCSI	1255	7		160 Mbyte	17 ms	$999
Miniscribe	7040S	3-1/2	SCSI				40.7 Mbyte	19 ms	$549
Miniscribe	7080S	3-1/2	SCSI				81.4 Mbyte	19 ms	$799
Miniscribe	8051S	3-1/2	SCSI	793	4	28	45 Mbyte	28 ms	
Miniscribe	8425S	3-1/2	SCSI	612	4		21 Mbyte	68 ms	$329
Miniscribe	9380S	5-1/4	SCSI	1224	15		347 Mbyte	16 ms	$1699
Miniscribe	9424S	5-1/4	SCSI	1661	8		355 Mbyte	17 ms	
Miniscribe	9780S	5-1/4	SCSI	1661	15		668 Mbyte	17 ms	
Mitsubishi	MR521	5-1/4	MFM	612	2	17	10 Mbyte	85 ms	

Manufacturer	Model Number	Form Factor	Interface	Cylinders	Heads	Sectors	Capacity Formatted	Access Time	Price
Mitsubishi	MR522	5-1/4	MFM	612	4	17	20 Mbyte	85 ms	
Mitsubishi	MR535	5-1/4	MFM	977	5	17	42 Mbyte	28 ms	$255
Mitsubishi	MR535	5-1/4	RLL	977	5	26	65 Mbyte	28 ms	$255
MMI	M 112	3-1/2	MFM	306	4	17	10 Mbyte	75 ms	
MMI	M 106	3-1/2	MFM	306	2	17	5 Mbyte	75 ms	
MMI	M 125	3-1/2	MFM	306	8	17	20 Mbyte	75 ms	
MMI	M 306	3-1/2	MFM	306	2	17	5 Mbyte	75 ms	
MMI	M 212	5-1/4	MFM	306	4	17	10 Mbyte	75 ms	
MMI	M 225	5-1/4	MFM	306	8	17	20 Mbyte	75 ms	
MMI	M 312	5-1/4	MFM	306	4	17	10 Mbyte	75 ms	
MMI	M 325	5-1/4	MFM	306	8	17	20 Mbyte	75 ms	
NEC	D3126	3-1/2	MFM	615	4	17	20 Mbyte	85 ms	
NEC	D3146H	3-1/2	MFM	615	8	32	40 Mbyte	35 ms	
NEC	D3142	3-1/2	MFM	642	8	32	42 Mbyte	28 ms	
NEC	D5124	5-1/4	MFM	309	4	17	10 Mbyte	85 ms	
NEC	D5126	5-1/4	MFM	612	4	17	20 Mbyte	85 ms	
NEC	D5126H		MFM	612	4	17	20 Mbyte	40 ms	
NEC	D5146	5-1/4	MFM	615	8	17	40 Mbyte	85 ms	
NEC	D5146H	5-1/4	MFM	615	8	17	40 Mbyte	40 ms	
NEC	D5652	5-1/4	ESDI	823	10		143 Mbyte	23 ms	
NEC	D5655	5-1/4	ESDI	1224	7	35	153 Mbyte	18 ms	$649
Newbury Data	NDR 340	3-1/2	MFM	615	8		42 Mbyte	40 ms	
Newbury Data	NDR 1065	5-1/4	MFM	918	7		55 Mbyte	25 ms	
Newbury Data	NDR 1085	5-1/4	MFM	1025	8		71 Mbyte	26 ms	
Newbury Data	NDR 1105	5-1/4	MFM	918	11		87 Mbyte	25 ms	
Newbury Data	NDR 1140	5-1/4	MFM	918	15		105 Mbyte	25 ms	
Newbury Data	NDR 2190	5-1/4	MFM	918	15		191 Mbyte	28 ms	
Newbury Data	NDR 4175	5-1/4	ESDI	1224	7	36	179 Mbyte	28 ms	

59

Manufacturer	Model Number	Form Factor	Interface	Cylinders	Heads	Sectors	Capacity Formatted	Access Time	Price
Newbury Data	NDR 4380	5-1/4	ESDI	1224	15	36	384 Mbyte	28 ms	
Newbury Data	NDR 3170S	5-1/4	SCSI	1224	9	26	146 Mbyte	28 ms	
Newbury Data	NDR 3280S	5-1/4	SCSI	1224	15	26	244 Mbyte	28 ms	
Newbury Data	NDR 4380S	5-1/4	SCSI	1224	15	34	319 Mbyte	28 ms	
Okidata	OD526		RLL	640	4	26	31 Mbyte		
Okidata	OD540		RLL	640	6	26	47 Mbyte		
Olivetti	HD662/11		MFM	612	2	17	10 Mbyte		
Olivetti	HD662/12		MFM	612	4	17	20 Mbyte		
Otari	C 214		MFM	306	4	17	10 Mbyte		
Otari	C 519		MFM	306	6	17			
Otari	C 526		MFM	306	8	17			
Panasonic	JU-116	3-1/2	MFM	615	4	17	20 Mbyte	85 ms	
Panasonic	JU-128	3-1/2	MFM	733	7	17	42 Mbyte	35 ms	
Priam	V-150		MFM	987	5	17	42 Mbyte		
Priam	V-160		MFM	1166	5	17	50 Mbyte		
Priam	V-170		MFM	987	7	17	60 Mbyte		
Priam	V-185		MFM	1166	7	17	71 Mbyte		
Priam	502		MFM	755	7	17	46 Mbyte		
Priam	504		MFM	755	7	17	46 Mbyte		
Priam	514	5-1/4	MFM	1224	11	17	117 Mbyte	22 ms	
Priam	519	5-1/4	MFM	1224	15	17	160 Mbyte	22 ms	
Priam	ED40	5-1/4	MFM	1018	5	17	42 Mbyte	23 ms	
Priam	ED60	5-1/4	MFM	1018	7	17	59 Mbyte	23 ms	
Priam	ED130	5-1/4	MFM	1218	15	17	132 Mbyte	13 ms	
Priam	ID45	5-1/4	MFM	1018	5	17	44 Mbyte	23 ms	
Priam	ID62	5-1/4	MFM	1018	7	17	62 Mbyte	23 ms	
Priam	ID130	5-1/4	MFM	1218	15	17	132 Mbyte	23 ms	
Priam	V-130		RLL	987	3	26	39 Mbyte	13 ms	

Manufacturer	Model Number	Form Factor	Interface	Cylinders	Heads	Sectors	Capacity Formatted	Access Time	Price
Priam	V-170	5-1/4	RLL	987	7	26	91 Mbyte	20 ms	
Priam	617	5-1/4	ESDI	1225	7		153 Mbyte	20 ms	
Priam	628	5-1/4	ESDI	1225	11		241 Mbyte	20 ms	
Priam	638	5-1/4	ESDI	1225	15		329 Mbyte	20 ms	
Priam	ED120	5-1/4	ESDI	1017	7	33	121 Mbyte	28 ms	
Priam	ED150	5-1/4	ESDI	1268	7	33	159 Mbyte	28 ms	
Priam	ED250	5-1/4	ESDI	1218	11	36	246 Mbyte	18 ms	
Priam	ED250	5-1/4	MCA	1195	11	36	241 Mbyte	18 ms	
Priam	ED330	5-1/4	ESDI	1218	15	36	336 Mbyte	18 ms	
Priam	ED330	5-1/4	MCA	1195	15	36	330 Mbyte	18 ms	
Priam	ID120	5-1/4	ESDI	1017	7	33	121 Mbyte	28 ms	
Priam	ID150	5-1/4	ESDI	1268	7	33	159 Mbyte	28 ms	
Priam	ID160	5-1/4	ESDI	1218	7	36	156 Mbyte	18 ms	
Priam	ID160	5-1/4	MCA	1195	7	36	152 Mbyte	18 ms	
Priam	ID250	5-1/4	ESDI	1218	11	36	246 Mbyte	18 ms	
Priam	ID250	5-1/4	MCA	1195	11	36	241 Mbyte	18 ms	
Priam	ID330	5-1/4	ESDI	1218	15	36	336 Mbyte	18 ms	
Priam	ID330	5-1/4	MCA	1195	15	36	330 Mbyte	18 ms	
Priam	717	5-1/4	SCSI	1225	7		153 Mbyte	20 ms	
Priam	728	5-1/4	SCSI	1225	11		241 Mbyte	20 ms	
Priam	738	5-1/4	SCSI	1225	15		329 Mbyte	20 ms	
Priam	ED160	5-1/4	SCSI	1218	7	36	158 Mbyte	18 ms	
Priam	ED250	5-1/4	SCSI	1218	11	36	248 Mbyte	18 ms	
Priam	ED330	5-1/4	SCSI	1218	15	36	338 Mbyte	18 ms	
Priam	ID160	5-1/4	SCSI	1218	7	36	158 Mbyte	18 ms	
Priam	ID250	5-1/4	SCSI	1218	11	36	248 Mbyte	18 ms	
Priam	ID330	5-1/4	SCSI	1218	15	36	338 Mbyte	18 ms	
PTI	PT-238A	3-1/2	AT	615	4		32 Mbyte	35 ms	

Manufacturer	Model Number	Form Factor	Interface	Cylinders	Heads	Sectors	Capacity Formatted	Access Time	Price
PTI	PT-251A	3-1/2	AT	820	4		43 Mbyte	35 ms	
PTI	PT-357A	3-1/2	AT	615	6		49 Mbyte	35 ms	
PTI	PT-376A	3-1/2	AT	820	6		65 Mbyte	35 ms	
PTI	PT-225	3-1/2	MFM	615	4	17	21 Mbyte	35 ms	
PTI	PT-234	3-1/2	MFM	820	4	17	28 Mbyte	35 ms	
PTI	PT-338	3-1/2	MFM	615	6	17	32 Mbyte	35 ms	
PTI	PT-351	3-1/2	MFM	820	6	17	42 Mbyte	35 ms	
PTI	PT-238R	3-1/2	RLL	615	4	26	32 Mbyte	35 ms	
PTI	PT-251R	3-1/2	RLL	820	4	26	43 Mbyte	35 ms	
PTI	PT-357R	3-1/2	RLL	615	6	26	49 Mbyte	35 ms	
PTI	PT-376R	3-1/2	RLL	820	6	26	65 Mbyte	35 ms	
PTI	PT-4102R	3-1/2	RLL	820	8	26	87 Mbyte	35 ms	
PTI	PT-238S	3-1/2	SCSI	615	4		32 Mbyte	35 ms	
PTI	PT-251S	3-1/2	SCSI	820	4		43 Mbyte	35 ms	
PTI	PT-357S	3-1/2	SCSI	615	6		49 Mbyte	35 ms	
PTI	PT-376S	3-1/2	SCSI	820	6		65 Mbyte	35 ms	
Quantum	PRO40	3-1/2	AT				42 Mbyte	19 ms	$390
Quantum	PRO80	3-1/2	AT				84 Mbyte	19 ms	$639
Quantum	PRO120	3-1/2	AT				120 Mbyte	14 ms	$779
Quantum	PRO170	3-1/2	AT				168 Mbyte	15 ms	$785
Quantum	Q-510		MFM	512	2	17	8 Mbyte		
Quantum	Q-520		MFM	512	4	17	18 Mbyte		
Quantum	Q-530		MFM	512	6	17	27 Mbyte		
Quantum	Q-540		MFM	512	8	17	36 Mbyte		
Quantum	PRO100	3-1/2	ESDI				103 Mbyte	19 ms	
Quantum	PRO145	3-1/2	ESDI				145 Mbyte	19 ms	
Quantum	Q-250	5-1/4	SCSI	823	4		53 Mbyte	26 ms	
Quantum	Q-280	5-1/4	SCSI	823	6		80 Mbyte	26 ms	

Manufacturer	Model Number	Form Factor	Interface	Cylinders	Heads	Sectors	Capacity Formatted	Access Time	Price
Quantum	Q-160	5-1/4	SCSI		12		200 Mbyte	26 ms	$249
Quantum	PRO40	3-1/2	SCSI				42 Mbyte	19 ms	$458
Quantum	PRO80	3-1/2	SCSI				84 Mbyte	19 ms	$639
Quantum	PRO120	3-1/2	SCSI				120 Mbyte	14 ms	$695
Quantum	PRO170	3-1/2	SCSI				168 Mbyte	15 ms	
Ricoh	RH-5130		MFM	612	2	17	10 Mbyte	85 ms	
Ricoh	RH-5260 (Remov.)		MFM	615	2	17	10 Mbyte	85 ms	
Ricoh	RH-5261 (Remov.)		SCSI	612	2		10 Mbyte	85 ms	
Rodime	RO 101	5-1/4	MFM	192	2	17	6 Mbyte		
Rodime	RO 102	5-1/4	MFM	192	4	17	12 Mbyte		
Rodime	RO 103	5-1/4	MFM	192	6	17	18 Mbyte	55 ms	
Rodime	RO 104	5-1/4	MFM	192	8	17	24 Mbyte		
Rodime	RO 201	5-1/4	MFM	321	2	17	5 Mbyte	85 ms	
Rodime	RO 201E	5-1/4	MFM	640	2	17	11 Mbyte	55 ms	
Rodime	RO 202	5-1/4	MFM	321	4	17	10 Mbyte	85 ms	
Rodime	RO 202E	5-1/4	MFM	640	4	17	21 Mbyte	55 ms	
Rodime	RO 203	5-1/4	MFM	321	6	17	15 Mbyte	85 ms	
Rodime	RO 203E	5-1/4	MFM	640	6	17	32 Mbyte	55 ms	
Rodime	RO 204	5-1/4	MFM	320	8	17	21 Mbyte	85 ms	
Rodime	RO 204E	5-1/4	MFM	640	8	17	43 Mbyte	55 ms	
Rodime	RO 251	5-1/4	MFM	306	2	17	5 Mbyte	85 ms	
Rodime	RO 252	5-1/4	MFM	306	4	17	11 Mbyte	85 ms	
Rodime	RO 351	5-1/4	MFM	306	2	17	5 Mbyte	85 ms	
Rodime	RO 352	3-1/2	MFM	306	4	17	11 Mbyte	85 ms	
Rodime	RO 365	3-1/2	MFM	612	4	17	21 Mbyte	85 ms	
Rodime	RO 3045		MFM	872	5	17	37 Mbyte	28 ms	
Rodime	RO 3055		MFM	872	6	17	45 Mbyte	28 ms	
Rodime	RO 3065		MFM	872	7	17	53 Mbyte	28 ms	

Manufacturer	Model Number	Form Factor	Interface	Cylinders	Heads	Sectors	Capacity Formatted	Access Time	Price
Rodime	RO 5065	5-1/4	MFM		5	17	63 Mbyte	28 ms	
Rodime	RO 5090	5-1/4	MFM	1224	7	17	89 Mbyte	28 ms	
Rodime	RO 652A		SCSI				20 Mbyte	85 ms	
Rodime	RO 652B		SCSI	306	4		20 Mbyte	85 ms	
Rodime	RO 752A	5-1/4	SCSI				25 Mbyte	85 ms	
Rodime	RO 3070S		SCSI				71 Mbyte	28 ms	
Rodime	RO 3085S		SCSI	750	7		85 Mbyte	28 ms	
Rodime	RO 3057S		SCSI	680	5		45 Mbyte	28 ms	
Rodime	RO 5040		MFM		3		38 Mbyte	28 ms	
Rodime	RO 5075S	5-1/4	SCSI				76 Mbyte	28 ms	
Rodime	RO 5125S	5-1/4	SCSI	1219	5		127 Mbyte	28 ms	
Rodime	RO 5180S	5-1/4	SCSI	1219	7		178 Mbyte	28 ms	
Seagate	ST-124	3-1/2	MFM	615	4	17	21.4 Mbyte	40 ms	$209
Seagate	ST-125-0	3-1/2	MFM	615	4	17	21.4 Mbyte	40 ms	$229
Seagate	ST-125-1	3-1/2	MFM	615	4	17	21.4 Mbyte	28 ms	$239
Seagate	ST-125A	3-1/2	AT	404	4	26	21.5 Mbyte	40 ms	$249
Seagate	ST-125A-1	3-1/2	AT	404	4	26	21.5 Mbyte	28 ms	
Seagate	ST-125N-0	3-1/2	SCSI	407	4	26	21.7 Mbyte	40 ms	$249
Seagate	ST-125N-1	3-1/2	SCSI	407	4	26	21.7 Mbyte	28 ms	$259
Seagate	ST-125-1	3-1/2	MFM	615	4	17	21.4 Mbyte	28 ms	$239
Seagate	ST-137R	3-1/2	RLL	615	6	26	49.1 Mbyte		
Seagate	ST-138-0	3-1/2	MFM	615	6	17	32.1 Mbyte	40 ms	$249
Seagate	ST-138-1	3-1/2	MFM	615	6	17	32.1 Mbyte	28 ms	$259
Seagate	ST-138N-0	3-1/2	SCSI	615	4	26	32.7 Mbyte	40 ms	$269
Seagate	ST-138N-1	3-1/2	SCSI	615	4	26	32.7 Mbyte	28 ms	$279
Seagate	ST-138R-0	3-1/2	RLL	615	4	26	32.7 Mbyte	40 ms	$239
Seagate	ST-138R-1	3-1/2	RLL	615	4	26	32.7 Mbyte	28 ms	$249
Seagate	ST-138A	3-1/2	AT	604	4	26	32.2 Mbyte	40 ms	$259

Manufacturer	Model Number	Form Factor	Interface	Cylinders	Heads	Sectors	Capacity Formatted	Access Time	Price
Seagate	ST-138A-1	3-1/2	AT	604	4	26	32 Mbyte	28 ms	$329
Seagate	ST-151	3-1/2	MFM	977	5	17	42.5 Mbyte	25 ms	$239
Seagate	ST-157A	3-1/2	AT	560	6	26	44.7 Mbyte	40 ms	
Seagate	ST-157A-1	3-1/2	AT	539	6	26	43 Mbyte	28 ms	$289
Seagate	ST-157N-0	3-1/2	SCSI	615	6	26	49.1 Mbyte	40 ms	$299
Seagate	ST-157N-1	3-1/2	SCSI	615	6	26	49.1 Mbyte	28 ms	$249
Seagate	ST-157R-0	3-1/2	RLL	615	6	26	49.1 Mbyte	40 ms	
Seagate	ST-157R-1	3-1/2	RLL	615	6	26	49.1 Mbyte	28 ms	$259
Seagate	ST-177N	3-1/2	SCSI	921	5	26	61.3 Mbyte	24 ms	$359
Seagate	ST-206	5-1/4	MFM	306	2		5 Mbyte		
Seagate	ST-212	5-1/4	MFM	306	4	17	10.7 Mbyte		
Seagate	ST-213	5-1/4	MFM	615	2	17	10.7 Mbyte		
Seagate	ST-224N	5-1/4	SCSI	615	2	17	10.7 Mbyte		
Seagate	ST-225	5-1/4	MFM	615	4	17	21.4 Mbyte	65 ms	$199
Seagate	ST-225N	5-1/4	SCSI	615	4	17	21.4 Mbyte	65 ms	$329
Seagate	ST-225R	5-1/4	RLL	667	2	31	21.2 Mbyte	70 ms	$183
Seagate	ST-238	5-1/4	RLL	615	4	26	32.7 Mbyte		$200
Seagate	ST-238R	5-1/4	RLL	615	4	26	32.7 Mbyte	65 ms	$209
Seagate	ST-250N	5-1/4	SCSI	667	4	31	42.3 Mbyte	70 ms	$279
Seagate	ST-250R	5-1/4	RLL	667	4	31	42.3 Mbyte	70 ms	$219
Seagate	ST-251	5-1/4	MFM	820	6	17	42 Mbyte	40 ms	
Seagate	ST-251-1	5-1/4	MFM	820	6	17	42.8 Mbyte	28 ms	$259
Seagate	ST-251N-0	5-1/4	SCSI	820	4	26	43.7 Mbyte	40 ms	$419
Seagate	ST-251N-1	5-1/4	SCSI	630	4	34	43.9 Mbyte	28 ms	
Seagate	ST-251R	5-1/4	RLL	820	4	26	43 Mbyte	40 ms	$249
Seagate	ST-252	5-1/4	MFM	820	6	17	42.8 Mbyte	40 ms	
Seagate	ST-253	5-1/4	MFM	989	5	17	43 Mbytes	28 ms	$299
Seagate	ST-274A	5-1/4	AT	948	5	27	65.5 Mbyte	29 ms	$369

Manufacturer	Model Number	Form Factor	Interface	Cylinders	Heads	Sectors	Capacity Formatted	Access Time	Price
Seagate	ST-277N-0	5-1/4	SCSI	820	6	26	65.5 Mbyte	40 ms	
Seagate	ST-277N-1	5-1/4	SCSI	628	6	34	65.6 Mbyte	28 ms	$329
Seagate	ST-277R	5-1/4	RLL	820	6	26	65 Mbyte	40 ms	
Seagate	ST-277R-1	5-1/4	RLL	820	6	26	65.5 Mbyte	28 ms	$289
Seagate	ST-278R	5-1/4	RLL	820	6	26	65.5 Mbyte	40 ms	$279
Seagate	ST-279R	5-1/4	RLL	989	5	26	65.8 Mbyte	28 ms	$329
Seagate	ST-280A	5-1/4	AT	1032	5	27	71.3 Mbyte	28 ms	$369
Seagate	ST-296N	5-1/4	SCSI	820	6	34	85.6 Mbyte	28 ms	$359
Seagate	ST-406	5-1/4	MFM	306	2	17	5.3 Mbyte		
Seagate	ST-412	5-1/4	MFM	306	4	17	10.7 Mbyte		
Seagate	ST-419	5-1/4	MFM	306	6	17	16 Mbyte		
Seagate	ST-425	5-1/4	MFM	306	8	17	21.3 Mbyte		
Seagate	ST-506	5-1/4	MFM	153	4	17	5.3 Mbyte		
Seagate	ST-706	5-1/4	MFM	306	2	17	5 Mbyte		
Seagate	ST-1057A			1024	6	17	53.3 Mbyte		
Seagate	ST-1090A			1072	5	29	79.6 Mbyte		
Seagate	ST-1090N		SCSI	1068	5	29	79.3 Mbyte		
Seagate	ST-1096N	3-1/2	SCSI	906	7	26	84.4 Mbyte	24 ms	$389
Seagate	ST-1100		MFM	1072	9	17	84 Mbyte	15 ms	$599
Seagate	ST-1102A		AT	1024	10	17	89.1 Mbyte	20 ms	$429
Seagate	ST-1106R			977	7	26	91 Mbyte		
Seagate	ST-1111E		ESDI	1072	5	36	98.8 Mbyte	15 ms	$639
Seagate	ST-1111A			1072	5	36	98.8 Mbyte		
Seagate	ST-1111N		SCSI	1068	5	36	98.4 Mbyte		
Seagate	ST-1126A		AT	1072	7	29	111.4 Mbyte	15 ms	$639
Seagate	ST-1126N		SCSI	1068	7	29	111 Mbyte		$655
Seagate	ST-1133A			1272	5	36	117.2 Mbyte		
Seagate	ST-1133N		SCSI	1268	5	36	116.9 Mbyte		

Manufacturer	Model Number	Form Factor	Interface	Cylinders	Heads	Sectors	Capacity Formatted	Access Time	Price
Seagate	ST-1144A		AT	1024	14	17	124.8 Mbyte	20 ms	$489
Seagate	ST-1150R			1072	9	26	128.4 Mbyte		
Seagate	ST-1156R			1072	7	36	138.3 Mbyte		
Seagate	ST-1156A			1072	7	36	138.3 Mbyte		
Seagate	ST-1156E			1072	7	36	138.3 Mbyte		$849
Seagate	ST-1156N, NS		SCSI	1068	7	36	137.8 Mbyte		
Seagate	ST-1162A	3-1/2	AT	1072	9	29	143.3 Mbyte	15 ms	$609
Seagate	ST-1162N	3-1/2	SCSI	1068	9	29	142.7 Mbyte	15 ms	$699
Seagate	ST-1182E			972	9	36	161.2 Mbyte		
Seagate	ST-1186A			1272	7	36	164.1 Mbyte		
Seagate	ST-1186N, NS		SCSI	1268	7	36	163.6 Mbyte		
Seagate	ST-1201E	3-1/2	ESDI	1072	9	36	177.8 Mbyte	15 ms	$953
Seagate	ST-1201A	3-1/2	AT	1072	9	36	177.8 Mbyte	15 ms	$689
Seagate	ST-1201N, NS	3-1/2	SCSI	1068	9	36	177.2 Mbyte	15 ms	$729
Seagate	ST-1239A	3-1/2	AT	1272	9	36	211 Mbyte	15 ms	$749
Seagate	ST-1239N, NS		SCSI	1268	9	36	210.3 Mbyte		$895
Seagate	ST-2106E		ESDI	1024	5	36	94.4 Mbyte	18 ms	$629
Seagate	ST-2106N		SCSI	1024	5	36	94.4 Mbyte	18 ms	$659
Seagate	ST-2125N		SCSI	1544	3	45	106.7 Mbyte	18 ms	$719
Seagate	ST-2182E		ESDI	1453	4	54	160.7 Mbyte	15 ms	$929
Seagate	ST-2209N, NM		SCSI	1544	5	45	177.9 Mbyte	18 ms	$939
Seagate	ST-2274A		AT	1747	5	54	241.5 Mbyte	16 ms	$1189
Seagate	ST-2383E		ESDI	1747	7	54	338.1 Mbyte	15 ms	$1259
Seagate	ST-2383A		AT	1747	7	54	338.1 Mbyte	16 ms	$1279
Seagate	ST-2383N		SCSI	1747	7	54	338.1 Mbyte	16 ms	$1299
Seagate	ST-2502N		SCSI	1755	7	70	440.3 Mbyte	16 ms	$1639
Seagate	ST-3144	3-1/2	SCSI-2				130 Mbyte	16 ms	$495
Seagate	ST-4026	5-1/4	MFM	615	4	17	21.4 Mbyte	16 ms	

Manufacturer	Model Number	Form Factor	Interface	Cylinders	Heads	Sectors	Capacity Formatted	Access Time	Price
Seagate	ST-4038, M	5-1/4	MFM	733	5	17	31.9 Mbyte	40 ms	$449
Seagate	ST-4051	5-1/4	MFM	977	5	17	42.5 Mbyte	40 ms	$479
Seagate	ST-4053	5-1/4	MFM	1024	5	17	44.6 Mbyte	28 ms	$499
Seagate	ST-4077R	5-1/4	RLL	1024	5	26	65 Mbyte	28 ms	
Seagate	ST-4077N	5-1/4	SCSI	1024	5	26	67 Mbyte	28 ms	
Seagate	ST-4085			1024	8	17	71.3 Mbyte		
Seagate	ST-4086, P			925	9	17	72.5 Mbyte		
Seagate	ST-4096	5-1/4	MFM	1024	9	17	80.2 Mbyte	28 ms	$549
Seagate	ST-4096N	5-1/4	SCSI				80 Mbyte	28 ms	$495
Seagate	ST-4097, P		MFM	1024	9	17	80.2 Mbyte	28 ms	$589
Seagate	ST-4135			960	9	26	115 Mbyte		
Seagate	ST-4144R	5-1/4	RLL	1024	9	26	122.7 Mbyte	28 ms	$589
Seagate	ST-4182E		ESDI	969	9	36	160.7 Mbyte	16.5 ms	$829
Seagate	ST-4182N		SCSI	967	9	36	160.4 Mbyte	16.5 ms	$899
Seagate	ST-4192E	5-1/4	ESDI	1147	8	36	169 Mbyte	17 ms	
Seagate	ST-4192N	5-1/4	SCSI	1147	8	36	169 Mbyte	17 ms	
Seagate	ST-4350N		SCSI	1412	9	46	299.3 Mbyte	16.5 ms	$1239
Seagate	ST-4376N		SCSI	1549	9	45	321.2 Mbyte	17.5 ms	$1289
Seagate	ST-4383E		ESDI	1412	13	36	338.3 Mbyte	18 ms	$1269
Seagate	ST-4384E		ESDI	1224	15	36	338.4 Mbyte	14.5 ms	$1329
Seagate	ST-4385N		SCSI	791	15	55	334.1 Mbyte	10.7 ms	$1489
Seagate	ST-4442E		ESDI	1412	15	36	390.4 Mbyte	16 ms	$1429
Seagate	ST-4702N		SCSI	1546	15	50	593.7 Mbyte	16.5 ms	$1779
Seagate	ST-4766E		ESDI	1632	15	54	676.8 Mbyte	15.5 ms	$1869
Seagate	ST-4766N		SCSI	1632	15	54	676.8 Mbyte	15.5 ms	$2029
Seagate	ST-4767N		SCSI	1356	15	64	666.5 Mbyte	11.9 ms	$2639
Seagate	ST-41651N	5-1/4	SCSI				1651 Mbyte	12.9 ms	$2350
Seagate	ST-41200N		SCSI	1931	15	71	1052.9 Mbyte	15 ms	$2939

Manufacturer	Model Number	Form Factor	Interface	Cylinders	Heads	Sectors	Capacity Formatted	Access Time	Price
Shugart	604		MFM	160	4	17	5 Mbyte		
Shugart	606		MFM	160	6	17	7 Mbyte		
Shugart	612		MFM	306	4	17	11 Mbyte		
Shugart	706		MFM	320	2	17	6 Mbyte		
Shugart	712		MFM	320	4	17			
Siemens	1200	5-1/4	ESDI	1216	8		174 Mbyte	25 ms	
Siemens	1300	5-1/4	ESDI	1216	12		261 Mbyte	25 ms	
Siemens	2300	5-1/4	ESDI	1216	12		261 Mbyte	25 ms	
Siemens	2200	5-1/4	ESDI	1216	8		174 Mbyte	25 ms	
Siemens	5710		ESDI		15		655 Mbyte	16 ms	
Siemens	5720		SCSI		15		655 Mbyte	16 ms	
Syquest	SQ 306RD (Remov.)		MFM	306	2	17	5 Mbyte		
Syquest	SQ 312RD (Remov.)		MFM	615	2	17	10 Mbyte		
Syquest	SQ 325F		MFM	615	4	17	20 Mbyte		
Syquest	SQ 338F		MFM	615	6	17	30 Mbyte		
Syquest	SQ 340AF		MFM	640	6	17	38 Mbyte		
Tandon	TM 252		MFM	306	4	17	10 Mbyte		
Tandon	TM 261		MFM	615	2	17	10 Mbyte		
Tandon	TM 262		MFM	615	4	17	21 Mbyte		
Tandon	TM 361		MFM	615	2	17	10 Mbyte		
Tandon	TM 362		MFM	615	4	17	21 Mbyte		
Tandon	TM 501		MFM	306	2	17	5 Mbyte		
Tandon	TM 502		MFM	306	4	17	10 Mbyte		
Tandon	TM 503		MFM	306	6	17	15 Mbyte		
Tandon	TM 702		RLL	615	4	26	20 Mbyte		
Tandon	TM 703		MFM	733	5	17	31 Mbyte		
Tandon	TM 755	5-1/4	MFM	981	5	17	43 Mbyte		
Tandon	TM 3085		MFM	1024	8	17	71 Mbyte	37 ms	

Manufacturer	Model Number	Form Factor	Interface	Cylinders	Heads	Sectors	Capacity Formatted	Access Time	Price
Tandon	TM 602S		MFM	153	4	17	10 Mbyte		
Tandon	TM 603S		MFM	153	6	17	10 Mbyte		
Tandon	TM 603SE		MFN	230	6	17	21 Mbyte		
Tandon	TM 244	3-1/2	RLL	782	4	26	41 Mbyte	37 ms	
Tandon	TM 246	3-1/2	RLL	782	6	26	62 Mbyte	37 ms	
Tandon	TM 262R	3-1/2	RLL	782	2	26	20 Mbyte		
Tandon	TM 264	3-1/2	RLL	782	4	26	41 Mbyte	85 ms	
Tandon	TM 344	3-1/2	RLL	782	4	26	41 Mbyte	37 ms	
Tandon	TM 346	3-1/2	RLL	782	6	26	62 Mbyte	37 ms	
Tandon	TM 362R	3-1/2	RLL	782	2	26	20 Mbyte	85 ms	
Tandon	TM 364	3-1/2	RLL	782	4	26	41 Mbyte	85 ms	
Tandon	TM 3085		RLL	1024	8	26	104 Mbyte	37 ms	
Tandon	TM 2085		SCSI	1004	9		74 Mbyte	25 ms	
Tandon	TM 2128		SCSI	1004	9		115 Mbyte	25 ms	
Tandon	TM 2170		SCSI	1344	9		154 Mbyte	25 ms	
Teac	SD 510		MFM	306	4	17	10 Mbyte		
Teac	SD 520		MFM	615	4	17	20 Mbyte		
Texas Instruments	ST-506	5-1/4	MFM	153	4	17	5 Mbyte		
Toshiba	MK 53FA	5-1/4	MFM	830	5	17	43 Mbyte	30 ms	
Toshiba	MK 53FB	5-1/4	RLL	830	5	17	64 Mbyte	25 ms	
Toshiba	MK 54FA	5-1/4	MFM	830	7	17	60 Mbyte	30 ms	
Toshiba	MK 54FB	5-1/4	RLL	830	7	17	90 Mbyte	25 ms	
Toshiba	MK 56FA	5-1/4	MFM	830	10	17	86 Mbyte	30 ms	
Toshiba	MK 56FB	5-1/4	RLL	830	10	17	130 Mbyte	25 ms	
Toshiba	MK 134FA	3-1/2	MFM	733	7	17	44 Mbyte	25 ms	$299
Toshiba	MK 53FA	5-1/4	RLL	830	5	26	43 Mbyte	30 ms	
Toshiba	MK 53FB	5-1/4	RLL	830	5	26	64 Mbyte	25 ms	
Toshiba	MK 54FA	5-1/4	RLL	830	5	26	60 Mbyte	30 ms	

Manufacturer	Model Number	Form Factor	Interface	Cylinders	Heads	Sectors	Capacity Formatted	Access Time	Price
Toshiba	MK 54FB	5-1/4	RLL	830	7	26	90 Mbyte	25 ms	
Toshiba	MK 56FA	5-1/4	RLL	830	10	26	86 Mbyte	30 ms	
Toshiba	MK 56FB	5-1/4	RLL	830	10	26	130 Mbyte	25 ms	
Toshiba	MK 153FA	5-1/4	ESDI	830	5	35	74 Mbyte	23 ms	
Toshiba	MK 154FA	5-1/4	ESDI	830	7	35	104 Mbyte	23 ms	
Toshiba	MK 156FA	5-1/4	ESDI	830	10	35	148 Mbyte	23 ms	
Toshiba	MK 250F	5-1/4	ESDI / SCSI	1224	10	35	382 Mbyte	18 ms	
Toshiba	MK 153FB	5-1/4	SCSI	830	5	35	74 Mbyte	23 ms	
Toshiba	MK 154FB	5-1/4	SCSI	830	7	35	104 Mbyte	23 ms	
Toshiba	MK 156FB	5-1/4	SCSI	830	10	35	148 Mbyte	23 ms	
Toshiba	MK 234FB	3-1/2	SCSI	845	3	35	45 Mbyte	25 ms	
Toshiba	MK 233FB	3-1/2	SCSI	845	5		75 Mbyte	25 ms	
Toshiba	MK 234FB	3-1/2	SCSI	845	7		106 Mbyte	25 ms	
Tulin	213		MFM	640	2	17	10 Mbyte		
Tulin	226		MFM	640	4	17	22 Mbyte		
Tulin	240		MFM	640	6	17	33 Mbyte		
Tulin	326		MFM	640	4	17	22 Mbyte		
Tulin	340		MFM	640	6	17	33 Mbyte		
Vertex (Priam)	V130		MFM	987	3	17	26 Mbyte		
Vertex (Priam)	V150		MFM	987	5	17	43 Mbyte		
Vertex (Priam)	V170		MFM	987	7	17	60 Mbyte		
Western Digital	WD93028-X	3-1/2	XT / RLL	782	2	27	20 Mbyte	80 ms	
Western Digital	WD93038-X	3-1/2	XT / RLL	782	3	27	30 Mbyte	80 ms	
Western Digital	WD93048-X	3-1/2	XT / RLL	782	4	27	40 Mbyte	80 ms	
Western Digital	WD95028-X	5-1/4	XT / RLL	782	2	27	20 Mbyte	80 ms	
Western Digital	WD95038-X	5-1/4	XT / RLL	782	3	27	30 Mbyte	80 ms	
Western Digital	WD95048-X	5-1/4	XT / RLL	782	4	27	40 Mbyte	80 ms	
Western Digital	WD93028-A	3-1/2	AT / RLL	782	2	27	20 Mbyte	80 ms	

Manufacturer	Model Number	Form Factor	Interface	Cylinders	Heads	Sectors	Capacity Formatted	Access Time	Price
Western Digital	WD93048-A	3-1/2	AT / RLL	782	4	27	40 Mbyte	80 ms	
Western Digital	WD95028-A	5-1/4	AT / RLL	782	2	27	20 Mbyte	80 ms	
Western Digital	WD95048-A	5-1/4	AT / RLL	782	4	27	40 Mbyte	80 ms	
Western Digital	WD 262	5-1/4	MFM	615	4	17	20 Mbyte	80 ms	
Western Digital	WD 362	3-1/2	MFM	615	4	17	20 Mbyte	80 ms	
Western Digital	WD 344R	3-1/2	RLL	782	4	26	40 Mbyte	40 ms	
Western Digital	WD 382R (TM262R)	3-1/2	RLL	782	2	26	20 Mbyte	85 ms	
Western Digital	WD 383R	3-1/2	RLL	615	4	26	30 Mbyte	85 ms	
Western Digital	WD 384R (TM364)	3-1/2	RLL	782	4	26	40 Mbyte	85 ms	
Western Digital	WD 544R	5-1/4	RLL	782	4	26	40 Mbyte	40 ms	
Western Digital	WD 582R	5-1/4	RLL	782	2	26	20 Mbyte	85 ms	
Western Digital	WD 583R	3-1/2	RLL	615	4	26	30 Mbyte	85 ms	
Western Digital	WD 584R	5-1/4	RLL	782	4	26	40 Mbyte	85 ms	
Xebec	OWL II	5-1/4	MFM		4		25 Mbyte	55 ms	
Xebec	OWL II	5-1/4	MFM		4		38 Mbyte	40 ms	
Xebec	OWL III	5-1/4	MFM		4		52 Mbyte	38 ms	

Sources: Western Digital Corp., Irvine, CA,
Seagate Technology, Inc., Scotts Valley, CA

when it is ready. In one revolution, six sectors of 512 bytes each will be read and stored. In three revolutions, all of the sectors will be read. Any interleave other than 3 will, in this example, cause drive access to increase.

XT HARD DRIVE TYPES

The original IBM PC did not support any hard drives at all, only floppies. When the IBM XT was introduced it contained the first hard drive controller with support for only 1 drive, even though the standard interface at the time (ST-506) could support up to four drives. Using INT 13h, the BIOS Fixed Disk Service provides the support for the reading, writing, formatting, initialization, and many other fixed disk functions. As the list of controllers provided at the end of this chapter confirms, most of the controllers sold today will support two hard drives and two floppies.

Data is moved by the BIOS from the system memory to the hard drive and from the hard drive to the system memory without the intervention of the CPU. The data movement is facilitated by channel 2 of the DMA controller. The BIOS Fixed Disk Service directs the disk controller by commands communicated to it from the CPU. The encoding or interface method used in a specific hard disk drive is not distinguished by the BIOS. However, the BIOS does use the fixed disk drive parameter table in the ROM BIOS data area.

The number of fixed disk drive types supported by an XT hard disk controller is limited to four and these types, as shown below, severely restrict the choices from the wide assortment of hard drives available in the marketplace. If the computer has an XT-type hard drive controller, only a physical installation process is required, unlike the software setup process for the AT-type hard drive controller.

Fixed Disk Drive 0 must be assigned disk identification number 80h and Fixed Disk Drive 1 must be assigned identification number 81h. If INT 13h, AH = 08h, "Return Disk Drive Parameters" is invoked, the caller can find out where the fixed disk parameter table is located.

If you have an XT-type fixed disk controller, the drive types supported are as follows:

Parameter	Type 0	Type 1	Type 2	Type 3
Maximum No. Cylinders	306	612	615	306
Maximum No. Heads	4	4	4	8
Reduced Write Current Cyl.	306	612	615	306
Write Precomp Cylinder	0	0	300	128
ECC Data Burst Length	11	11	11	11
Control Byte	5	5	5	5
Standard Time-Out	12	32	24	12
Format Drive Time-Out	180	180	180	180
Check Drive Time-Out	40	40	40	40

AT HARD DRIVE TYPES

The first fifteen AT hard drive types were defined by IBM in the original AT. Since then, additional types have been defined by IBM and others, so that the table in your computer may vary. If you install a different BIOS in an AT-type computer and have difficulty booting, inspect or print the drive tables to ensure that the correct type has been selected. The address of the drive table is at locations 0000:0118–0000:011B when only one (1) hard drive has been selected during the configuration "Setup" routine. This location may not be valid if two (2) hard drives are selected. With some BIOS's the Drive Table may be displayed with the SysVue "TYPES" command.

The following program, written in GWBASIC, is used to display your AT Hard Drive Types Table on the video monitor. The program assumes that the table is stored in the ROM BIOS. If you cannot match the parameters of your disk drive exactly to a type listing in your computer's table, select a hard drive type with the same number of heads, the same pre-compensation, and a smaller number of tracks. Try to pick a drive type from your table with the number of tracks closest (on the low side) to the disk drive you have. By choosing a drive type from the table with just slightly fewer tracks, you will simply reduce the amount of information you can store on your drive by a small percentage.

```
1     REM — PROGRAM IN GWBASIC TO PRINT THE AT HARD DRIVE TABLE
10    REM — The table is stored in the ROM BIOS
20    CLS   'Clear the screen
30    KEY OFF 'Erase the key display from the 25th line
40    SCREEN 0 'Text Mode only
50    WIDTH 80 '80 characters per line
100   PRINT "Program To Display The Hard Disk Drive Types In
The AT BIOS"
110   PRINT
120   DEF SEG=&HF000 'Assign the current segment address to be
referenced by a subsequent PEEK
125   REM—Examine location FFFF:000E for the IBM Machine
Identification; It should be HFC = 25 2₁₀
130   IF PEEK (&HFFFE) <> 252 THEN BEEP
140   LET LINENUM = 0 'Counter for output position on the
screen
150   FOR TYPE = 0 TO 56
160   ADR% = TYPE * 16 + &HE401 'Start of list
170   IF LINENUM > 0 THEN GOTO 200
180   PRINT
185   REM — Print the heading
190   PRINT "TYPE CYLINDERS HEADS PRE-COMPENSATION PARK-
```

```
CYLINDER SECTORS CAPACITY IN MBYTES"
195  PRINT "--------------------------------------------------
------------------------------"
198  REM — Get the information from the ROM
200  IF PEEK(ADR%) = 0 THEN 400
210  LINENUM = LINENUM + 1
220  CYL = PEEK(ADR%) + 256 * PEEK(ADR%+1)
230  HEAD = PEEK(ADR%+2)
240  PARK = PEEK(ADR%+12) + 256 * PEEK(ADR%+13)
250  PRE = PEEK(ADR%+5) + 256 * PEEK(ADR%+6)
260  SEC = PEEK(ADR%+14)
270  CAPA =(PEEK(ADR%)+PEEK(ADR%+1)*256)*PEEK(ADR%+2)*SEC*512/
(1024*1024)
300  PRINT USING" ##      ####       ##          ######
####      ## ###.#";TYPE+1,CYL,HEAD,PRE,PARK,SEC,CAPA
400  IF LINENUM < 15 THEN 500
410  PRINT "Press any key to continue" 'End of screen page
420  KB$ = INKEY$ 'Get typed key
430  IF KB$ = "" THEN 420 'Loop until you get the key
490  LINENUM = 0
500  NLXT TYPE 'Get next line of disk data
1000 END
```

GENERAL INFORMATION

Hard drive and fixed drive are really other names for a Winchester disk drive, whose technology was developed at IBM in 1973. These disk drives have almost become necessities as additions to personal computers. Unlike the floppy disk drive, the Winchester disk drive has a sealed unit that contains the recording media (platter) and the recording heads. The platter is a rigid metal, circular disk coated with magnetic metal oxide on both sides. The magnetic material is often covered with a protective coating to insure against abrasions and dings to the surface. The platter rotates on a spindle at 3,600 RPM. Newer drives have rotation speeds of 4,800 RPM. In comparison, the floppy disk drive has a rotation speed of 360 RPM. On some units the spindle is directly connected to the motor and on others the spindle is connected to the motor via a drive belt.

Because the platter and heads make up a sealed unit that is permanently attached to the spindle, the Winchester disk drive is also called a non-removable disk drive. As in a floppy disk, the heads move radially across the spinning platter. Whereas the floppy disk drive heads are in contact with the recording media, the Winchester disk drive heads "fly" above the surface of the recording media at a height of less than 0.005

Drive Type	Number of Cylinders	Number of Heads	Pre-Compensation	Landing Zone	Number of Sectors	Approximate Capacity
1	306	4	128	305	17	10.1 Mbytes
2	615	4	300	615	17	20.4 Mbytes
3	615	6	300	615	17	30.6 Mbytes
4	940	8	512	940	17	62.4 Mbytes
5	940	6	512	940	17	46.8 Mbytes
6	615	4	−1	615	17	20.4 Mbytes
7	462	8	256	511	17	30.6 Mbytes
8	733	5	−1	733	17	30.4 Mbytes
9	900	15	−1	901	17	112.0 Mbytes
10	820	3	−1	820	17	20.4 Mbytes
11	855	5	−1	855	17	35.4 Mbytes
12	855	7	−1	855	17	49.6 Mbytes
13	306	8	128	319	17	20.3 Mbytes
14	733	7	−1	733	17	42.5 Mbytes
15	0	0	0	0	0	

Type 1:   IBM 5.25" 10Mb;   CMI 5412; MiniScribe 2012; Seagate ST412
Type 2:   IBM 5.25" 20Mb;   Seagate ST225, ST4026; CDC Wren II 94155-25, -28; MiniScribe 8438F
Type 3:   IBM 5.25" 30Mb;   Hitachi DK511-3
Type 4:   IBM 5.25" 62Mb
Type 5:   IBM 5.25" 46Mb
Type 6:   IBM 5.25" 20Mb;   MiniScribe MS 8425; Tandon TM 262; Tandon TM 702AT
Type 7:   IBM 5.25" 30Mb
Type 8:   IBM 5.25" 30Mb;   Seagate ST4038; CDC Wren II 9415-5-38; Tandon TM 703AT
Type 9:   IBM 5.25" 112Mb;   Priam IDED 130
Type 10: IBM 5.25" 20Mb;   Priam IDED 75, 100, 120, 150, 160, 230, 330; CDC 94155-48
Type 11: IBM 5.25" 35Mb;   Priam IDED 40, 45, 45H; Priam ID 45T-S, ID 45T-Q
Type 12: IBM 5.25" 49Mb
Type 13: IBM 5.25" 20Mb
Type 14: IBM 5.25" 42Mb

On some drives it may be necessary to disable connector J1, pin 2 when the drive is used on an AT.
On some drives it may be necessary to remove jumper W3.
Values for Write Pre-compensation of −1, 0, or the last track are assumed to be equivalent.

THE FOLLOWING ENTRIES MAY VARY.

Drive Type	Number of Cylinders	Number of Heads	Pre-Compensation	Landing Zone	Number of Sectors	Approximate Capacity
16	612	4	0	663	17	20 Mbytes
17	977	5	300	977	17	40 Mbytes
18	977	7	−1	977	17	56 Mbytes
19	1024	7	512	1023	17	60 Mbytes
20	733	5	300	732	17	30 Mbytes
21	733	7	300	733	17	42 Mbytes
22	733	5	300	733	17	30 Mbytes
23	306	4	0	336	17	10 Mbytes
24	925	7	0	925	17	53 Mbytes
25	925	9	0	925	17	70 Mbytes
26	754	7	0	754	17	43 Mbytes
27	754	11	0	754	17	68 Mbytes
28	699	7	0	699	17	40 Mbytes
29	823	10	0	823	17	68 Mbytes
30	918	7	0	918	17	53 Mbytes
31	1024	11	0	1024	17	93 Mbytes
32	1024	15	0	1024	17	127 Mbytes
33	1024	5	0	1024	17	42 Mbytes
34	612	2	0	611	17	10 Mbytes
35	1024	9	0	1024	17	76 Mbytes

Drive Type	Number of Cylinders	Number of Heads	Pre-Compensation	Landing Zone	Number of Sectors	Approximate Capacity
36	1024	8	0	1024	17	68 Mbytes
37	615	8	0	615	17	40 Mbytes
38	987	3	0	987	17	24 Mbytes
39	987	7	0	987	17	57 Mbytes
40	820	6	0	820	17	40 Mbytes
41	977	4	0	977	17	32 Mbytes
42	981	4	0	981	17	32 Mbytes
43	830	7	0	830	17	48 Mbytes
44	830	10	0	830	17	68 Mbytes
45	612	4	305	663	17	20 Mbytes
46	306	4	-1	340	17	10 Mbytes
47	612	4	-1	670	17	20 Mbytes
48	698	7	300	732	17	40 Mbytes
49	976	5	488	977	17	40 Mbytes
50	306	4	0	340	17	10 Mbytes
51	611	4	306	363	17	20 Mbytes
52	732	7	300	732	17	42 Mbytes
53	1023	5	-1	1023	17	42 Mbytes
54	306	2	-1	305	17	5 Mbytes
55	1024	8	512	1024	17	58 Mbytes

THE FOLLOWING ENTRIES MAY VARY. (For NEC 286 Plus)

Drive Type	Number of Cylinders	Number of Heads	Pre-Compensation	Landing Zone	Number of Sectors	Approximate Capacity
16	612	4	0	663	17	20.3 Mbytes
17	977	5	300	977	17	40.5 Mbytes
18	977	7	−1	977	17	56.7 Mbytes
19	1024	7	512	1023	17	59.5 Mbytes
20	733	5	300	732	17	30.4 Mbytes
21	733	7	300	732	17	42.5 Mbytes
22	733	5	300	733	17	30.4 Mbytes
23	306	4	0	336	17	10.1 Mbytes
24	286	16	−1	−1	63	140.7 Mbytes
25	980	5	−1	−1	17	40.7 Mbytes
26	805	4	−1	−1	26	40.9 Mbytes
27	1024	5	−1	1024	17	42.5 Mbytes
28	1024	8	−1	1024	17	68.0 Mbytes
29	615	4	−1	−1	17	20.4 Mbytes
30	776	8	−1	−1	33	100.0 Mbytes
31	823	6	−1	823	34	81.9 Mbytes
32	1020	15	−1	1024	17	127.0 Mbytes
33	611	16	−1	−1	63	300.7 Mbytes
34	823	10	−1	823	34	136.6 Mbytes
35	1024	9	1024	1024	17	76.5 Mbytes
36	1024	5	512	1024	17	42.5 Mbytes

Drive Type	Number of Cylinders	Number of Heads	Pre-Compensation	Landing Zone	Number of Sectors	Approximate Capacity
37	830	10	−1	830	17	68.8 Mbytes
38	214	16	−1	−1	63	105.3 Mbytes
39	615	4	128	664	17	20.4 Mbytes
40	615	8	128	664	17	40.8 Mbytes
41	745	2	−1	320	28	20.4 Mbytes
42	745	4	−1	−1	28	40.7 Mbytes
43	823	10	512	823	17	68.3 Mbytes
44	820	6	−1	820	17	40.8 Mbytes
45	642	8	256	664	17	42.6 Mbytes
46	925	9	−1	925	17	69.1 Mbytes
47	699	7	256	700	17	40.6 Mbytes

Type 14: Panasonic 3.5" 40Mb
Type 17: Seagate 3.5" ST151
Type 24: NEC 140 Mb
Type 38: NEC 100 Mb
Type 39: NEC 20 Mb
Type 40: NEC 40 Mb
Type 45: NEC 42 Mb

Source: NEC Information Systems, Inc., Boxborough, MA

THE FOLLOWING ENTRIES MAY VARY. (For American Megatrends 386)

Drive Type	Number of Cylinders	Number of Heads	Pre-Compensation	Landing Zone	Number of Sectors	Approximate Capacity
16	612	4	0	663	17	20.3 Mbytes
17	977	5	300	977	17	40.5 Mbytes
18	977	7	-1	977	17	56.8 Mbytes
20	733	5	300	732	17	30.4 Mbytes
21	733	7	300	732	17	42.6 Mbytes
22	733	5	300	733	17	30.4 Mbytes
23	306	4	0	336	17	10.2 Mbytes
24	925	7	0	925	17	53.7 Mbytes
25	925	9	-1	925	17	69.1 Mbytes
26	754	7	754	754	17	43.8 Mbytes
27	754	11	-1	754	17	68.8 Mbytes
28	699	7	256	699	17	40.6 Mbytes
29	823	10	-1	823	17	68.3 Mbytes
30	918	7	918	918	17	53.3 Mbytes
34	612	2	128	612	17	10.2 Mbytes
37	615	8	128	615	17	40.8 Mbytes
38	987	3	987	987	17	24.6 Mbytes
39	987	7	987	987	17	57.4 Mbytes
40	820	6	820	820	17	40.8 Mbytes
41	977	5	977	977	17	40.5 Mbytes
42	981	5	981	981	17	40.7 Mbytes
43	830	7	512	830	17	48.2 Mbytes
44	830	10	-1	830	17	68.9 Mbytes
45	917	15	-1	918	17	114.2 Mbytes
46	1224	15	-1	1223	17	152.4 Mbytes

inches. Winchester disk drives are available in platter diameters of 14 inches, 9 inches, 8 inches, 5.25 inches, 3.5 inches, and 2.5 inches. The most common diameter platters for personal computers are 5.25 inches and 3.5 inches. Capacities of Winchester disk drives currently range from 5 Megabytes to over 3,000 Megabytes (3 Gigabytes).

Because the tracks are closer together and the platters are spinning faster, the Winchester disk drive controllers utilize sophisticated error detection and correction techniques.

Because their heads are "flying" above the surface of the platters, the Winchester disk drives are particularly sensitive to contaminants such as dust, hair, and fingerprints, which can disturb the "flying" height and cause head crashes. Do *not*, under any circumstances, open the sealed units; this must be done only in a "clean room." Opening the sealed unit will void the warranty. The low "flying" height also makes the Winchester disk drive sensitive to physical shocks and jolts.

Under normal useage the mean time between failures (MTBF) of a typical Winchester disk drive is at least five years. A Winchester disk drive failure is unpredictable. Frequent backup of all programs and data is essential. Consult the DOS programs called "BACKUP" and "RESTORE." A more efficient backup program is available called "FASTBACK PLUS," manufactured by Fifth Generation Systems, 10049 North Reiger Road, Baton Rouge, LA 70809, telephone (800) 873-4384, FAX (804) 295-3268. The list price is $189.00.

Prior to each time a Winchester disk drive is powered down, its heads should be moved to a safe landing area. This process is called "parking" the disk drive. Some of the newer disk drives have circuitry built into the drive to automatically park the heads on power down without operator intervention.

There are five popular interface/encoding systems in use today for writing the data on the Winchester disk drive. These are MFM (Modified Frequency Modulation), SCSI (Small Computer Systems Interface), RLL(2,7) (Run Length Limited), ESDI (Enhanced Small Device Interface), and IDE (Integrated Drive Electronics). Each disk drive must be run with the encoding system for which it was designed. Though MFM and RLL(2,7) have just a few minor differences (extra amplifier in disk drive controller circuit) an MFM drive will not necessarily run under RLL(2,7). Operation of an MFM drive with an RLL(2,7) controller will void the warranty.

MFM encoding places 17 sectors on each track and RLL(2,7) encoding places 26 sectors on each track, so an RLL(2,7) disk drive with the same number of heads and cylinders will hold about 50% more data. The SCSI interface works with the RLL(2,7) recording method and generally will have an internal transfer rate of 7.5 Megabytes per second. The ESDI interface works with the RLL(2,7) recording method, places 36 sectors on each track, and has an internal transfer rate of 10 Megabytes per second. An MFM-encoded Winchester disk drive with an ST506/ST412 interface has an internal transfer rate of 5.0 Megabytes per second.

The MFM interface (ST506/ST412) is the most common. To connect the disk drive to its controller there are two cables—a 34-pin cable for drive control and a 20-pin cable for data. The control cable is "daisy chained" from one drive to the next (serially linked together) while each drive has a separate cable run from the controller to the drive for its data. When two drives are "daisy chained" together only the last drive in the chain must have a terminating resistor. The terminating resistor in the first drive in the chain must be removed.

Regardless of the size of your first Winchester disk drive, you will always want a larger one. Before rushing out to replace your first disk drive or add a second disk drive there are a few things you should do.

1.   Delete all old .BAK, .OLD, .TMP, .BK!, etc. files or transfer them to floppy disk.
2.   Delete all old program files or transfer them to floppy disk.
3.   Delete runtime Windows.
4.   Archive all seldomly used files.
5.   Pack databases.
6.   Defragment the Winchester disk drive.
7.   Store programs and data on the network server, if you have one.

You will be amazed at how much room you have freed up. This process should probably be performed once a month.

THE SECOND HARD DISK DRIVE

When you have finally decided to add a second disk drive there are some important points to consider.

1.   Is there adequate capacity in the power supply?
2.   Can your controller support a second disk drive?
3.   Do you need new cables?
4.   Do you need a "Y" cable for power?
5.   Do you have a copy of "DISK MANAGER"?
6.   Do you have a copy of "SpinRite II"?
7.   Have you planned the mounting of the new drive?
8.   Are you going to buy a new or a reconditioned disk drive?
9.   Have you planned the partitioning?
10.   Do you know the new drive's type number?

These questions should be answered before you spend your first dollar on a second disk drive.

The interface and encoding of the second drive must match the first drive. Often it is advisable that both drives have the same model number, but this is not required. Check the Model Number Table. Perhaps you want to replace your controller with a new one at this time and obtain two new drives. Be sure the new controller matches your computer bus (XT, AT, MCA) (i.e., 8-bit bus or 16-bit bus).

As a special note, XT controllers have their own BIOS and these controllers may be installed in XT, AT, and 386 computers. If a BIOS is included on the controller card you must answer "0" to the number of installed hard drives in Step 2, below. With ATs, the tables listed previously contain the hard disk specifications so that a BIOS on the controller card is not necessary. Run the BASIC program supplied to get the Drive Number Table in your AT.

If you are adding a second drive for the first time, you might want the company of an acquaintance who has performed this operation before. The process is not complicated and should take no more than one hour (with the exception of running the quality verification check on the drive for at least 24 hours). Do not be upset if your new disk drive has a number of defective tracks. On a Seagate ST251 or ST252 (42.8 Megabytes per drive, formatted capacity), the manufacturer states there will be no more than forty-two (42) defects total per drive. Cylinders 0, 1, and 2 are defect-free.

Once you have all your ducks in a row (all the pieces gathered together), be sure the power to your computer system is off and disconnected from the wall. Disassemble the computer as described in Chapter 13 under the instructions for replacing the power supply.

Once you have installed the new disk drive and the cables, reassemble the computer. Don't forget to connect the LED on the front panel, which indicates hard disk access. If it doesn't light during checkout, try reversing the LED connector. The LED cannot be damaged if it is connected backwards. Check your work carefully.

Supply power to the computer and boot up DOS on the original drive. Now is the time for "DISK MANAGER" from ONTRACK Computer Systems, Inc., 6321 Bury Drive, Suite 15-19, Eden Prairie, MN 55346, telephone (800) 752-1333 or (612) 937-1107, FAX (612) 937-5815. The procedure is as follows:

1. Perform the low-level format on your new drive using "DISK MANAGER". You must know the drive type number.
2. Using either "SETUP" (if your computer has such a program) or "FDISK" (from DOS), partition the new disk drive. If the new disk drive is bigger than 32 Megabytes and you are running a version of

DOS prior to 3.3 you must install "DMDRIVER.BIN", which comes with "DISK MANAGER". Remember, with some exceptions (NEC computers and others) DOS Version 3.3 does not allow partitions greater than 32 Megabytes. DOS Version 4.01 fixes this.

3. After being certain that you have the correct drive letter for your new disk drive, format the new disk drive using "FORMAT" or "PC TOOLS".
4. Run "SpinRite II" on the new drive to test its data handling and reliability for 24 hours.
5. Make your directories. Install your software, and you're on your way.

Now, that wasn't difficult, was it? If you get into trouble the suppliers who sold you the drive (see Appendix A), the drive manufacturer, and the controller manufacturer all have technical support telephone lines. Seagate Technology's telephone number for technical support is (800) 468-3472.

CONTROLLERS FOR HARD DRIVES AND FLOPPIES

The controller interface *must* match the drive interface because the selection of controller and drive go hand in hand. The choices are MFM (ST506/412), ESDI, SCSI, RLL, or AT (IDE). In addition, you must have information about the slot available in the computer (i.e., is it for an 8-bit bus or for a 16-bit bus?). If you select an XT-type (8-bit bus) controller, there is a BIOS for the hard disk on the controller card. If there is a slot available in your computer for a 16-bit controller, make that selection in preference to an 8-bit controller. The 16-bit controllers transfer data faster across the computer bus than 8-bit controllers.

ST-506 GENERAL INFORMATION

A disk controller provides the interconnection path between the disk drive and its host computer. The disk controller facilitates the flow of commands, status, and data between the PC bus (described in Chapter 12) and the disk drive interface. The most commonly used interface to a Winchester disk drive is the ST-506, MFM interface.

The ST-506 interface was originally developed by Shugart Corporation for their floppy disk drives and has been popularized for use on Winchester disk drives by the Seagate Corporation. The interface specification imposes a fixed data transfer rate, MFM data encoding, a specific written format on the disk media, and a specified signal/connector arrangement. Implementation of the ST-506 interface is straightforward, moderate in cost, and provides an intermediate level of performance.

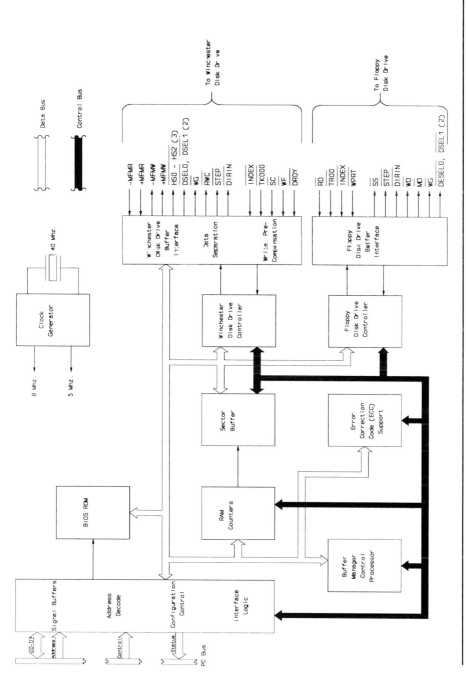

Block diagram of a typical floppy/Winchester disk controller.

87

Manufacturer	Model No.	Format	BUS	Use	BIOS	Interleave	Price
Adaptec	ADA1520	SCSI	16-bit	2HD/2FD			$129
Adaptec	ADA1542	SCSI	16-bit	2HD/2FD			$319
Adaptec	ADA2372	RLL	16-bit			1:1	$149
Adaptec	ACB-2322B8	ESDI				1:1	$295
Adaptec	ACB-2322D	ESDI					$225
Always Technology	AT2000	SCSI	16-bit	HD/FD	NOVELL		$189
AMS	1100 SM4	MFM		2HD/4FD			$87
AMS	1100 SR4	RLL		2HD/4FD			$96
DataStor	DS208	ESDI		HD/FD	(8K)		$169
DataStor	DS264	ESDI		HD/FD	(64K)		$189
Data Technology	DTC3150	SCSI		HD			$95
Data Technology	DTC3250	SCSI	8-bit	HD/FD			$112
Data Technology	DTC3280	SCSI		HD/FD			$165
Data Technology	DTC5150CRH	MFM	8-bit	HD	Yes		$49
Data Technology	DTC5160CRH	RLL	8-bit	HD	Yes		$56
Data Technology	DTC5280(-2)	MFM		HD/FD			
Data Technology	DTC6180	ESDI	16-bit	2HD		1:1	$120
Data Technology	DTC6280	ESDI	16-bit	2HD/2FD		1:1	$139
Data Technology	DTC6280-15T	ESDI	16-bit	HD/FD			$170
Data Technology	DTC7187	RLL	16-bit	2HD		1:1	$100
Data Technology	DTC7287	RLL	16-bit	2HD/2FD		1:1	$109
Data Technology	DTC7180	MFM	16-bit	2HD		1:1	$79
Data Technology	DTC7280	MFM	16-bit	2HD/2FD		1:1	$89
Future Domain	TMC-850	SCSI	8-bit				$79
Future Domain	TMC-860DNK	SCSI	16-bit	HD			$265
Future Domain	TMC-875	SCSI	8-bit	HD/FD			$119
Future Domain	TMC-885	SCSI	16-bit	HD/FD			$139
Future Domain	TMC-1660	SCSI-2	16-bit	HD			$149

Manufacturer	Model No.	Format	BUS	Use	BIOS	Interleave	Price
Future Domain	TMC-1680	SCSI-2	16-bit	HD/FD			$179
Future Domain	MCS350	SCSI	MCR				$209
Future Domain	MCS700	SCSI-2	MCR				$269
Longshine	LCS6210	MFM	8-bit	2HD			$48
Longshine	LCS6220		8-bit	2HD/2FD			$79
Longshine	LCS6622	MFM	16-bit	HD/FD		1:1	$79
Morse Technology	KP3000	MFM	16-bit	HD/FD		1:1	$65
Perstor	PS180-16F		16-bit	2HD/2FD			$205
Procomp USA	MDCBISA	SCSI		16HD	(16K)		$349
Seagate	ST11M	MFM	8-bit	2HD	Yes		$44
Seagate	ST11R	RLL	8-bit	2HD	Yes	3:1	$45
Seagate	ST01	SCSI	8-bit	2HD	Yes	3:1	$29
Seagate	ST02	SCSI	8-bit	2HD/2FD	Yes	3:1	$58
Seagate	ST05X	SCSI	8-bit	2HD	Yes		$29
Seagate	ST07A	AT	16-bit	2HD			$58
Seagate	ST08A	AT	16-bit	2HD/2FD			$65
Seagate	ST21R	RLL	16-bit	2HD	Yes	1:1	$55
Seagate	ST21M	MFM	16-bit	2HD/2FD	Yes	1:1	$75
Seagate	ST22R	RLL	16-bit	2HD/2FD	Yes	1:1	$65
Seagate	ST22M	MFM	16-bit	2HD/2FD	Yes	1:1	$219
UltraStor	ULTRA-12F	ESDI	16-bit	HD/FD	(32K)	1:1	$47
Western Digital	XT-GEN2	MFM	8-bit	2HD		3:1	$52
Western Digital	WD4A-27X	RLL	8-bit	2HD			$55
Western Digital	WD-27X	RLL	8-bit	2HD			$88
Western Digital	WD-MM1	MFM	16-bit	2HD			$101
Western Digital	WD-MM2	MFM	16-bit	2HD/2FD			$98
Western Digital	WD-MM1-6	MFM	16-bit	2HD		1:1	$108
Western Digital	WD-MM2-6	MFM	16-bit	2HD/2FD		1:1	

Manufacturer	Model No.	Format	BUS	Use	BIOS	Interleave	Price
Western Digital	WD-SR1	RLL	16-bit	2HD			$102
Western Digital	WD-SR2	RLL	16-bit	2HD/2FD			$111
Western Digital	WD-SR1-6	RLL	16-bit	2HD		1:1	$109
Western Digital	WD-SR2-6	RLL	16-bit	2HD/2FD		1:1	$123
Western Digital	WD7-WAH	ESDI	16-bit	2HD		1:1	$155
Western Digital	WD1003V-MM1	MFM	16-bit	2HD		2:1	$73
Western Digital	WD1003V-MM2	MFM	16-bit	2HD/2FD		2:1	$76
Western Digital	WD1003V-SR1	RLL	16-bit	2HD		2:1	$83
Western Digital	WD1003V-SR2	RLL	16-bit	2HD/2FD		2:1	$86
Western Digital	WD1004-A27X	RLL	8-bit	2HD		3:1	$45
Western Digital	WD1006V-MM1	MFM	16-bit	2HD		1:1	$84
Western Digital	WD1006V-MM2	MFM	16-bit	2HD/2FD		1:1	$89
Western Digital	WD1006V-MM2	MFM	16-bit		(8K)	1:1	$125
Western Digital	WD1006V-SR1	RLL	16-bit	2HD		1:1	$82
Western Digital	WD1006V-SR2	RLL	16-bit	2HD/2FD		1:1	$99
Western Digital	WD1006-MC1	MFM	MCR				$269
Western Digital	WD1007-MC1	ESDI	MCR				$279
Western Digital	WD1007-WAH	ESDI	16-bit	2HD			$255
Western Digital	WD1007-WA2	ESDI	16-bit	2HD/2FD		1:1	$295
Western Digital	WD1007A	ESDI	16-bit	2HD/2FD		1:1	$189
Western Digital	WD1007V-SE1	ESDI	16-bit	2HD	(32K)	1:1	$169
Western Digital	WD1007V-SE2	ESDI	16-bit	2HD/2FD	(32K)	1:1	$179
Western Digital	WD7000FASST	SCSI	16-bit	2HD/2FD		1:1	$299
Western Digital	WDMC1-7	MCR	16-bit	2HD			$319
Western Digital	WDAT140	AT	HD				$29
Western Digital	WDAT240	AT	HD	HD/FD			$40

Sources: Seagate Technology, Inc., Scotts Valley, CA 95066, Western Digital Corp. Irvine, CA 92718

The ST-506 serial data rate at the interface to the disk drive is set at 5 Megabits per second when the disk platters are spinning at 3,600 RPM and a track contains 10,416 bytes (or 83,328 bits) of data. Do not confuse this number (10,416 bytes) with the number of *data bytes* per track (8,704 = 512 × 17). At 3,600 RPM (60 revolutions per second) and 83,328 bits per revolution you end up with 4,999,680 bits per second. For the ST-506 interface, a disk drive like the Seagate ST-225, with 615 cylinders, 4 heads, and 10,416 bytes per track, will have a capacity of approximately 25,623,360 bytes, unformatted or 21.4 Megabytes, formatted.

The serial data rate at the interface is fixed at 5,000,000 bits per second. If more than 83,328 bits were stored on a track it would be necessary to slow down the rotation speed of the drive to keep the serial data rate at a constant 5,000,000 bits per second. Similarly, if less than 83,328 bits were stored on a track it would be necessary to speed up the rotation speed of the drive to maintain the constant serial data rate. Therefore, to increase the storage capacity of an ST-506 type disk drive more tracks are added by either increasing the number of tracks per surface or by increasing the number of recording surfaces.

The ST-506 Interface requires that the serial data transmitted between the disk drive and the controller be MFM (Modified Frequency Modulation) encoded. MFM encoding is derived from FM encoding, the original method of combining clock and data information into a single serial bit stream. When constructing an FM encoded signal, the data stream of "1's" and "0's" is divided into bit cells, each cell containing a single bit. At the starting boundry of each bit cell there is a clock bit which is the same frequency as the data to be encoded. If the bit cell contains a binary "1", an extra pulse (or bit) is inserted into the center of the bit cell. If the bit cell contains a binary "0", no transition occurs in the center of the bit cell. By observing the bit stream that results from FM encoding we see that a long stream of binary "1's" will produce a waveform that is double the frequency of the clock frequency, hence the term for FM encoding is "double frequency encoding".

MFM encoding also utilizes a Write Clock which is the same frequency as the serial data. The Write Clock is combined with the data, as in FM encoding, so that a single serial bit stream is transmitted. However, in MFM encoding the rules for producing the serial bit stream are different than those for producing the serial bit stream in FM recording. If the bit cell contains a binary "1", a pulse (or bit) is written into the center of the bit cell. If the bit cell contains a binary "0", and the previous bit cell also contains a binary "0", a clock pulse (or bit) is written into the leading portion of the bit cell. It follows that if the bit cell contains a binary "0" and the previous bit cell contains a binary "1", nothing is written into that bit cell. It may be observed from the diagram that MFM recording transmits the same amount of data but the data stream flowing down the cable is at half the frequency of that produced by FM recording. Synchronization fields composed of strings of binary "0's" are added to the data stream and they produce a series of bits in the clock position of the data stream.

The MFM is decoded into a data stream of binary "1's" and "0's" using either a phase locked loop circuit or a digital delay (one-shot) circuit. The MFM Read Clock need not be synchronized with the MFM Write Clock. Data is written (and also read) with the most significant bit (MSB) first.

Prior to utilizing the disk drive for the recording of data, the magnetic media must be written with the *format*. The *format* serves to partition the magnetic media into sectors so that the data may be reliably recorded and read. A sector of data on a track is the smallest set of recorded bits which may be accessed by the disk controller. The sector typically contains a synchronization field, an identification field, a data field, and a buffer field. Formatting the disk drive is a function of the controller and will usually destroy all the data stored on the magnetic surface of the platters.

Formatting divides each sector into the following:

   a.   Synchronization (00H)
   b.   Identification (ID)
   c.   Write Splice Gap
   d.   Data
   e.   Post Data Field Gap

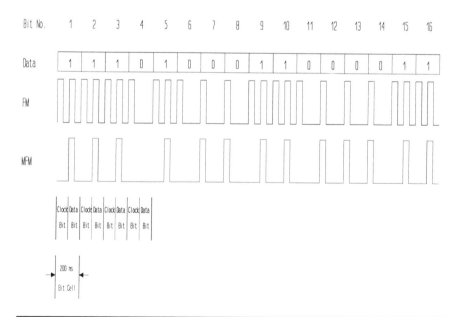

FM and MFM serial data encoding.

In addition, the Index Gap (GAP 1) and Track Buffer GAP (GAP 4) occur once per revolution (per track).

The Index Gap, GAP 1, occurs each time the platter makes a full revolution and consists of 22 bytes of 4EH. The occurrence of the Index Gap is timed from the Index indicator on the disk drive. The Index Gap is used to compensate for variations in the index pulse timing which occur because of motor speed variations. The Index Gap also allows a small delay time during which a choice of disk drive heads may be made without missing a sector and causing a wait of a full rotation of the disk. In this manner, data transfer is optimized when the last sector of a track has been read and the next logical sector in the file occurs on another platter.

7

Memory Maps

Typical Memory Map

Hex Address Range	Size	Use
00000–9FFFF	640K	System Dynamic RAM
00000–001DF	480_{10}	Interrupt Vectors
001E0–002FF	288_{10}	User Vectors
00300–003FF	256_{10}	BIOS Stack/User Vectors
00400–004FF	256_{10}	BIOS Data
00500–005FF	256_{10}	DOS and BASIC Use
00600–9FFFF	638K	User RAM
A0000–BFFFF	128K	Video Buffer RAM Area
A0000–BFFFF	128K	EGA/VGA Video Buffer
B0000–B7FFF	32K	MDA Video Buffer
B8000–BFFFF	32K	CGA Video Buffer
C0000–DFFFF	128K	ROM Expansion Area
C0000–C3FFF	16K	EGA BIOS
C6000–C63FF	1K	PGA Communication Area
C8000–CBFFF	16K	XT Hard Disk BIOS
D0000–D7FFF	32K	Cluster Adapter BIOS
E0000–EFFFF	64K	ROM Expansion (XT) BIOS Expansion (AT)
F0000–FFFFF	64K	ROM BIOS and Diagnostics
100000–FDFFFF	14.9 MBytes	AT Extended RAM
FE0000–FFFFFF	128K	AT ROM BIOS Area

95

Detailed Memory Map For A PC Using DOS Version 2.1 With No CONFIG.SYS and No AUTOEXEC.BAT and 384K RAM

Hex Address Range	Approximate Size	Use
00000–003FF	1K	8088 Vectors INT 0-7
		8259 Vectors INT 8-F
		BIOS Vectors INT 10-1F
		DOS Vectors INT 20-2F
		Assignable INT 40-FF
00400–004FF	256	ROM BIOS Communications Area
00500–006FF	512	DOS Data Area
00700–00E2F	1.8K	IBMBIO
00E30–04DB9	16K	IBMDOS
04DBA–053F0	2K	Device Drivers
		ANSI.SYS
		CONFIG.SYS
		Extensions of IBMBIO
		User Buffers
		Files
05F3F1–05FD0	3K	Resident COMMAND
05FD1–06080	160	Master Environment for COMMAND
06081–060B0	160	Environment For Next Program
060B1–1C000	80K	BASIC Extensions
		Advanced BASIC
		BASIC Workspace
		Communications Buffers
		RS-232 Routines
		File Control Blocks
		File Random Buffers
		BASIC Program Text
		Scalars
		Arrays
		Strings
		Stack
1C001–1FFFF	16K	Video Buffer In 128K PCjr
20000–9FFFF	up to 524K	Unused and Available To Top Of Expansion RAM
		At Top Of Expansion RAM
		Transient COMMAND
		Error Messages
		Internal Command Table
		Last Command Text
		Length of Last Command
		Formatted File Specification

Hex Address Range	Approximate Size	Use
A0000–AFFFF	64K	Reserved For Future Video Buffers
B0000–B0FFF	4K	Monochrome Video Buffer
B1000–B7FFF	24K	Reserved For Future Video Buffers
B8000–BBFFF	16K	Color Video Buffer(s)
BC000–BFFFF	16K	Reserved For Future Video Buffers
C0000–C7FFF	32K	ROM Expansion or Cartridge on PCjr
C8000–CFFFF	32K	Hard Disk ROM on XT or Cartridge on PCjr
D0000–D7FFF	32K	ROM Expansion or Cartridge on PCjr
D8000–DFFFF	32K	ROM Expansion or Cartridge on PCjr
E0000–E7FFF	32K	ROM Expansion or Cartridge on PCjr
E8000–EFFFF	32K	ROM Expansion or BASIC Cartridge on PCjr
F0000–F5FFF	24K	ROM Expansion or POST on PCjr
F6000–FDFFF	32K	Cassette BASIC or Cartridge on PCjr
FE000–FFFFF	8K	ROM BIOS or Cartridge on PCjr

FORMING THE MEMORY ADDRESS

The 8086 microprocessor is a 16-bit CPU. Data is handled at the integrated circuit level on pins connected to a multiplexed address bus/data bus. The 8086 sends and/or receives the data in 16-bit units, treated as a low-order byte and a high-order byte.

Because the 8086 CPU can actually directly address one million bytes (1 Megabyte) of memory, twenty (20) bits of address information are necessary. Addresses are handled at the integrated circuit level on pins connected to the multiplexed address bus/data bus for the lowest 16 bits of the address and on four pins multiplexed with the status information for the 4 most significant bits of the address. The address pins are labeled AD0 to AD15 and A16/S3, A17/S4, A18/S5, and A19/S6.

During the first clock period of a bus cycle, lines AD0 to AD15 hold the 16 low-order address bits. During all other clock cycles, these lines are used as the data bus. These lines are placed in the high-impedance state when the 8086 is performing an "interrupt acknowledge" cycle or a "hold acknowledge" cycle. During the first clock period of a bus cycle, lines A16/S3, A17/S4, A18/S5, and A19/S6 serve as address lines 16, 17, 18, and 19 respectively. If an I/O instruction is performed, these lines are low during the first clock period.

During all other clock periods but the first, lines A16/S3 and A17/S4 are utilized to specify which segment register is producing the segment portion of the 8086 address in accordance with the following table:

A17/S4	A16/S3	Interpretation
0	0	Extra Segment
0	1	Stack Segment
1	0	Code Segment or No Segment
1	1	Data Segment

During all other clock periods except the first, line A18/S5 indicates the state of the 8086's interrupt enable flag. During all other clock periods except the first, line A19/S6 is held low by the 8086 if it is controlling the system bus. During a "hold acknowledge" clock period the 8086 will cause this line to float, thus allowing another bus master to obtain control of the system bus.

As we have seen, the registers in the CPU are only 16 bits wide, and in particular the instruction pointer (IP) is also only 16 bits wide. This means that only $2^{16} = 65,536$ different memory locations can be accessed by the instruction pointer register. How then does the PC address a megabyte of memory?

The answer is that whenever the CPU sends out a memory address, it is always a 20-bit address formed from the sum of a segment register and one of the other registers (or in some cases a 16-bit address obtained from an instruction or memory). The sum is formed by shifting the segment register 4 bits to the left and then adding the shifted contents to the other register. The formation of the 20-bit address is performed automatically by the hardware and is not under control of the programmer. Such addresses are written CS:IP and the DEBUG program displays all addresses in this manner. If a microprocessor had 32-bit wide internal registers, larger memory would be directly addressable but it would take more room to store the code.

Remember, IP is always added to CS and SP is always added to SS. BP is added to SS and all other registers are added to DS but these segment register assignments can be changed with a segment register override prefix. An exception to the above is that DI is always added to ES for string primitive instructions.

Therefore, each segment register can point to a 64 Kbyte block of memory (called a segment). The 64 Kilobyte segment can begin at any address that is a multiple of 16 (because of the 4-bit shift to the left used to form the 20-bit address). The memory segments pointed to by the CS, DS, SS, and ES registers can fully or partially overlap, or the segments may be in completely different areas of memory. There are no restrictions to segment locations.

Most of the time the existence of segment registers may be ignored as the operating system initializes the segment register values for you when your program is loaded into memory for execution. Therefore, unless the program and data are greater than 64 Kilobytes in size all the addresses can be thought of as being 16 bits long and the segment registers will simply provide a fixed offset into the memory address space. In this manner whatever is stored below the user area in memory (such as the operating system) does not change the program's 16-bit addresses, it just changes the segment registers.

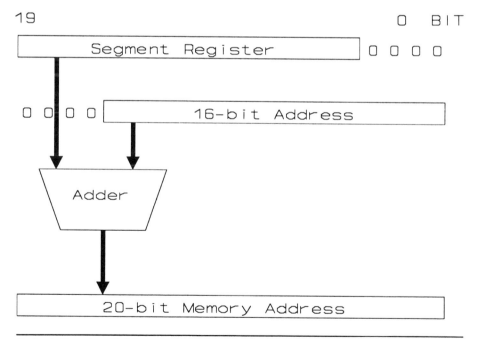

Calculating the 20-bit memory address.

For example, if the segment register is 1111h and the address is 4444h then:

$$11110$$
$$+ \quad 04444$$

15554h is the 20-bit memory address

ADDING MEMORY BEYOND 640K

There are three kinds of memory available beyond 640K. The time to think about adding memory to your CPU is long before a message stating "INSUFFICIENT MEMORY" appears on your screen.

1. **3.x Expanded Memory**   3.x Expanded Memory is used for data storage as originally proposed by Lotus, Intel, and Microsoft. It is non-linear memory beyond 1 Megabyte that is accessible on a revolving basis in blocks made available by an Expanded Memory Manager (EMM).
2. **4.x Expanded Memory**   Can do all that 3.x Expanded Memory will do. In addition, 4.x can run full-sized programs. 4.x can also provide multitasking and one or more operating environments.
3. **Extended Memory**   Extended Memory is directly accessible memory at addresses 640K to 1 Megabyte and above 1 Megabyte. It is accessible and directly usable only with 80286 and higher processors; it may also be used to emulate expanded memory.

To diverge briefly, the price today of a 256 Kbit, 100-nanosecond memory chip is about $2.00. This works out to $8/megabit, or $64/megabyte for the memory integrated circuits (chips) alone, that is, not counting the support circuitry to build a memory. For a gigabyte memory (that is, 32,000 256 Kbit chips) we have to come up with $64,000 plus. As the 80386 will support 4 Gigabytes, to buy all those 128,000 integrated circuits will cost $256,000. Adding power supplies, error detection and correction circuitry, drivers, and printed circuit board mounting takes care of this week's allowance. From the above it is clear to see that the hard drive will be with us for at least a few more years.

Before rushing out to purchase more memory for your CPU, you should be sure that the memory you have is being used efficiently. In order to free up the largest space possible below 640K so that your application programs will fit, a utility is provided in DOS Version 4.0 and above that will assist in mapping your memory. It is called MEM.COM. Typing MEM, MEM/PROGRAM, or MEM/DEBUG will provide much useful information on what is stored in your CPU memory. You should try to move everything possible to locations above 640K, remembering that no two programs can occupy the same address space at the same time. The moving of programs to locations above 640K works on all the processors from the 8088 to the 80486.

AT CMOS MEMORY

Real-Time Clock/Complementary Metal Oxide Semiconductor (RT/CMOS) RAM

The RT/CMOS RAM integrated circuit (Motorola MC 146818) contains the real-time clock and 64 bytes of CMOS RAM. The internal clock circuitry uses 14 bytes of this RAM, and the rest is allocated to configuration information.

Writing to CMOS RAM involves two steps:

1. OUT to port 70, hexadecimal, with the CMOS address that will be written to.
2. OUT to port 71, hexadecimal, with the data to be written.

Reading CMOS RAM also requires two steps:

1. OUT to port 70, hexadecimal, with the CMOS address that is to be read from.
2. IN from port 71, hexadecimal, and the data read is returned in the AL register.

CMOS RAM Address Map

Addresses	Description
00–0D	Real-Time Clock information*
0E	Diagnostic Status byte*
0F	Shutdown Status byte*
10	Diskette Drive Type byte—drives A and B
11	Reserved
12	Fixed Disk Type byte—drives C and D
13	Reserved
14	Equipment byte
15	Low Base Memory byte
16	High Base Memory byte
17	Low Expansion Memory byte
18	High Expansion Memory byte
19–2D	Reserved
2E–2F	2-byte CMOS Checksum
30	Low Expansion Memory byte*

Addresses	Description
31	High Expansion Memory byte*
32	Date Century byte*
33	Information flags (set during power on)*
34–3F	Reserved

*These bytes are not included in the checksum calculation and are not part of the configuration record.

The following describes the real-time bytes and specifies their addresses:

Byte	Function	Address
0	Seconds	00
1	Second Alarm	01
2	Minutes	02
3	Minute Alarm	03
4	Hours	04
5	Hour Alarm	05
6	Day Of Week	06
7	Day Of Month	07
8	Month	08
9	Year	09
10	Status Register A	0A
11	Status Register B	0B
12	Status Register C	0C
13	Status Register D	0D

The Setup Program initializes registers A, B, C, and D when the time and date are set. Interrupt 1A is the BIOS's interface to read/set the time and date. It initializes the status bytes the same as the Setup Program.

Status Register A

Bit 7	Update In Progress (UIP)—A "1" indicates the time update cycle is in progress. A "0" indicates the current date and time is available to be read.
Bit 6–Bit 4	22-Stage Divider (DV2 through DV0)—These three divider-selection bits identify which time-base frequency is being used. The system initializes the stage divider to 010, which selects a 32.768 kHz time base.

Bit 3–Bit 0	Rate Selection Bits (RS3 through RS0)—These bits allow the selection of a divider output frequency. The system initializes the rate selection bits to 0110, which selects a 1.024 kHz square wave output frequency and a 976.562 microsecond periodic interrupt rate.

Status Register B

Bit 7	Set—A "0" updates the cycle normally by advancing the counts at one-per-second. A "1" aborts any update cycle in progress and the program can initialize the 14 time-bytes without any further updates occurring until a "0" is written to this bit.
Bit 6	Periodic Interrupt Enable (PIE)—This bit is a read/write bit that allows an interrupt to occur at a rate specified by the rate and divider bits in register A. A "1" enables an interrupt, and a "0" disables it. The system initializes this bit to "0".
Bit 5	Alarm Interrupt Enable (AIE)—A "1" enables the alarm interrupt, and a "0" disables it. The system initializes this bit to "0".
Bit 4	Update-Ended Interrupt Enabled (UIE)—A "1" enables the update-ended interrupt, and a "0" disables it. The system initializes this bit to "0".
Bit 3	Square Wave Enabled (SQWE)—A "1" enables the square-wave frequency as set by the rate selection bits in register A, and a "0" disables the square wave. The system initializes this bit to "0".
Bit 2	Data Mode (DM)—This bit indicates whether the time and date calendar updates are to use binary or binary-coded-decimal (BCD) formats. A "1" indicates binary, and a "0" indicates BCD. The system initializes this bit to "0".
Bit 1	24 / 12—This bit establishes whether the hours byte is in the 24-hour or the 12-hour mode. A "1" indicates the 24-hour mode and a "0" indicates the 12-hour mode. The system initializes this bit to "1".
Bit 0	Daylight Savings Enabled (DSE)—A "1" enables daylight savings and a "0" disables daylight savings (standard time). The system enables this bit to "0".

Status Register C

Bit 7–Bit 4   IRQF, PF, AF, UF—These flag bits are read only and are affected when the "AIE", "PIE", and "UIE" interrupts are enabled in register B.

Bit 3–Bit 0   Reserved

CMOS RAM Configuration

The following shows the bit definition for the CMOS configuration bytes (addresses 0E–3F).

Diagnostic Status Byte (0E hexadecimal)

Bit 7   Real-time clock chip has lost power. A "0" indicates that the chip has not lost power and a "1" indicates that the chip has lost power.

Bit 6   Configuration Record—Checksum Status Indicator—A "0" indicates that the checksum is good, and a "1" indicates that it is bad.

Bit 5   Incorrect Configuration Information—This is a check, at power on time, of the equipment byte of the configuration record. A "0" indicates that the configuration information is valid, and a "1" indicates it is invalid. Power-on checks require:

                                    a.   At least one diskette drive to be installed (Bit 0 of the equipment byte set to "1").

                                    b.   The primary display adapter setting in the configuration matches the system board's display switch setting and the actual display hardware in the system.

Bit 4   Memory Size Miscompare—A "0" indicates that the power-on check determined the same memory size as in the configuration record and a "1" indicates that the memory size is different.

Bit 3   Fixed Disk Adapter/Drive C Initialization Status—A "0" indicates that the adapter and drive are functioning properly and the system can attempt "boot-up". A "1" indicates that the adapter and/or drive C failed initialization, which prevents the system from attempting to "boot-up".

Bit 2   Time Status Indicator—(POST validity check) A
                         "0" indicates that the time is valid and a "1"
                         indicates that the time is invalid.

Bit 1–Bit 0   Reserved

Shutdown Status Byte (0F hexadecimal)

The bits in this byte are defined by the power on diagnostics. For more
information about this byte, see the BIOS listing.

Diskette Drive Type Byte (10 hexadecimal)

Bit 7–Bit 4   Type of first diskette drive installed:
                         0000   No drive is present.
                         0001   Double Sided Diskette Drive (48
                                     TPI)
                         0010   High Capacity Diskette Drive (96
                                     TPI)
                         0011–1111   are reserved

Bit 3–Bit 0   Type of second diskette drive installed:
                         0000   No drive is present.
                         0001   Double Sided Diskette Drive (48
                                     TPI)
                         0010   High Capacity Diskette Drivre (96
                                     TPI)
                         0011–1111   are reserved

Hexadecimal address 11 contains a reserved byte.

Fixed Disk Type Byte (12 hexadecimal)

Bit 7–Bit 4   Defines the type of first fixed disk drive installed
                         (drive C:)
                         0000   No fixed disk drive is
                                          present.
                         0001 through 1111   define type 1 through type
                                             15. (See BIOS listing at
                                             label FD_TBL and Chap-
                                             ter 6)

Bit 3–Bit 0   Defines the type of second fixed disk drive in-
                         stalled (drive D:)
                         0000   No fixed disk drive is
                                          present.

0001 through 1111 define type 1 through type 15. (See BIOS listing at label FD_TBL and Chapter 6)

Hexadecimal address 13 contains a reserved byte.

Equipment Byte (14 hexadecimal)

The equipment byte defines the basic equipment in the system for the power-on diagnostics.

Bit 7–Bit 6	Indicates the number of diskette drives installed	
	00	1 drive
	01	2 drives
	10	Reserved
	11	Reserved
Bit 5–Bit 4	Primary display	
	00	Reserved
	01	Primary display is attached to the Color/Graphics Monitor Adapter in the 40-column mode.
	10	Primary display is attached to the Color/Graphics Monitor Adapter in the 80-column mode.
	11	Primary display is attached to the Monochrome Display and Printer Adapter.
Bit 3–Bit 2	Not used	
Bit 1	Mathematics Coprocessor presence bit	
	0	Mathematics Coprocessor not installed
	1	Mathematics Coprocessor installed
Bit 0	The set condition of this bit indicates that diskette drives are installed.	

Low and High Base Memory Bytes (15 and 16 hexadecimal)

Bit 7–Bit 0	Address hexadecimal 15—Low-byte base size	
Bit 7–Bit 0	Address hexadecimal 16—High-byte base size	
	Valid sizes:	
	0100h	256 Kbyte System Board RAM

0200h	512 Kbyte System Board RAM
0280h	640 Kbyte. 512 Kbyte System Board RAM and the IBM Personal Computer AT 128 Kbyte Memory Expansion Option

Low and High Memory Expansion Bytes (17 and 18 hexadecimal)

Bit 7–Bit 0   Address hexadecimal 17—Low-byte expansion size

Bit 7–Bit 0   Address hexadecimal 18—High-byte expansion size

Valid sizes:

0200h	512 Kbyte I/O adapter
0400h	1024 Kbyte I/O adapter (2 adapters)
0600h	1536 Kbyte I/O adapter (3 adapters)
to	
3C00h	15360 Kbyte I/O adapter (15 Mbytes maximum)

Hexadecimal addresses 19 through 2D are reserved.

Checksum (2E and 2F hexadecimal)

Checksum is on addresses hexadecimal 10–20

    Address 2E hexadecimal—High Byte of checksum

    Address 2F hexadecimal—Low Byte of checksum

Low and High Expansion Memory Bytes (30 and 31 hexadecimal)

This word reflects the total expansion memory above the 1 Mbyte address space as determined at power-on time. This expansion memory size can be determined through system interrupt 15 (see the BIOS listing). The base memory at power-on time is determined through the system memory-size-determine interrupt.

Bit 7–Bit 0   Address hexadecimal 30—Low-byte expansion size

Bit 7–Bit 0   Address hexadecimal 31—High-byte expansion size

Valid sizes:

0200h	512 Kbyte I/O adapter
0400h	1024 Kbyte I/O adapter
0600h	1536 Kbyte I/O adapter
to	
3C00h	15360 Kbyte I/O adapter (15 Mbytes maximum)

Date Century Byte (32 hexadecimal)

Bit 7–Bit 0   BCD value for the century (BIOS interface to
                                     read and set)

Information Flag (33 hexadecimal)

Bit 7   Set if the IBM Personal Computer AT 128 Kbyte
                                     Memory Expansion Option is installed.

Bit 6   This bit used by the setup utility to put out a first
                                     user message after initial setup.

Bit 5–Bit 0   Reserved

Hexadecimal addresses 34 through 3F are reserved.

8

I/O Address Map

The installation of adapters using ports not listed below may result in conflicting assignments due to the wide variety of third-party adapters available for the PC bus. Users are cautioned that problems usually occur if ports collide.

I/O addresses, hex 000 to 0FF, are reserved for the system board I/O. Hex 100 to 3FF are available on the I/O channel.

Hex Range	Device
000–01F	DMA Controller 1, 8237A-5
020–03F	Interrupt Controller 1, 8259A, Master
040–05F	Timer 8254.2 (8253)
060–06F	8042 (Keyboard)
060–063	8255 PPI (XT)
060–064	8742 Controller (AT)
070–07F	Real-time Clock, NMI (non-maskable interrupt) mask
070–071	CMOS RAM and NMI Mask Register (AT)
080–09F	DMA Page Registers, 74LS612
0A0–0BF	Interrupt Controller 2, 8259A (AT)
0A0–0AF	NMI Mask Register (XT)
0C0–0DF	DMA Controller 2, 8237A-5 (AT—word mapped)
0F0	Clear Math Coprocessor Busy
0F1	Reset Math Coprocessor
0F8–0FF	Math Coprocessor
1F0–1FF	Hard Disk (AT)

Hex Range	Device
200–20F	Game Control I/O
210–21F	Expansion Unit (XT)
238–23B	Bus Mouse
23C–23F	Alternate Bus Mouse
278–27F	Parallel Printer Port 2
2B0–2BF	EGA
2C0–2CF	EGA
2D0–2DF	EGA
2E0–2E7	GPIB (AT)
2E8–2EF	Serial Port
2F8–2FF	Serial Port 2
300–30F	Prototype Card
310–31F	Prototype Card
320–32F	Hard Disk (XT)
360–36F	Reserved
378–37F	Parallel Printer Port 1
380–38F	SDLC Bisynchronous 2
3A0–3AF	Bisynchronous 2
3B0–3BB	Monochrome Display
3BC–3BF	Parallel Printer
3C0–3CF	Reserved
3C0–3CF	EGA
3D0–3DF	Color/Graphics Monitor Adapter (CGA)
3E8–3EF	Serial Port
3F0–3F7	Floppy Diskette Controller
3F8–3FF	Serial Port 1

9

I/O Bus—62-Pin Connector

In the PC and the XT the I/O bus uses only the 62-pin connector. In the AT the I/O bus uses both the 62-pin and the 36-pin connectors. There is some variation in the signal names but the functionality remains the same.

Arrows pointing toward the connector pin designation indicate signals into the system board (from the devices on the bus). Arrows pointing away from the connector pin designation indicate signals out of the system board. When both arrows are used this indicates a bi-directional signal.

Pins A1 and B1 are closest to the end of the printed circuit board where the bracket is attached. Pin B4 is used as IRQ2 in an XT and used as IRQ9 in an AT, where it is redirected as IRQ2.

	Solder Side			Component Side	
Description	Signal Direction	Pin Number	Pin Number	Signal Direction	Description
Ground	<	B1	A1	<	−I/O CHCK
+Reset	<	B2	A2	< >	SD 7
+5 Volts	<	B3	A3	< >	SD 6
+IRQ2/9	>	B4	A4	< >	SD 5
−5 Volts	<	B5	A5	< >	SD 4
+DRQ2	>	B6	A6	< >	SD 3
−12 Volts		B7	A7	< >	SD 2
0WS	>	B8	A8	< >	SD 1
+12 Volts	>	B9	A9	< >	SD 0
Ground	<	B10	A10	<	I/O CHRDY
−SMEMW	<	B11	A11	>	AEN
−SMEMR	<	B12	A12	< >	SA 19
−IOW	< >	B13	A13	< >	SA 18
−IOR	< >	B14	A14	< >	SA 17
−DACK3	< >	B15	A15	< >	SA 16
+DRQ3	>	B16	A16	< >	SA 15
−DACK1	<	B17	A17	< >	SA 14

	Solder Side			Component Side	
Description	Signal Direction	Pin Number	Pin Number	Signal Direction	Description
+DRQ1	>	B18	A18	<>	SA 13
–DACK0	<	B19	A19	<>	SA 12
CLK	<	B20	A20	<>	SA 11
+IRQ7	>	B21	A21	<>	SA 10
+IRQ6	>	B22	A22	<>	SA 9
+IRQ5	>	B23	A23	<>	SA 8
+IRQ4	>	B24	A24	<>	SA 7
+IRQ3	>	B25	A25	<>	SA 6
–DACK2	<	B26	A26	<>	SA 5
+T/C	<	B27	A27	<>	SA 4
+BALE	<	B28	A28	<>	SA 3
+5 Volts	<	B29	A29	<>	SA 2
OSC	<	B30	A30	<>	SA 1
Ground	<	B31	A31	<>	SA 0

10

I/O Bus—36-Pin Connector

In the PC and the XT the I/O bus uses only the 62-pin connector. In the AT the I/O bus uses both the 62-pin and the 36-pin connectors. There is some variation in the signal names but the functionality remains the same.

Arrows pointing toward the connector pin designation indicate signals into the system board (from the devices on the bus). Arrows pointing away from the connector pin designation indicate signals out of the system board. When both arrows are used this indicates a bi-directional signal.

Pins C1 and D1 are closest to pins A31 and B31 on the printed circuit board.

Solder Side			Component Side		
Description	Signal Direction	Pin Number	Pin Number	Signal Direction	Description
-MEMCS16	^	D1	C1	^	SBHE
-I/OCS16	^	D2	C2	v	LA 23
+IRQ10	^	D3	C3	v	LA 22
+IRQ11	^	D4	C4	v	LA 21
+IRQ12	^	D5	C5	v	LA 20
+IRQ15	^	D6	C6	v	LA 19
+IRQ14	^	D7	C7	v	LA 18
-DACK0	v	D8	C8	v	LA 17
+DRQ0	^	D9	C9	^	-MEMR
-DACK5	v	D10	C10	^	-MEMW
+DRQ5	^	D11	C11	v	SD 08
-DACK6	v	D12	C12	v	SD 09
+DRQ6	^	D13	C13	v	SD 10
-DACK7	v	D14	C14	v	SD 11
+DRQ7	^	D15	C15	v	SD 12
+5 Volts		D16	C16	v	SD 13
-MASTER	^	D17	C17	v	SD 14
Ground		D18	C18	v	SD 15

11

Cables

The PC and its many clones use a variety of cables. Not every clone manufacturer has standardized on the scheme selected by IBM. The following information is furnished as a guide. Check the data with the particular manufacturer of your computer before connecting any equipment.

Legend:

         <   Signal into CPU
         >   Signal out of CPU
         <> Bi-directional signal
         NC No Connection

a. *RS-232C—25-Pin, Asynchronous Adapter Connector (Connector Male, 25-Pin D-Subminiature; Cable requires female)*

Pin Number	Signal Direction	Description
1		NC (Shield Ground Other End)
2	>	TX (Transmit Data)
3	<	RX (Receive Data)
4	>	RTS (Request To Send)
5	<	CTS (Clear To Send)
6	<	DSR (Data Set Ready)
7		GND (Signal Ground)

Pin Number	Signal Direction		Description
8	<		DCD (Data Carrier Detect)
9		>	+ Transmit Current Loop Data
10			NC
11		>	− Transmit Current Loop Data
12			NC
13			NC
14			NC
15			NC
16			NC
17			NC
18	<		+ Receive Current Loop Data
19			NC
20		>	DTR (Data Terminal Ready)
21			NC
22	<		RI (Ring Indicator)
23			NC
24			NC
25	<		− Receive Current Loop Data

b. *RS-232C—9-Pin, Alternate Asychronous Adapter Connector (Connector Male, 9-Pin D-Subminiature; Cable requires female)*

Pin Number	Signal Direction		Description
1	<		DCD (Data Carrier Detect)
2	<		RX (Receive Data)
3		>	TX (Transmit Data)
4		>	DTR (Data Terminal Ready)
5			GND (Signal Ground)
6	<		DSR (Data Set Ready)
7		>	RTS (Request To Send)
8	<		CTS (Clear To Send)
9	<		RI (Ring Indicator)

c. RS-232C—25-Pin To 9-Pin Cable
To wire a 25-pin connector to a 9-pin connector,
use the following table.

DB 9 Pin	DB 25 Pin	Description
1	8	DCD (Data Carrier Detect)
2	3	RX (Receive Data)
3	2	TX (Transmit Data)
4	20	DTR (Data Terminal Ready)
5	7	GND (Signal Ground)
6	6	DSR (Data Set Ready)
7	4	RTS (Request To Send)
8	5	CTS (Clear To Send)
9	22	RI (Ring Indicator)

d. Parallel Printer Cable (Connector Female, 25-Pin
D-Subminiature; Cable requires male)

Pin Number	Signal Direction	Description
1	<	– Strobe
2	>	+ Data Bit 0
3	>	+ Data Bit 1
4	>	+ Data Bit 2
5	>	+ Data Bit 3
6	>	+ Data Bit 4
7	>	+ Data Bit 5
8	>	+ Data Bit 6
9	>	+ Data Bit 7
10	<	– Acknowledge
11	<	+ Busy
12	<	+ Paper End
13	<	+ Select
14	<	– Auto Feed
15	< >	– Error
16	<	– Initialize Printer
17	<	– Select Input
18–25		Ground

e. *Monochrome Display Adapter (Hercules) Cable (Connector Female, 9-Pin D-Subminiature; Cable requires male)*

Pin Number	Signal Direction	Description
1		Ground
2		Ground
3		NC
4		NC
5		NC
6	>	+ Intensity
7	>	+ Video
8	>	+ Horizontal
9	>	− Vertical

f. *CGA Display Adapter Cable (Connector Female, 9-Pin D-Subminiature; Cable requires male)*

Pin Number	Signal Direction	Description
1		Ground
2		Ground
3	>	Red
4	>	Green
5	>	Blue
6	>	Intensity
7	>	Reserved
8	>	Horizontal Drive
9	>	Vertical Drive

g. *CGA Composite Video Cable (Connector Female, RCA Phonograph Jack; Cable requires male)*

Pin Number	Signal Direction	Description
1 (Pin)	>	1.5 Volts Composite Video
2 (Shell)	>	Ground

h. EGA RGB Display Adapter Cable (Connector Female, 9-Pin D-Subminiature; Cable requires male)

Pin Number	Signal Direction	Description
1		Ground
2	>	S. Red
3	>	Red
4	>	Green
5	>	Blue
6	>	S. Green/Intensity
7	>	S. Blue/Mono Video
8	>	Horizontal Drive
9	>	Vertical Drive

i. VGA RGB Display Adapter Cable (Connector Female, 15-Pin D-Subminiature; Cable requires male)

Pin Number	Signal Direction	Description	Monochrome Use	Color Use
1	>	Red		Red
2	>	Green	Monochrome	Green
3	>	Blue		Blue
4		Reserved		
5		Digital Ground	Self Test	Self Test
6	<	Red Return	Key	Red Return
7	<	Green Return	Monochrome Return	Green Return
8	<	Blue Return		
9		Plug		
10		Digital Ground	Ground	Ground
11		Reserved		Ground
12		Reserved	Ground	
13	>	Horizontal Drive	Horizontal Drive	Horizontal Drive
14	>	Vertical Drive	Vertical Drive	Vertical Drive
15		Reserved		

j. Game Control Adapter Cable (Connector Female, 15-Pin D-Subminiature; Cable requires male)

Pin Number	Signal Direction	Description
1	>	+5 Volts
2	<	Button No. 4
3	<	Position No. 0
4		Ground
5		Ground
6	<	Position No. 1
7	<	Button No. 5
8	>	+5 Volts
9	>	+5 Volts
10	<	Button No. 6
11	<	Position No. 2
12		Ground
13	<	Position No. 3
14	<	Button No. 7
15	>	+5 Volts

k. Keyboard Cable (Connector Female, 5-Pin DIN; Cable requires male)

Pin Number	Description
1	+ Keyboard Clock
2	+ Keyboard Data
3	– Keyboard Reset
4	Ground
5	+5 Volts

l. XT Speaker Cable (Connector, 4-Pin Berg)

Pin Number	Description
1	Audio
2	Key
3	Ground
4	+5 Volts

m. Power Cable PS-8 (Connector, 6-Pin Molex)

Pin Number	XT	AT
1	Power Ground	Power Good
2	Key	+5 Volts
3	+12 Volts	+12 Volts
4	−12 Volts	−12 Volts
5	Ground	Ground
6	Ground	Ground

n. Power Cable PS-9 (Connector, 6-Pin Molex)

Pin Number	XT	AT
1	Ground	Ground
2	Ground	Ground
3	−5 Volts	−5 Volts
4	+5 Volts	+5 Volts
5	+5 Volts	+5 Volts
6	+5 Volts	+5 Volts

o. Disk Drive Power Cable (Connector, 4-Pin Molex)

Pin Number	Description
1	+12 Volts
2	Ground
3	Ground
4	+5 Volts

p. AT Battery Cable (Connector, 4-Pin Berg)

Pin Number	Description
1	Ground
2	NC
3	Key
4	+6 Volts

q. *Floppy Disk Drive Cable (34 Conductor, Ribbon)*

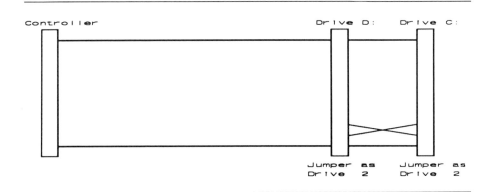

r. *Hard Disk Drive Cables (34 Conductor, Ribbon; Two variations)*

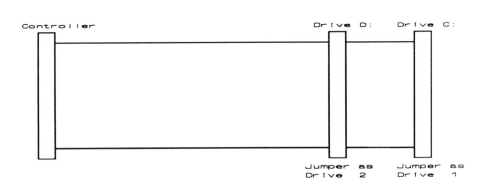

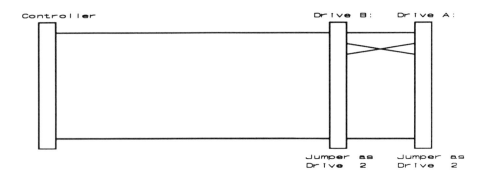

s.   AT LED and Keylock Cable (Connector, 5-Pin Berg)

Pin Number	Description
1	LED Power (+5 Volts)
2	Key
3	Ground
4	Keyboard Inhibit
5	Ground

RECOMMENDED CONNECTORS

9-pin, D-shell (male)	AMP P/N 205865-1
9-pin, D-shell (female)	AMP P/N 205866-1
15-pin, D-shell (male)	AMP P/N 205867-1
15-pin, D-shell (female)	AMP P/N 205868-1
25-pin, D-shell (male)	AMP P/N 205857-1
25-pin, D-shell (female)	AMP P/N 205858-1
37-pin, D-shell (male)	AMP P/N 205859-1
37-pin, D-shell (female)	AMP P/N 205860-1

12

Bus Signal Summary

The signal names used in this table are for the AT bus. When appropriate, the older names used for the PC/XT are shown in parentheses. "I" indicates that the signal is an input to the system board from the bus, and "O" indicates an output from the system board to the bus. All signal lines are TTL compatible. I/O adapters should be designed with a maximum of two low-power Shottky (LS) loads per line.

0WS   I

The "Zero Wait State" signal tells the microprocessor that it can complete the present bus cycle without inserting any additional wait cycles. In order to run a memory cycle to a 16-bit device without wait cycles, "0WS" is dervied from an address decode gated with a Read or Write command. In order to run a memory cycle to an 8-bit device with a minimum of two wait states, "0WS" should be driven active one system clock after the Read or Write command is active gated with the address decode for the device. Memory Read and Write commands to an 8-bit device are active on the falling edge of the system clock. "0WS" is active low and should be driven with an open collector or tri-state driver capable of sinking 20 milliamperes.

AEN   O

"Address Enable" is used to degate the microprocessor and other devices from the I/O channel to allow DMA transfers to take place. When this line is active, the DMA controller has control of the address bus, the data bus Read command lines (memory and I/O), and the Write command lines (memory and I/O).

BALE (ALE)   O

"Address Latch Enable" (buffered) is provided by the 82288 bus controller and is used on the system board to latch valid addresses and memory decodes from the microprocessor. It is available to the I/O channel as an indicator of a valid microprocessor or DMA address (when used with "AEN"). Microprocessor addresses SA0 through SA19 are latched with the falling edge of "BALE". "BALE" is forced high during DMA cycles.

CLK   O

This is the 6 Mhz system clock. It is a synchronous microprocessor cycle clock with a cycle time of 167 nanoseconds. The clock has a 50% duty cycle. This signal should only be used for synchronization. It is not intended for uses requiring a fixed frequency. The system clock in the XT is 4.77 Mhz.

–DACK0 to –DACK3 and –DACK5 to –DACK7 (–DACK1–3)   O

–DMA Acknowledge 0 to 3 and 5 to 7 are used to acknowledge DMA requests (DRQ0 through DRQ7). They are active low.

DRQ0 to DRQ3 and DRQ5 to DRQ7 (DRQ0-3)   I

DMA Requests 0 through 3 and 5 through 7 are asynchronous channel requests used by peripheral devices and the I/O channel microprocessors to gain DMA service (or control of the system). They are prioritized, with "DRQ0" having the highest priority and "DRQ7" having the lowest. A request is generated by bringing a DRQ line to an active level. A DRQ line must be held high until the corresponding "DMA Request Acknowledge" (DACK) line goes active. "DRQ0" through "DRQ3" will perform 8-bit transfers; "DRQ5" through "DRQ7" will perform 16-bit transfers. "DRQ4" is used on the system board and is not available on the I/O channel.

–I/O CH CK   I

"–I/O Channel Check" provides the system board with parity (error) information about memory or devices on the I/O channel. When this signal is active, it indicates an uncorrectable system error.

I/O CH RDY   I

"I/O Channel Ready" is pulled low (not ready) by a memory or I/O device to lengthen I/O or memory cycles. Any slow device using this line should drive it low immediately upon detecting its valid address and a Read or Write command. Machine cycles are extended by an integral number of clock cycles (167 nanoseconds for a 6 Mhz system clock). The signal should be held low for no more than 2.5 microseconds.

–I/O CS16   I

"–I/O 16-bit Chip Select" signals the system board that the present data transfer is a 16-bit, 1 wait state I/O cycle. It is derived from an address decode. "–I/O CS16" is active low and should be driven with an open collector or tri-state driver capable of sinking 20 milliamperes.

–IOR   I O

"–I/O Read" instructs an I/O device to drive its data onto the data bus. It may be driven by the system microprocessor or DMA controller, or by a microprocessor or DMA controller resident on the I/O channel. This signal is active low.

–IOW   I O

"–I/O Write" instructs an I/O device to read the data on the data bus. It may be driven by any microprocessor or DMA controller in the system. The signal is active low.

IRQ3 to IRQ7, IRQ9 to IRQ12, and IRQ14 through IRQ15 (IRQ2-7)   I

Interrupt Requests 3 through 7, 9 through 12, and 14 through 15 are used to signal the microprocessor that an I/O device needs attention. The interrupt requests are prioritized, with IRQ9 through IRQ12 and IRQ14 through IRQ15 having the highest priority (IRQ9 is the highest) and IRQ3 through IRQ7 having the lowest (IRQ7 is the lowest). An interrupt request is generated when an IRQ line is raised from low to high. The line must be held high until the microprocessor acknowledges the interrupt request (Interrupt Service Routine). Interrupt 13 is used on the system board and is not available on the I/O channel. Interrupt 8 is used for the real-time clock.

LA17 thru LA23   I O

These signals (unlatched) are used to address memory and I/O devices within the system. They give the system up to 16 Mbyte of addressability. These signals are valid when "BALE" is high. LA17 through LA23 are not latched during microprocessor cycles and therefore do not stay valid for the whole cycle. Their purpose is to generate memory decodes for 1 wait-state. These decodes should be latched by I/O adapters on the falling edge of "BALE". These signals also may be driven by other microprocessors or DMA controllers that reside on the I/O channel.

–MASTER   I

This signal is used with a DRQ line to gain control of the system. A processor or DMA controller on the I/O channel may issue a DRQ to a DMA channel in cascade mode and receive a "–DACK". Upon receiving the "–DACK", an I/O microprocessor may pull "–MASTER" low, which will allow it to control the system address, data, and control lines (a condition known as *tri-state*). After "–MASTER" is low, the I/O microprocessor must wait one system clock period before driving the address and data lines, and two clock periods before issuing a Read or Write command. If this signal is held low for more than 15 microseconds, system memory may be lost because of a lack of refresh.

–MEM CS16   I

"MEM 16 Chip Select" signals the system board if the present data transfer is a 1 wait-state, 16-bit, memory cycle. It must be derived from the decode of LA17 through LA23. "–MEM CS16" should be driven with an open collector or tri-state driver capable of sinking 20 milliamperes.

–SMEMR   O
–MEMR   I O

These signals instruct the memory devices to drive data onto the data bus. "–SMEMR" is active only when the memory decode is within the low 1 Mbyte of memory space. "–MEMR" is active on all memory read cycles. "–MEMR" may be driven by any microprocessor or DMA controller in the system. "–SMEMR" is derived from "–MEMR" and the decode of the low 1 Mbyte of memory. When a microprocessor on the I/O channel wishes to drive "–MEMR", it must have the address lines valid on the bus for one system clock period before driving "–MEMR" active. Both signals are active LOW.

–SMEMW   O
–MEMW   I O

These signals instruct the memory devices to store the data present on the data bus. "–SMEMW" is active only when the memory decode is within the low 1 Mbyte of the memory space. "–MEMW" is active on all memory read cycles. "–MEMW" may be driven by any microprocessor or DMA controller in the system. "–SMEMW" is derived from "–MEMW" and the decode of the low 1 Mbyte of memory. When a microprocessor on the I/O channel wishes to drive "–MEMW", it must have the address lines valid on the bus for one system clock period before driving "–MEMW" active. Both signals are active LOW.

OSC   O

"Oscillator" (OSC) is a high-speed clock with a 70-nanosecond period (14.31818 Mhz). This signal is not synchronized with the system clock. It has a 50% duty cycle.

–REFRESH   I O

This signal is used to indicate a refresh cycle and can be driven by a microprocessor in the I/O channel.

RESET DRV   O

"Reset Drive" is used to reset or initialize system logic at power-up time or during a low line-voltage outage. This signal is active HIGH.

SA0 thru SA19 (A0-19)   I O

Address bits 0 through 19 are used to address memory and I/O devices within the system. These 20 address lines, in addition to LA17 through LA23, allow access of up to 16 Mbyte of memory. SA0 through SA19 are gated on to the system bus when "BALE" is high and are latched on the falling edge of "BALE". These signals are generated by the microprocessor or DMA controller. They also may be driven by other microprocessors or DMA controllers that reside on the I/O channel.

SBHE   I O

"Bus High Enable" (system) indicates a transfer of data on the upper byte of the data bus, SD8 through SD15. Sixteen-bit devices use "SBHE" to condition data bus buffers tied to SD8 through SD15.

SD0 thru SD15 (D0-7)   I O

These signals provide bus bits 0 through 15 for the microprocessor, memory, and I/O devices. D0 is the least significant bit and D15 is the most significant bit. All 8-bit devices on the I/O channel should use D0 through D7 for communications to the microprocessor. The 16-bit devices will use D0 through D15. To support 8-bit devices, the data on D8 through D15 will be gated to D0 through D7 during 8-bit transfers to these devices; 16-bit microprocessor transfers to 8-bit devices will be converted to two 8-bit transfers.

T/C   O

"Terminal Count" provides a pulse when the terminal count for any DMA channel is reached.

13

Power-On Self Tests (Post)

The POST (Power-On Self Test) system test routines are included in the BIOS. The function of the POST is to initialize the circuitry of the motherboard and the peripheral adapter boards and perform a variety of tests to check for proper functioning of the computer and its peripheral circuitry. Execution of the POST requires between 13 and 90 seconds depending on the microprocessor speed and the total amount of system memory. The POST is executed each time power is applied to the system and each time the system is reset from the keyboard during a reboot ("CTL-ALT-DEL").

Program execution from the reset state begins at the highest paragraph of memory (F000:FFF0 for the 8088 microprocessor, FFFFF:0000 for the 80286 microprocessor) with a long jump to E000:E05B where the code for the POST is located (in ROM). The program code for the POST is BIOS manufacturer-specific and therefore the system initialization and testing will proceed along lines particular to the BIOS installed. One short "BEEP" from the speaker announces the sucessful completion of the POST.

The typical sequence of operations is as follows:

1. Some CPU register checks.
2. Set up the 8253/8254 timer for RAM refresh timing.
3. Set up the DMA for RAM refresh on Channel 0.
4. Verify that refresh is operating.
5. Test the low RAM (16K–64K).
6. Load the interrupt vectors and assign a stack in the low RAM area.
7. Initialize the primary video display and keyboard devices.

133

8. Determine the size of and test the remaining RAM.
9. Initialize the COM, LPT, and game ports.
10. Initialize the floppy disk sub-system.
11. Initialize the hard disk sub-system.
12. Initialize the mathematics coprocessor (if there is one).
13. Initialize the SDLC communication adapter (if there is one).
14. Check the expansion unit (if there is one).
15. Scan the user ROM area.
16. Call the bootstrap interrupt.

THE SYSTEM POWER SUPPLY

If the microprocessor CPU is the brains of the computer, the power supply may be considered to be the heart. The power supply pumps the electric current throughout the computer system. The capacity of the power supply is measured in watts as is the load to the power supply presented by each and every board and peripheral that is plugged into it.

The power supply derives its power from the wall plug, which, in theory at least, provides a direct connection to Hoover Dam. The function of the power supply is conversion of a certain amount of that power to levels useful by the computer components. The basic question is "What should the capacity of the power supply be?" None of the following numbers are exact. In general, older boards are less efficient and use more power than newer ones, and the more complicated the board the more power it uses. The faster, more powerful processors have more transistors in their integrated circuits and use more power.

In general, it is safer to overestimate power consumption than to underestimate it. In the final analysis, overestimation of consumption offers a worst-case policy and tends to provide a margin of reserves for future expansion when it occurs.

System Board	20 to 40 watts
Expansion Board	5 to 15 watts
Floppy Disk (each)	5 to 15 watts
Hard Disk (each)	10 to 25 watts
Tape Drive	15 watts
CD-ROM Drive	10 watts
Adequate For Most Configurations	200 watts
For 386 or 486 Systems	250 watts

Most power supplies today include load monitoring circuitry, which will shut down the power supply before it can be damaged by overload.

This, of course, does not help matters when the shutdown occurs at some critical time.

One of the biggest causes of power supply failure is inadequate cooling caused by poor air circulation. Because the computer generally has only one fan and that fan is located in the power supply, the air path to that fan should not be obstructed or allowed to become clogged with dirt or dust. The air path should be checked every month or so.

Replacement or upgrading of a power supply is a fairly straightforward process. The physical size of the replacement unit is the most critical issue. Does the new unit fit in the place where the old one was? There are two basic physical sizes available; those designed to fit in the original IBM PC and XT and their clones, and those designed for the AT and its clones. The AT units are about 10% larger and include a voltage selector switch, which allows you to select the input voltage between 115 volts AC and 230 volts AC, or between 120 volts AC and 240 volts AC. Four power distribution connectors are usually standard on the AT power supplies whereas only two distribution connectors come with the XT models. This is not a large handicap as most computer stores sell power distribution "Y" (splitter) cables in various lengths for under $5.00.

Before undertaking the replacement of a power supply you should equip yourself with two items. The first is a screwdriver and the second some sticky-back labels which are used to mark each connector and its mate before disconnecting them. Particularly note the orientation of the connector mating by examining the color of the wires in each connector half. Also check to see if the connectors are keyed.

Power supplies have been built with two kinds of connectors. The first kind has small square pins (Molex) and those are not as common as the second kind, which has rectangular pins (Burndy). You should check your original power supply in a dry run and order the replacement power supply with the proper kind of pins. In addition, you should negotiate a no-charge return if for some reason the replacement unit doesn't fit. Some clones (such as COMPAQ) used odd-shaped power supplies for which replacements are difficult to find.

Pricing of replacement power supplies is based on a variety of factors. The first is capacity in watts. The second, and equally important, is quality of manufacture. The fan also represents an important cost factor insofar as the quantity of air it moves, its reliability, and whether it can move the air quietly.

Access to the power supply is gained by removing the computer chassis cover, which is generally held in place by five screws. After removing the screws set them in a safe place so you can find them when the time comes to replace the cover. Again, note connector location and orientation before disconnecting anything and record this information. The power supply is generally held in place by four screws accessed at the computer back panel. In addition, after removal of the four screws the power supply is often still held in place by two tabs in the bottom of the system chassis. These tabs are released by sliding the power supply gently toward the front panel.

When the connectors are all removed the power supply may be lifted free of the system chassis. This process should take less than 15 minutes.

Installing the new power supply is simply the reversal of the removal process. Remember to properly engage the tabs in the bottom of the chassis. Route the cables carefully so they do not get pinched when installing the power supply or when replacing the computer cover. Perhaps some nylon cable ties will help in cable routing. When installing the screws, don't tighten them until they have all been started, so that final position adjustments may be made.

A final check should be made to see that all the connectors are properly oriented and that the voltage selector switch (if there is one) on the new supply is set for the desired primary power. Some final light dusting might be in order at this point.

You might want to check for proper operation before replacing the cover. Be careful not to drop anything into the uncovered chassis. If all is well, replace the cover.

14

Audible Diagnostic Codes

You may have wondered why your PC emits a single short "BEEP" while DOS is in the process of booting up. The purpose of the beep is to indicate to the user that the Power-On Self Tests (POST) (see Chapter 13) have been successfully completed. If the tests fail or find errors, a variety of other audible signals are generated to indicate which area of the computer has failed to respond in the expected manner. The audible signals are particularly useful in the cases where it has not been possible to initialize the display system and provide a visual display of the problem.

Some of the audible diagnostic codes are listed below as an aid to pinpointing the problem. The notation used is a number for the quantity of short beeps, and a dash for a pause between beeps, unless otherwise specified.

It is noted that the audible diagnostic codes are ROM BIOS dependent, and each manufacturer's ROM might not have every code.

Audible Code	Port 80h Contents	Fatal Error
No Beep	01h	CPU Register Test In Progress
Continuous Beep		Power Failure
No Beep		Power Failure
Repeating Short Beeps		Power Failure
1–1–1	02h	CMOS Read/Write Failure
1–1–2	03h	ROM BIOS Checksum Failure
1–1–3		CMOS Read/Write Test Failure

137

Audible Code	Port 80h Contents	Fatal Error
1–1–4		BIOS Checksum Failure
1–2–1	06h	DMA Page Register R/W Failure
1–2–1		8253 Timer Failure
1–2–2		DMA Initialization Failure
1–2–3	04h	Programmable Interval Timer Failure
1–2–3		DMA Page Register Failure
1–2–4	05h	DMA Initialization Failure
1–3–1		RAM Refresh Not Verified
1–3–1	08h	1st 64K RAM odd/even logic Failure
1–3–2	08h	RAM Refresh Verification Failure
1–3–3	0Ah	1st 64K RAM–Data Line (multi-bit)
None	09h	1st 64K RAM Test In Progress
1–3–4	0Bh	Low 64K RAM Even/Odd Failure
1–4–1	0Ch	Low 64K RAM Address Line Failure
1–4–2	0Ch	Low 64K RAM Parity Error
1–4–3	0Dh	Parity Failure 1st 64K RAM
2–1–1	10h	Low 64K RAM Bit 0 Error
2–1–2	11h	Low 64K RAM Bit 1 Error
2–1–3	12h	Low 64K RAM Bit 2 Error
2–1–4	13h	Low 64K RAM Bit 3 Error
2–2–1	14h	Low 64K RAM Bit 4 Error
2–2–2	15h	Low 64K RAM Bit 5 Error
2–2–3	16h	Low 64K RAM Bit 6 Error
2–2–4	17h	Low 64K RAM Bit 7 Error
2–3–1	18h	Low 64K RAM Bit 8 Error
2–3–2	19h	Low 64K RAM Bit 9 Error
2–3–3	1Ah	Low 64K RAM Bit 10 Error
2–3–4	1Bh	Low 64K RAM Bit 11 Error
2–4–1	1Ch	Low 64K RAM Bit 12 Error
2–4–2	1Dh	Low 64K RAM Bit 13 Error
2–4–3	1Eh	Low 64K RAM Bit 14 Error
2–4–4	1Fh	Low 64K RAM Bit 15 Error
3–1–1	20h	DMA No. 2 (Slave) Register Error
3–1–2	21h	DMA No. 1 (Master) Register Error
3–1–3	22h	8259 Interrupt Mask No. 1 Error
3–1–4	23h	8259 Interrupt Mask No. 2 Error

Audible Code	Port 80h Contents	Fatal Error
None	25h	Interrupt Vector Loading In Progress
3–2–4	27h	8042 Keyboard Controller Error
None	28h	CMOS Power Failure And Checksum Calculation In Progress
None	29h	CMOS Configuration Validation In Progress
3–3–4	2Bh	Screen Memory Test Failure
3–3–4		Video Initialization Error
3–4–1	2Ch	Screen Initialization Failure
3–4–1		Video Retrace Failure
3–4–2	2Dh	Screen Retrace Test Failure
3–4–2		Video ROM–Scan In Progress
3–4–3		Video ROM–Scan Error
1 Long, 2 Short		Display Error
2 Short		Display Error
None	2Eh	Search For Video ROM In Progress
None	30h	Screen Believed Operable And Running With Video ROM
None	31h	Monochrome Monitor Believed OK
None	32h	Color Monitor (40 col.) Believed OK
None	33h	Color Monitor (80 col.) Believed OK

Audible Code	Port 80th Contents	Non-Fatal Error (if manufacturing jumper installed on 8042)
4–2–1	34h	8253 Timer Tick Test
4–2–2	35h	Shutdown/Restart Sequence
4–2–3	36h	Gate A20 Failure
4–2–4	37h	Unexpected Virtual Mode Interrupt
4–3–1		RAM Test In Progress
4–3–1	38h	Memory High Address Line Failure At 010000h–0A0000h
4–3–3	3Ah	8253 Timer Channel No. 2 Test
4–3–4	3Bh	Time Of Day Clock Test
4–4–1	3Ch	Serial Port Test
4–4–2	3Dh	Parallel Port Test
4–4–3	3Eh	Mathematics Coprocessor Test
4–4–4		Try Draining CMOS

Audible Code	Interpretation
1 Short	Tests Completed Satisfactorily

Source: Phoenix Technologies, Ltd. Norwood, MA

15

Displayed Problem Isolation Codes (PIC)

The Power-On Self Tests (POST) (Chapter 13) and other diagnostics check various portions of your PC and display on the monitor (or beep) a problem isolation code (PIC) if an error has been detected. Note that *not* all errors or failures in the hardware are detectable with a software test routine.

The following list of problem isolation codes has been assembled by consulting various sources. Each of the codes may not be applicable to each type of computer (PC, XT, or AT) or to a specific peripheral type. In addition, in some cases a code may have a different interpretation in different PC's or options.

In general, the display of a problem isolation code ending with "00" indicates that the tests in a particular group have been completed successfully. A problem isolation code terminating in other than "00" indicates an error or failure during that group of tests.

Test Groups With Error Messages (If Any) Displayed On The Monitor

010	Start—Undetermined Problem
020	Power Supply
100	System Board
101	8259 Interrupt Failure
102	8253 Timer Failure
103	8253 Timer Interrupt Failure
104	Protected Mode Failure
105	8742 Command Not Accepted
106	Logic Test Failure

107	Non-Maskable Interrupt Test Failure
108	8253 Timer Failure
109	LMCS Test Failure or DMA Test Failure
114	Option ROM Checksum Error
121	Unexpected Hardware Interrupt
130	Shutdown/Restart Error
131	Cassette Wrap Failure
161	Battery Failure (Run Setup)
162	Configuration Incorrect (Run Setup)
163	Time and/or Date Incorrect (Run Setup)
164	Memory Size Incorrect (Run Setup)
165	Invalid Adapter Configuration
166	Nonexistent Adapter Configuration
167	Invalid Diskette Adapter Configuration
168	Invalid System Configuration
199	User Configuration Incorrect (Run Setup)
200	System Memory
201	Memory Error
202	Memory Address Lines 00–15
203	Memory Address Lines 16–23
300	Keyboard
301	Bad Reset; If Stuck Key—Scan Code Is Displayed
302	Keyswitch Is Locked
303	Keyboard or System Error
304	Keyboard Clock Line Error
306	Keyboard Data Line Error
307	Keyboard Stuck Key Error
400	Monochrome Display Adapter (MDA)
401	MDA Memory or Horizontal Syncronization Failed
408	Display Attributes Failure
416	Character Set Failure
424	80 × 25 Mode Failure
432	Parallel Port Test On MDA Failed
500	Color/Graphics Adapter
501	CGA Memory or Horizontal Synchronization Failed
508	Display Attribute Failure
516	Character Set Failure
524	80 × 25 Mode Failure
532	40 × 25 Mode Failure
540	320 × 200 Graphics Mode Failure
548	640 × 200 Graphics Mode Failure
600	Floppy Disk Adapter
601	Disk Power On Diagnostics Failed
602	Floppy Disk Boot Error

605	Disk Test Failed
606	Disk Verify Function Failed
607	Write Protected Disk
608	Bad Command Disk Status Returned
610	Disk Initialization Failed
611	Timeout—Disk Status Returned
612	Bad NEC—Disk Status Returned
613	Bad DMA—Disk Status Returned
621	Bad SEEK—Disk Status Returned
622	Bad CRC—Disk Status Returned
623	Record Not Found—Disk Status Returned
624	Bad Address Mark—Disk Status Returned
625	Bad NEC Seek—Disk Status Returned
626	Disk Data Compare Error
700	8087 Mathematics Coprocessor
800	Reserved
900	Parallel Printer Adapter
901	Parallel Printer Adapter Test Failed
1000	Alternate Parallel Printer Adapter
1100	Asynchronous Adapter
1101	Asynchronous Adapter Failed
1200	Alternate Asynchronous Adapter
1201	Alternate Asynchronous Adapter Failed
1300	Game Control Adapter
1301	Game Control Adapter Failed
1302	Joystick Failed
1400	Matrix Printer
1401	Printer Failed
1500	SDLC Communication Adapter
1510	8255 Port B Failure
1511	8255 Port A Failure
1512	8255 Port C Failure
1513	8253 Timer 1 Did Not Reach Terminal Count
1514	8253 Timer 1 Stuck On
1515	8253 Timer 0 Did Not Reach Terminal Count
1516	8253 Timer 0 Stuck On
1517	8253 Timer 2 Did Not Reach Terminal Count
1518	8253 Timer 2 Stuck On
1519	8273 Port B Error
1520	8273 Port A Error
1521	8273 Command/Read Timeout
1522	Interrupt Level 4 Failure
1523	Ring Indicate Stuck On

1524	Receive Clock Stuck On
1525	Transmit Clock Stuck On
1526	Test Indicate Stuck On
1527	Ring Indicate Not On
1528	Receive Clock Not On
1529	Transmit Clock Not On
1530	Test Indicate Not On
1531	Data Set Ready Not On
1532	Carrier Detect Not On
1533	Clear To Send Not On
1534	Data Set Ready Stuck On
1536	Clear To Send Stuck On
1537	Level 3 Interrupt Failure
1538	Receive Interrupt Results Error
1539	Wrap Data Miscompare
1540	DMA Channel 1 Error
1541	DMA Channel 1 Error
1542	Error In 8273 Status
1547	Stray Interrupt Level 4
1548	Stray Interrupt Level 3
1549	Interrupt Timeout
16XX	Display Emulation Error (327X, 5520, 525X)
1700	Hard Disk Drive
1701	Hard Disk POST Error
1702	Hard Disk Adapter Error
1703	Hard Disk Drive Error
1704	Hard Disk Adapter or Drive Error
1780	Hard Disk 0 Failed
1781	Hard Disk 1 Failed
1782	Hard Disk Controller Error
1790	Hard Disk 0 Error
1791	Hard Disk 1 Error
1800	Expansion Unit
1801	I/O Expansion Unit POST Error
1810	Enable/Disable Error
1811	Extender Card Wrap Test Failed (disabled)
1812	High Order Address Lines Failure (disabled)
1813	Wait State Failure (disabled)
1814	Enable/Disable Could Not Be Set On
1815	Wait State Failure (enabled)
1816	Extender Card Wrap Test Failed (enabled)
1817	High Order Address Line Failure (enabled)
1818	Disable Not Functioning
1819	Wait Request Switch Not Set Correctly

1820	Receiver Card Wrap Test Failure
1821	Receiver High Order Address Lines Failure
19XX	3270 PC Attachment Card Errors
2000	Bisync Communications Adapter Errors
2010	8255 Port A Failure
2011	8255 Port B Failure
2012	8255 Port C Failure
2013	8253 Timer 1 Did Not Reach Terminal Count
2014	8253 Timer 1 Stuck On
2016	8253 Timer 2 Did Not Reach Terminal Count Or Stuck On
2017	8251 Data Set Ready Failed To Come On
2018	8251 Clear To Send Not Sensed
2019	8251 Data Set Ready Stuck On
2020	8251 Clear To Send Stuck On
2021	8251 Hardware Reset Failed
2022	8251 Software Reset Failed
2023	8251 Software "Error Reset" Failed
2024	8251 Transmit Ready Did Not Come On
2025	8251 Receive Ready Did Not Come On
2026	8251 Could Not Force "Overrun" Error Status
2027	Interrupt Failure—No Timer Interrupt
2028	Interrupt Failure—Transmit; Replace Card Or Planar
2029	Interrupt Failure—Transmit; Replace Card
2030	Interrupt Failure—Receive; Replace Card Or Planar
2031	Interrupt Failure—Receive; Replace Card
2033	Ring Indicate Stuck On
2034	Receive Clock Stuck On
2035	Transmit Clock Stuck On
2036	Test Indicate Stuck On
2037	Ring Indicate Stuck On
2038	Receive Clock Not On
2039	Transmit Clock Not On
2040	Test Indicate Not On
2041	Data Set Ready Not On
2042	Carrier Detect Not On
2043	Clear To Send Not On
2044	Data Set Ready Stuck On
2045	Carrier Detect Stuck On
2046	Clear To Send Stuck On
2047	Unexpected Transmit Interrupt
2048	Unexpected Receive Interrupt
2049	Transmit Data Did Not Equal Receive Data
2050	8251 Detected Overrun Error
2051	Lost Data Set Ready During Data Wrap

2052	Receive Timeout During Data Wrap
2100	Alternate Bisync Communications Adapter Errors
2110	8255 Port A Failure
2111	8255 Port B Failure
2112	8255 Port C Failure
2113	8253 Timer 1 Did Not Reach Terminal Count
2114	8253 Timer 1 Stuck On
2116	8253 Timer 2 Did Not Reach Terminal Count Or Stuck On
2117	8251 Data Set Ready Failed To Come On
2118	8251 Clear To Send Not Sensed
2119	8251 Data Set Ready Stuck On
2120	8251 Clear To Send Stuck On
2121	8251 Hardware Reset Failed
2122	8251 Software Reset Failed
2123	8251 Software "Error Reset" Failed
2124	8251 Transmit Ready Did Not Come On
2125	8251 Receive Ready Did Not Come On
2126	8251 Could Not Force "Overrun" Error Status
2127	Interrupt Failure—No Timer Interrupt
2128	Interrupt Failure—Transmit; Replace Card Or Planar
2129	Interrupt Failure—Transmit; Replace Card
2130	Interrupt Failure—Receive; Replace Card Or Planar
2131	Interrupt Failure—Receive; Replace Card
2133	Ring Indicator Stuck On
2134	Receive Clock Stuck On
2135	Transmit Clock Stuck On
2136	Test Indicate Stuck On
2137	Ring Indicate Stuck On
2138	Receive Clock Not On
2139	Transmit Clock Not On
2140	Test Indicate Not On
2141	Data Set Ready Not On
2142	Carrier Detect Not On
2143	Clear To Send Not On
2144	Data Set Ready Stuck On
2145	Carrier Detect Stuck On
2146	Clear To Send Stuck On
2147	Unexpected Transmit Interrupt
2148	Unexpected Receive Interrupt
2149	Transmit Data Did Not Equal Receive Data
2150	8251 Detected Overrun Error
2151	Lost Data Set Ready During Data Wrap
2152	Receive Timeout During Data Wrap
22XX	Cluster Adapter Errors

24XX	EGA Errors
2401	Video Error
29XX	Color Matrix Printer Errors
30XX	VGA Errors
3001	Video Error
33XX	Compact Printer Errors
7000	Chipset CMOS RAM
7001	Chipset Shadow RAM Error
7002	Chipset CMOS RAM Configuration Error
8600	Mouse Interface
8601	Mouse Interface Command Error
8602	Mouse Interface Test Error
8603	Mouse Interface Timeout Error
C8000	Fixed Disk Adapter
F0000–FE000	System Board
XXXXX	ROM

16

Interrupts

80286 Program Interrupt Listing (Real Mode Only)

Address	Interrupt	Name	BIOS Entry
0–3	0	Divide By Zero	D11
4–7	1	Single Step	D11
8–B	2	Nonmaskable	NMI_INT
C–F	3	Breakpoint	D11
10–13	4	Overflow	D11
14–17	5	Print Screen	PRINT_SCREEN
18–1B	6	Reserved	D11
1D–1F	7	Reserved	D11
20–23	8	Time Of Day	TIMER_INT (0)*
24–27	9	Keyboard	KB_INT (1)*
28–2B	A	Reserved	D11 Reserved (XT), Int. 8-15 (AT), IRQ2
2C–2F	B	Communications	D11 (COM or SDLC), IRQ3
30–33	C	Communications	D11 (COM or SDLC), IRQ4
34–37	D	Alternate Printer	D11 (Hard Disk [XT], LPT [AT]), IRQ5
38–3B	E	Diskette	DISK_INT (Floppy Disk), IRQ6
3C–3F	F	Printer	D11 (LPT), IRQ7

149

Address	Interrupt	Name	BIOS Entry
40–43	10	Video	VIDEO_IO
44–47	11	Equipment Check	EQUIPMENT
48–4B	12	Memory	MEMORY_SIZE_ DETERMINE
4C–4F	13	Diskette/Disk	DISKETTE_IO
50–53	14	Communications	RS232_IO
54–57	15	Cassette	CASSETTE_IO System Extensions
58–5B	16	Keyboard	KEYBOARD_IO
5C–5F	17	Printer	PRINTER_IO
60–63	18	Resident BASIC	F600:0000
64–67	19	Bootstrap	BOOT_STRAP
68–6B	1A	Time Of Day	TIME_OF_DAY
6C–6F	1B	Keyboard Break	DUMMY_RETURN
70–73	1C	Timer Tick	DUMMY_RETURN
74–77	1D	Video Initialization	VIDEO_PARMS
78–7B	1E	Diskette Parameters	DISK_BASE
7C–7F	1F	Video Graphics Chars	0
	—		NMI_INT (Parity)*

*These interrupts exist on the system board and are not available on the bus connector.

Hardware, BASIC, and DOS Reserved Interrupts

Address	Interrupt	Function
80–83	20	DOS Program Terminate
84–87	21	DOS Function Call
88–8B	22	DOS Terminate Address
8C–8F	23	DOS Control-Break Exit Address
90–93	24	DOS Fatal Error Vector
94–97	25	DOS Absolute Disk Read
98–9B	26	DOS Absolute Disk Write
9C–9F	27	DOS Terminate, Fix In Storage
A0–FF	28–3F	Reserved For DOS
100–17F	40–5F	Reserved
180–19F	60–67	Reserved For User Program Interrupts
1A0–1BF	68–6F	Not Used
1C0–1C3	70	IRQ 8 Real Time Clock INT (BIOS Entry RTC_INT)

Address	Interrupt	Name	BIOS Entry
1C4–1C7	71	IRQ 9 (BIOS Entry RE_DIRECT) (Redirected To IRQ 2)	
1C8–1CB	72	IRQ 10 (BIOS Entry D11)	
1CC–1CF	73	IRQ 11 (BIOS Entry D11)	
1D0–1D3	74	IRQ 12 (BIOS Entry D11)	
1D4–1D7	75	IRQ 13 BIOS Redirect To NMI Interrupt (BIOS Entry INT_287), 80287 Coprocessor	
1D8–1DB	76	IRQ 14 (BIOS Entry D11), Hard Disk	
1DC–1DF	77	IRQ 15 (BIOS Entry D11)	
1E0–1FF	78–7F	Not Used	
200–217	80–85	Reserved By BASIC	
218–3C3	86–F0	Used By BASIC Interpreter While BASIC Is Running	
3C4–3FF	F1–FF	Not Used	

The 80286 microprocessor NMI and two 8259A interrupt controller integrated circuits provide 16 levels of system interrupts. Any or all interrupts may be masked (including the microprocessor's NMI). The following shows the interrupt-level assignments in decreasing priority.

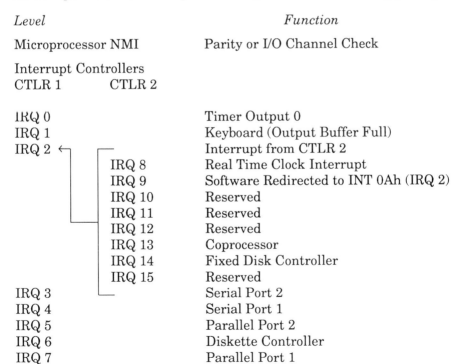

Level	*Function*
Microprocessor NMI	Parity or I/O Channel Check
Interrupt Controllers	
CTLR 1 CTLR 2	
IRQ 0	Timer Output 0
IRQ 1	Keyboard (Output Buffer Full)
IRQ 2 ←	Interrupt from CTLR 2
IRQ 8	Real Time Clock Interrupt
IRQ 9	Software Redirected to INT 0Ah (IRQ 2)
IRQ 10	Reserved
IRQ 11	Reserved
IRQ 12	Reserved
IRQ 13	Coprocessor
IRQ 14	Fixed Disk Controller
IRQ 15	Reserved
IRQ 3	Serial Port 2
IRQ 4	Serial Port 1
IRQ 5	Parallel Port 2
IRQ 6	Diskette Controller
IRQ 7	Parallel Port 1

17

BIOS Entry Points

IBM warns programmers not to use the actual entry points in calling BIOS routines, because they may change from version to version. The proper entry to the BIOS is through the software interrupt system. In practice, usually in the interest of maximizing speed, there are those who violate the rules. The entry points marked with an asterisk (*) have remained constant on all, or nearly all, of the PC- and XT-compatible BIOS versions. Be aware of the risk to future compatibility if your software uses them. The following data applies to the IBM AT.

Address	Publics By Name
0000:E729*	A1
0000:3792	ACT_DISP_PAGE
0000:E137	ADERR
0000:E11C	ADERR1
0000:17AA	BEEP
0000:0000	BEGIN
0000:16B9	BLINK_INT
0000:E372	BOOT_INVA
0000:E6F2*	BOOT_STRAP
0000:1B66	BOOT_STRAP_1
0000:E05E	C1
0000:0222	C11
0000:E060	C2
0000:0C3F	C21
0000:0454	C30
0000:0405	C8042
0000:E062	C8042A
0000:E066	C8042B
0000:E068	C8042C
0000:F859*	CASSETTE_IO
0000:3FE2	CASSETTE_IO_1
0000:09FB	CHK_VIDEO
0000:E234	CM1
0000:E25D	CM2
0000:E286	CM3
0000:E0D0	CM4
0000:E2C6	CM4_A
0000:E2DF	CM4_B
0000:E2F8	CM4_C
0000:E311	CM4_D
0000:FA6E*	CRT_CHAR_GEN
0000:E164	D1
0000:1805	D11
0000:E174	D2
0000:E184	D2A
0000:17FD	DDS
0000:EC59*	DISKETTE_IO
0000:20A5	DISKETTE_IO_1
0000:EFC7*	DISK_BASE
0000:EF57*	DISK_INT
0000:260E	DISK_INT_1
0000:2A71	DISK_IO
0000:28DA	DISK_SETUP

Address	Publics By Name
0000:2816	DSKETTE_SETUP
0000:FF53*	DUMMY_RETURN
0000:1851	DUMMY_RETURN_1
0000:E06C	E0
0000:E085	E0_A
0000:E09E	E0_B
0000:E0E9	E1
0000:E32A	E1_A
0000:E0FC	E1_B
0000:E10C	E1_C
0000:03E5	E30B
0000:03EB	E30C
0000:F84D*	EQUIPMENT
0000:3E6C	EQUIPMENT_1
0000:177A	ERR_BEEP
0000:187F	EXC_00
0000:1884	EXC_01
0000:1889	EXC_02
0000:188E	EXC_03
0000:1893	EXC_04
0000:1898	EXC_05
0000:18B1	EXC_06
0000:18B6	EXC_07
0000:18BB	EXC_08
0000:18C0	EXC_09
0000:18C5	EXC_10
0000:18CA	EXC_11
0000:18CF	EXC_12
0000:18D4	EXC_13
0000:18D9	EXC_14
0000:18DE	EXC_15
0000:18E3	EXC_16
0000:18E8	EXC_17
0000:18ED	EXC_18
0000:18F2	EXC_19
0000:18F7	EXC_20
0000:18FC	EXC_21
0000:1901	EXC_22
0000:1906	EXC_23
0000:190B	EXC_24
0000:1910	EXC_25
0000:1915	EXC_26
0000:191A	EXC_27

Address		Publics By Name
0000:191F		EXC_28
0000:1924		EXC_29
0000:1929		EXC_30
0000:192E		EXC_31
0000:1753		E_MSG
0000:E1C2		F1
0000:E393		F1780
0000:E3A8		F1781
0000:E3BD		F1782
0000:E3DB		F1790
0000:E3EE		F1791
0000:E1FB		F1_A
0000:E34E		F1_B
0000:E21F		F3
0000:E152		F3A
0000:E15D		F3B
0000:E18B		F3D
0000:E1A1		F3D1
0000:E2AC		F4
0000:E2B2		F4E
0000:E401		FD_TBL
0000:4752		FILL
0000:4392		GATE_A20
0000:1FF0		GDT_BLD
0000:1BC6		H5
0000:2FA4		HD_INT
0000:1852		INT_287
0000:E8E1		K10
0000:E91B		K11
0000:E955		K12
0000:E95F		K13
0000:E969		K14
0000:E976		K15
0000:30A9		K16
0000:E87E		K6
0000:0008	Abs	K6L
0000:E886		K7
0000:E88E		K8
0000:E8C8		K9
0000:17D2		KBD_RESET
0000:E987*		KB_INT
0000:3054		KB_INT_1
0000:E82E*		KEYBOARD_IO

Address		Publics By Name
0000:2FC8		KEYBOARD_IO_1
0000:E1D7		LOCK
0000:0010	Abs	M4
0000:F0E4		M5
0000:F0EC		M6
0000:F0F4		M7
0000:F841*		MEMORY_SIZE_DETERMINE
0000:3E62		MEMORY_SIZE_DETERMINE_1
0000:E2C3*		NMI_INT
0000:3E76		NMI_INT_1
0000:0411		OBF_42
0000:E064		OBF_42A
0000:E06A		OBF_42B
0000:002C		POST1
0000:0C3F		POST2
0000:16AD		POST3
0000:1753		POST4
0000:187F		POST5
0000:199C		POST6
0000:1C2D		POST7
0000:EFD2*		PRINTER_IO
0000:346F		PRINTER_IO_1
0000:FF54*		PRINT_SCREEN
0000:46CC		PRINT_SCREEN_1
0000:174C		PROC_SHUTDOWN
0000:1720		PROT_PRT_HEX
0000:1719		PRT_HEX
0000:186A		PRT_SEG
0000:176C		P_MSG
0000:FFF0*		P_O_R
0000:38F5		READ_AC_CURRENT
0000:377B		READ_CURSOR
0000:3A3B		READ_DOT
0000:3DBC		READ_LPEN
0000:1861		RE_DIRECT
0000:16D0		ROM_CHECK
0000:1AF9		ROM_ERR
0000:16AD		ROS_CHECKSUM
0000:E739*		RS232_IO
0000:34F5		RS232_IO_1
0000:462A		RTC_INT
0000:38A3		SCROLL_DOWN
0000:37FF		SCROLL_UP
0000:24C1		SEEK

Address	Publics By Name
0000:37B6	SET_COLOR
0000:3751	SET_CPOS
0000:372A	SET_CTYPE
0000:364E	SET_MODE
0000:3F2F	SET_TOD
0000:1197	SHUT2
0000:114A	SHUT3
0000:169B	SHUT4
0000:11BC	SHUT6
0000:119A	SHUT7
0000:4252	SHUT9
0000:1FF9	SIDT_BLD
0000:FF23	SLAVE_VECTOR_TABLE
0000:E05B*	START
0000:00A6	START_1
0000:199C	STGTST_CNT
0000:1F1A	SYSINIT1
0000:1933	SYS_32
0000:1938	SYS_33
0000:193D	SYS_34
0000:1942	SYS_35
0000:1947	SYS_36
0000:194C	SYS_37
0000:1951	SYS_38
0000:FEA5*	TIMER_INT
0000:4684	TIMER_INT_1
0000:FE6E*	TIME_OF_DAY
0000:445C	TIME_OF_DAY_1
0000:03C7	TST4_B
0000:03D3	TST4_C
0000:03F7	TST4_D
0000:FEF3*	VECTOR_TABLE
0000:F065*	VIDEO_IO
0000:3605	VIDEO_IO_1
0000:F0A4*	VIDEO_PARMS
0000:37DC	VIDEO_STATE
0000:E0B7	VIR_ERR
0000:393B	WRITE_AC_CURRENT
0000:396E	WRITE_C_CURRENT
0000:3A4C	WRITE_DOT
0000:3D38	WRITE_TTY
0000:1713	XLAT_PR
0000:1B25	XMIT_8042
0000:1708	XPC_BYTE

Address		Publics By Value
0000:0000		BEGIN
0000:0008	Abs	K6L
0000:0010	Abs	M4
0000:002C		POST1
0000:00A6		START_1
0000:0222		C11
0000:03C7		TST4_B
0000:03D3		TST4_C
0000:03E5		E30B
0000:03EB		E30C
0000:03F7		TST4_D
0000:0405		C8042
0000:0411		OBF_42
0000:0454		C30
0000:09FB		CHK_VIDEO
0000:0C3F		POST2
0000:0C3F		C21
0000:114A		SHUT3
0000:1197		SHUT2
0000:119A		SHUT7
0000:11BC		SHUT6
0000:169B		SHUT4
0000:16AD		ROS_CHECKSUM
0000:16AD		POST3
0000:16B9		BLINK_INT
0000:16D0		ROM_CHECK
0000:1708		XPC_BYTE
0000:1713		XLAT_PR
0000:1719		PRT_HEX
0000:1720		PROT_PRT_HEX
0000:174C		PROC_SHUTDOWN
0000:1753		POST4
0000:1753		E_MSG
0000:176C		P_MSG
0000:177A		ERR_BEEP
0000:17AA		BEEP
0000:17D2		KBD_RESET
0000:17FD		DDS
0000:1805		D11
0000:1851		DUMMY_RETURN_1
0000:1852		INT_287

Address	Publics By Value
0000:1861	RE_DIRECT
0000:186A	PRT_SEG
0000:187F	EXC_00
0000:187F	POST5
0000:1884	EXC_01
0000:1889	EXC_02
0000:188E	EXC_03
0000:1893	EXC_04
0000:1898	EXC_05
0000:18B1	EXC_06
0000:18B6	EXC_07
0000:18BB	EXC_08
0000:18C0	EXC_09
0000:18C5	EXC_10
0000:18CA	EXC_11
0000:18CF	EXC_12
0000:18D4	EXC_13
0000:18D9	EXC_14
0000:18DE	EXC_15
0000:18E3	EXC_16
0000:18E8	EXC_17
0000:18ED	EXC_18
0000:18F2	EXC_19
0000:18F7	EXC_20
0000:18FC	EXC_21
0000:1901	EXC_22
0000:1906	EXC_23
0000:190B	EXC_24
0000:1910	EXC_25
0000:1915	EXC_26
0000:191A	EXC_27
0000:191F	EXC_28
0000:1924	EXC_29
0000:1929	EXC_30
0000:192E	EXC_31
0000:1933	SYS_32
0000:1938	SYS_33
0000:193D	SYS_34
0000:1942	SYS_35
0000:1947	SYS_36
0000:194C	SYS_37

Address	Publics By Value
0000:1951	SYS_38
0000:199C	POST6
0000:199C	STGTST_CNT
0000:1AF9	ROM_ERR
0000:1B25	XMIT_8042
0000:1B66	BOOT_STRAP_1
0000:1BC6	H5
0000:1C2D	POST7
0000:1F1A	SYSINIT1
0000:1FF0	GDT_BLD
0000:1FF9	SIDT_BLD
0000:20A5	DISKETTE_IO_1
0000:24C1	SEEK
0000:260E	DISK_INT_1
0000:2816	DSKETTE_SETUP
0000:28DA	DISK_SETUP
0000:2A71	DISK_IO
0000:2FA4	HD_INT
0000:2FC8	KEYBOARD_IO_1
0000:3054	KB_INT_1
0000:30A9	K16
0000:346F	PRINTER_IO_1
0000:34F5	RS232_IO_1
0000:3605	VIDEO_IO_1
0000:364E	SET_MODE
0000:372A	SET_CTYPE
0000:3751	SET_CPOS
0000:377B	READ_CURSOR
0000:3792	ACT_DISP_PAGE
0000:37B6	SET_COLOR
0000:37DC	VIDEO_STATE
0000:37FF	SCROLL_UP
0000:38A3	SCROLL_DOWN
0000:38F5	READ_AC_CURRENT
0000:393B	WRITE_AC_CURRENT
0000:396E	WRITE_C_CURRENT
0000:3A3B	READ_DOT
0000:3A4C	WRITE_DOT
0000:3D38	WRITE_TTY
0000:3DBC	READ_LPEN
0000:3E62	MEMORY_SIZE_DETERMINE_1

Address	Publics By Value
0000:3E6C	EQUIPMENT_1
0000:3E76	NMI_INT_1
0000:3F2F	SET_TOD
0000:3FE2	CASSETTE_IO_1
0000:4252	SHUT9
0000:4392	GATE_A20
0000:445C	TIME_OF_DAY_1
0000:462A	RTC_INT
0000:4684	TIMER_INT_1
0000:46CC	PRINT_SCREEN_1
0000:4752	FILL
0000:E05B*	START
0000:E05E	C1
0000:E060	C2
0000:E062	C8042A
0000:E064	OBF_42A
0000:E066	C8042B
0000:E068	C8042C
0000:E06A	OBF_42B
0000:E06C	E0
0000:E085	E0_A
0000:E09E	E0_B
0000:E0B7	VIR_ERR
0000:E0D0	CM4
0000:E0E9	E1
0000:E0FC	E1_B
0000:E10C	E1_C
0000:E11C	ADERR1
0000:E137	ADERR
0000:E152	F3A
0000:E15D	F3B
0000:E164	D1
0000:E174	D2
0000:E184	D2A
0000:E18B	F3D
0000:E1A1	F3D1
0000:E1C2	F1
0000:E1D7	LOCK
0000:E1FB	F1_A
0000:E21F	F3
0000:E234	CM1

Address	Publics By Value
0000:E25D	CM2
0000:E286	CM3
0000:E2AC	F4
0000:E2B2	F4E
0000:E2C3*	NMI_INT
0000:E2C6	CM4_A
0000:E2DF	CM4_B
0000:E2F8	CM4_C
0000:E311	CM4_D
0000:E32A	E1_A
0000:E34E	F1_B
0000:E372	BOOT_INVA
0000:E393	F1780
0000:E3A8	F1781
0000:E3BD	F1782
0000:E3DB	F1790
0000:E3EE	F1791
0000:E401	FD_TBL
0000:E6F2*	BOOT_STRAP
0000:E729*	A1 (UART Parameters for Overlaying Drivers)
0000:E739*	RS232_IO
0000:E82E*	KEYBOARD_IO
0000:E87E	K6
0000:E886	K7
0000:E88E	K8
0000:E8C8	K9
0000:E8E1	K10
0000:E91B	K11
0000:E955	K12
0000:E95F	K13
0000:E969	K14
0000:E976	K15
0000:E987*	KB_INT
0000:EC59*	DISKETTE_IO
0000:EF57*	DISK_INT (Floppy Disk ISR)
0000:EFC7*	DISK_BASE (Floppy Disk Parameter Table)
0000:EFD2*	PRINTER_IO
0000:F065*	VIDEO_IO
0000:F0A4*	VIDEO_PARMS

Address	Publics By Value
0000:F0E4	M5
0000:F0EC	M6
0000:F0F4	M7
0000:F841*	MEMORY_SIZE_DETERMINE
0000:F84D*	EQUIPMENT
0000:F859*	CASSETTE_IO
0000:FA6E*	CRT_CHAR_GEN
0000:FE6E*	TIME_OF_DAY
0000:FEA5*	TIMER_INT
0000:FEF3*	VECTOR_TABLE
0000:FF23	SLAVE_VECTOR_TABLE
0000:FF53*	DUMMY_RETURN
0000:FF54*	PRINT_SCREEN
0000:FFF0*	P_O_R
0000:FFF5*	Date Stamp of BIOS
0000:FFFE*	Hardware ID Byte (Model Number)

Source: IBM Corporation, Boca Raton, Florida 33432

18

BIOS Data Area

The BIOS data area is located at 00400–004FF and is commonly referenced as 0040:0000–0040:00FF. The actual use of this area may vary between BIOSes, and may also vary between different releases of a particular manufacturer's BIOS. The table below shows a typical usage. Locations shown as "not used" or "reserved" may in fact be used in some instances.

Location	Size	Description
00	word	COM1 Port Address
02	word	COM2 Port Address
04	word	COM3 Port Address
06	word	COM4 Port Address
08	word	LPT1 Port Address
0A	word	LPT2 Port Address
0C	word	LPT3 Port Address
0E	word	Not Used (PS/2 Extended BIOS Data Pointer)
10	word	Equipment Variable (Installed Hardware)
12	byte	Not Used (Manufacturing Test— Initialization Flag)
13	word	Memory Size In 1K Blocks
15	word	Not Used (Manufacturing Error Flag— Scratchpad)
17	byte	Keyboard Flag 1

Location	Size	Description
18	byte	Keyboard Flag 2
19	byte	Storage For Alternate Keyboard Entry
1A	word	Pointer To Head Of Keyboard Buffer
1C	word	Pointer To Tail Of Keyboard Buffer
1E	16 words	Keyboard Buffer—Room For 15 Entries
3E	byte	Floppy Recalibrate Flag
3F	byte	Floppy Motor Status
40	byte	Time Out Counter For Drive Motor Turn Off
41	byte	Floppy Status Byte
42	7 bytes	Floppy Controller Status Bytes
49	byte	Current CRT Display Mode
4A	word	Number Of Columns On Screen
4C	word	Video Buffer Length (bytes)
4E	word	Starting Address In Regen Buffer
50	8 words	Cursor Position For Each Of Up To 8 pages
60	word	Current Cursor Mode Setting
62	byte	Current Page Being Displayed
63	word	Base Address For Active Display Controller
65	byte	Current 3×8 Register Value
66	byte	Current Pallette Setting Color Card (3×9 Register)
67	double word	Virtual Save For Segment:Offset (Opt I/O ROM Init)
6B	byte	Virtual Mode Save (Pointer To I/O ROM Segment)
6C	double word	Timer Counter (Low Word Then High Word)
70	byte	Timer Overflow Flag (Timer Has Rolled Over)
71	byte	Break Key Flag (Bit 7 = 1)
72	word	Reset Flag (1234h = Warm Boot—Keyboard Reset)
74	byte	Hard Disk Status
75	byte	Number Of Hard Drives
76	byte	XT Hard Disk Control Byte
77	byte	XT Hard Disk Controller Port
78	byte	LPT1 Timeout Value
79	byte	LPT2 Timeout Value
7A	byte	LPT3 Timeout Value

Location	Size	Description
7B	byte	Not Used
7C	byte	COM1 Timeout Value
7D	byte	COM2 Timeout Value
7E	byte	COM3 Timeout Value
7F	byte	COM4 Timeout Value
80	word	Keyboard Buffer Start Pointer
82	word	Keyboard Buffer End Pointer
84	byte	Number Of Video Rows (−1)
85	word	Character Height In Bytes/Character
87	byte	Video Control State 1
88	byte	Video Control State 2
89	word	Not Used
8B	byte	Floppy Data and Step Rates
8C	byte	Hard Disk Controller Status Register
8D	byte	Hard Disk Error Status Register
8E	byte	Hard Disk Interrupt Control Flag
8F	byte	Combo Hard File/Floppy Card Bit 0 = 1
90	byte	Floppy Drive 0 Media State
91	byte	Floppy Drive 1 Media State
92	byte	Floppy Drive 0 Operation Start State
93	byte	Floppy Drive 1 Operation Start State
94	byte	Floppy Drive 0 Current Cylinder
95	byte	Floppy Drive 1 Current Cylinder
96	byte	Keyboard Flag 3
97	byte	Keyboard LED Flags
98	double word	Offset Address Vector To User Wait Flag
9A	double word	Segment Address Of User Wait Flag
9C	double word	Low Word Of User Wait Flag
9E	double word	High Word Of User Wait Flag
A0	byte	Wait Active Flag
A1	7 bytes	Reserved
A8	double word	EGA Parameter Table Pointer
AC	double word	EGA Save Area 1 Pointer
B0	double word	EGA Alpha Font Pointer
B4	double word	EGA Graphics Font Pointer
B8	double word	PS/2 Save Area 2 Pointer
BC	72 bytes	Reserved

0050:0000 is the Print_Screen Status Byte

The following tables contain data referred to by the BIOS. They include information describing the modes and status of the various peripherals attached to the CPU.

a. Video Display (See also Chapter 42)

Mode	Type	Adapter	Resolution	Box	Character	Colors
00h	Text	CGA [3]	320 × 200	8 × 8	40 × 25	16
		EGA [2,3]	320 × 350	8 × 14	40 × 25	16
		MCGA	320 × 400	8 × 16	40 × 25	16
		VGA [1]	360 × 400	9 × 16	40 × 25	16
01h	Text	CGA	320 × 200	8 × 8	40 × 25	16
		EGA [2]	320 × 350	8 × 14	40 × 25	16
		MCGA	320 × 400	8 × 16	40 × 25	16
		VGA [1]	360 × 400	9 × 16	40 × 25	16
02h	Text	CGA [3]	640 × 200	8 × 8	80 × 25	16
		EGA [2,3]	640 × 350	8 × 14	80 × 25	16
		MCGA	640 × 400	8 × 16	80 × 25	16
		VGA [1]	720 × 400	9 × 16	80 × 25	16
03h	Text	CGA	640 × 200	8 × 8	80 × 25	16
		EGA [2]	640 × 350	8 × 14	80 × 25	16
		MCGA	640 × 400	8 × 16	80 × 25	16
		VGA [1]	720 × 400	9 × 16	80 × 25	16
04h	Graph	CGA/EGA/MCGA/VGA	320 × 200	8 × 8	40 × 25	4
05h	Graph	CGA/EGA[3]/MCGA/VGA	320 × 200	8 × 8	40 × 25	4
06h	Graph	CGA/EGA/MCGA/VGA	640 × 200	8 × 8	80 × 25	2

Mode	Type	Adapter	Resolution	Box	Character	Colors
07h	Text	MDA/EGA	720×350	9×14	80×25	Mono
		VGA [1]	720×400	9×16	80×25	Mono
08h	Graph	PCjr	160×200	8×8	20×25	16
09h	Graph	PCjr	320×200	8×8	40×25	16
0Ah	Graph	PCjr	640×200	8×8	80×25	4
0Bh	——RESERVED——					
0Ch	——RESERVED——					
0Dh	Graph	EGA/VGA	320×200	8×8	40×25	16
0Eh	Graph	EGA/VGA	640×200	8×8	80×25	16
0Fh	Graph	EGA/VGA	640×350	8×14	80×25	Mono
10h	Graph	EGA/VGA	640×350	8×14	80×25	16
11h	Graph	MCGA/VGA	640×480	8×16	80×30	2
12h	Graph	VGA	640×480	9×16	80×30	16
13h	Graph	MCGA/VGA	320×200	8×8	40×25	256

[1] Enhanced VGA mode; otherwise the VGA can emulate either CGA or EGA characteristics in this mode.
[2] EGA mode when connected to an enhanced color display; otherwise emulates CGA characteristics in this mode.
[3] Denotes shades of gray.

b. Equipment Status Word

Bits	Description
0	Disk Drive Installed = 1
1	Mathematics Coprocessor Installed = 1
2–3	System Board RAM
	00 = 16K
	01 = 32K
	10 = 48K
	11 = 64K
2	Pointing Device Installed = 1 (PS/2)
3	Not Used (PS/2)
4–5	Initial Video Mode
	01 = 40 × 25 color
	10 = 80 × 25 color
	11 = 80 × 25 monochrome
6–7	Number of disk drives (If bit 0 = 1)
	00 = 1 drive attached
	01 = 2 drives attached
	10 = 3 drives attached
	11 = 4 drives attached
8	Not Used
9–11	Number Of Serial Cards Attached
12	Game Adapter Installed = 1
12	Not Used (PS/2)
13	Not Used
13	Internal Modem Installed = 1 (PS/2)
14–15	Number Of Printers Attached

c. Disk Controller Status Bits

7	6	5	4	3	2	1	0	Description
.	.	.	.	.	.	.	1	Illegal Command To Driver
.	.	.	.	.	.	1	.	Address Mark Not Found (Bad Sector)
.	.	.	.	.	.	1	1	Write-Protected Disk
.	.	.	.	.	1	.	.	Requested Sector Not Found
.	.	.	.	.	1	1	.	Diskette Change Line Active
.	.	.	.	1	.	.	.	DMA Overrun
.	.	.	.	1	.	.	1	DMA Attempt Across 64K Boundary
.	.	.	.	1	1	.	.	Invalid Media
.	.	.	1	.	.	.	.	CRC Error On Disk Read
.	.	1	.	.	.	.	.	Controller Error
.	1	.	.	.	.	.	.	Seek Failure
1	.	.	.	.	.	.	.	Disk Time Out (Drive Not Ready)

d. Port Status Bits

7	6	5	4	3	2	1	0	Description
.	.	.	.	.	.	.	1	Data Ready
.	.	.	.	.	.	1	.	Overrun Error
.	.	.	.	.	1	.	.	Parity Error
.	.	.	.	1	.	.	.	Framing Error
.	.	.	1	.	.	.	.	Break Detected
.	.	1	.	.	.	.	.	Transmit Holding Register (THR) Empty
.	1	.	.	.	.	.	.	Transmit Shift Register (TSR) Empty
1	.	.	.	.	.	.	.	Time Out

e. Modem Status Bits

7	6	5	4	3	2	1	0	Description
.	.	.	.	.	.	.	1	Change In Clear To Send (CTS) Status
.	.	.	.	.	.	1	.	Change In Data Set Ready (DSR) Status
.	.	.	.	.	1	.	.	Trailing Edge Ring Indicator
.	.	.	.	1	.	.	.	Change In Receive Line Signal
.	.	.	1	.	.	.	.	Clear To Send (CTS)
.	.	1	.	.	.	.	.	Data Set Ready (DSR)
.	1	.	.	.	.	.	.	Ring Indicator
1	.	.	.	.	.	.	.	Receive Line Signal Detected

f. Print Status Bits

7	6	5	4	3	2	1	0	Description
.	.	.	.	.	.	.	1	Time Out
.	.	.	.	.	x	x	.	Unused
.	.	.	.	1	.	.	.	I / O Error
.	.	.	1	.	.	.	.	Printer Selected
.	.	1	.	.	.	.	.	Out Of Paper
.	1	.	.	.	.	.	.	Acknowledged
1	.	.	.	.	.	.	.	Printer Not Busy

g. Cassette Services Return Codes

Code	Description
00h	Invalid Command
01h	CRC Error
02h	Data Transitions Lost
03h	No Data Located On Tape
04h	Data Not Found (PCjr only)
86h	No Cassette Port Available

h. The Global Descriptor Table

Offset	Description
00h	Dummy (Set To Zero)
08h	GDT Data Segment Location (Set To Zero)
10h	Source GDT Pointer
18h	Target GDT Pointer
20h	Pointer to BIOS code segment, initialized to zero. BIOS will use this area to create the protected-mode code segment.
28h	Pointer to BIOS stack segment, initialized to zero. BIOS will use this area to create the protected-mode stack segment.

i. Source/Target Global Descriptor Table Layout

Offset	Description
00h	Segment Limit
02h	24-bit Segment Physical Address
05h	Data Access Rights (set to 93h)
06h	Reserved Word (Must Be Zero)

19

BIOS and DOS Functions

In the following list of BIOS and DOS functions all numbers are hexadecimal. Interrupts may be caused by a signal on the INTR pin of the CPU. The CPU detects the interrupt at the end of execution of the current instruction. The flag register, CS (code segment), and IP (instruction pointer) are pushed on the stack to save the current state of the system. The trap and interrupt bits of the flag register are cleared to prevent any further interrupts while the interrupt is being handled. The interrupt vector selected is based on the interrupt number, and the vector is used to proceed to the interrupt routine. The routine issues an IRET instruction when it has finished processing the interrupt condition. This causes the saved system state to be restored, and the interrupted process continues. Interrupts may be ignored by using the CLI operation code, which clears the interrupt enable bit in the flag register. The NMI interrupt cannot be ignored. It is triggered by a signal on the CPU NMI pin.

BIOS	DOS	Interrupt Number	Memory	(AH)	(AL)	Description
X		00	00			Divide by Zero Error
X		01	04			Single Step
X		02	08			Non-Maskable Interrupt (NMI)
X		03	0C			Breakpoint Interrupt
X		04	10			Arithmetic Overflow
X		05	14			Print Screen Image
X		06	18			Reserved For Future Use
X		07	1C			Reserved For Future Use
X		08	20			System Timer-Tick (IRQ0)
X		09	24			Keyboard Attention (IRQ1)
X		0A	28			Reserved For Future Use
X		0B	2C			Communications COM2 (IRQ3)
X		0C	30			Communications COM1 (IRQ4)
X		0D	34			Hard Disk Attention (IRQ5)
X		0E	38			Floppy Disk (IRQ6)
X		0F	3C			Parallel Printer (IRQ7)
X		10	40	00		Set Video Mode
X				01		Set Cursor Type
X				02		Set Cursor Position
X				03		Get Cursor Position, Config
X				04		Get Light Pen Position
X				05		Set Active Display Page
X				06		Scroll Window Up
X				07		Scroll Window Down

BIOS	DOS	Interrupt Number	Memory	(AH)	(AL)	Description
X				08		Get Character & Attribute
X				09		Put Character & Attribute
X				0A		Write Character at Cursor
X				0B		Set Color Palette
X				0C		Write Graphics Pixel
X				0D		Read Graphics Pixel
X				0E		Write Text in Teletype Mode
X				0F		Get Status-Cols. Mode Page
X				10		Set Palette Registers
X				11		Character Generator
X				13		Write String
X		11	44			Get Equipment Status
X		12	48			Memory Size Determination
X		13	4C	00		Reset Floppy Disk System
X				01		Get Floppy Disk System Status
X				02		Read Floppy Disk
X				03		Write Disk Sectors
X				04		Verify Disk Sectors
X				05		Format Disk Track
X				06		Reserved
X				07		Reserved
X				08		Return Disk Drive Parameters
X				09		Initialize Fixed Disk Table
X				0A		Read Long Sector

BIOS	DOS	Interrupt Number	Memory	(AH)	(AL)	Description
X				0B		Write Long Sector
X				0C		Seek Cylinder
X				0D		Alternate Disk Reset
X				0E		Reserved
X				0F		Reserved
X				10		Reserved
X				11		Reserved
X				12		Reserved
X				13		Reserved
X				14		Reserved
X				15		Return DASD Type
X				16		Read Disk Change Line Status
X				17		Set DASD Type for Disk Format
X				18		Set Media Type For Format
X		14	50	00		Initialize Communication Port
X				01		Write Character to Comm Port
X				02		Read Character from Comm Port
X				03		Request Comm Port Status
X				04		Extended Initialization (PS/2)
X				05		Extended Comm Port Control (PS/2)
X		15	54	00		Turn On Cassette Motor
X				01		Turn Off Cassette Motor
X				02		Read Data Blocks from Cassette
X				03		Write Data Blocks to Cassette Drive

BIOS	DOS	Interrupt Number	Memory	(AH)	(AL)	Description
X				0F		Format Unit Periodic Interrupt (PS/2)
X				21		Power-On Self-Test Error Log (PS/2)
X				4F		Keyboard Intercept
X				80		Device Open
X				81		Device Close
X				82		Program Termination
X				83		Event Wait
X				84		Joystick Support
X				85		System Request Key Pressed
X				86		Wait
X				87		Move Block
X				88		Get Extended Memory Size
X				89		Switch Processor To Protected Mode
X				90		Device Busy
X				91		Interrupt Complete
X				C0		Return System-Configuration Param
X		15	54	C1		Return EBDA Segment Address
X				C2		Pointing Device BIOS Interface
X				C3		Enable/Disable Watchdog Timeout
X				C4		Programmable Option Select
X		16	58	00		Read Keyboard Character
X				01		Read Keyboard Status
X				05		Write to Keyboard Buffer
X				10		Get Keystroke
X				11		Check Keyboard
X				12		Get Keyboard Status Flag

BIOS	DOS	Interrupt Number	Memory	(AH)	(AL)	Description
X		17	5C	00		Write Character To Printer
X				01		Initialize Printer Port
X				02		Request Printer Port Status
X		18	60			Execute ROM BASIC
X		19	64			System Warm Boot
X		1A	68	00		Get Clock Counter
X				01		Set Clock Counter
X				02		Read Real-Time Clock
X				03		Set Real-Time Clock
X				04		Read Date from Real-Time Clock
X				05		Set Date of Real-Time Clock
X				06		Set System Alarm
X				07		Disable Real-Time Clock Alarm
X		1B	6C			Ctrl-Break Handler Address
X		1C	70			Timer Tick Interrupt
X		1D	74			Video-Initialization Parameter Table
X		1E	78			Floppy Disk-Init Param Table Pointer
X		1F	7C			Graphics Display Char Bit-Map Table
	X	20	80			Terminate Program
	X	21	84	00		Terminate Program
	X			01		Keyboard Input With Echo
	X			02		Display Output
	X			03		Auxiliary Input
	X			04		Auxiliary Output

BIOS	DOS	Interrupt Number	Memory	(AH)	(AL)	Description
	X			05		Printer Output
	X			06		Direct Console I/O
	X			07		Direct STDIN Input
	X			08		STDIN Input
	X			09		Display String
	X			0A		Buffered STDIN Onput
	X			0B		Check STDIN Status
	X			0C		Clear Buffer and Input
	X			0D		Reset Disk
	X			0E		Select Disk
	X			0F		Open File (File Control Block)
	X			10		Close File (File Control Block)
	X			11		Search For First Entry (FCB)
	X			12		Search For Next Entry (FCB)
	X			13		Delete File (File Control Block)
	X			14		Read Sequential File (FCB)
	X			15		Write Sequential File (FCB)
	X			16		Create File (File Control Block)
	X			17		Rename File (File Control Block)
	X	21	84	18		Reserved
	X			19		Get Default Drive
	X			1A		Get DTA Address
	X			1B		Get Allocation Table Information
	X			1C		Get Allocation Table Information For Specific Drive

BIOS	DOS	Interrupt Number	Memory	(AH)	(AL)	Description
	X			1D		Reserved
	X			1E		Reserved
	X			1F		Reserved
	X			20		Reserved
	X			21		Random File Read (File Control Block)
	X			22		Random File Write (File Control Block)
	X			23		Get File Size (File Control Block)
	X			24		Set Random-Record Field (FCB)
	X			25		Set Interrupt Vector
	X			26		Create PSP
	X			27		Random Block Read (FCB)
	X			28		Random Block Write (FCB)
	X			29		Parse File Name
	X			2A		Get System Date
	X			2B		Set System Date
	X			2C		Get System Time
	X			2D		Set System Time
	X			2E		Set Verify Flag
	X			2F		Get DTA Address
	X			30		Get DOS Version Number
	X			31		Terminate and Stay Resident
	X			32		Reserved
	X			33		Get/Set System Values
	X			34		Reserved

BIOS	DOS	Interrupt Number (AH)	Memory	(AL)	Description
	X	35			Get Interrupt Vector
	X	36			Get Free Disk Space
	X	37			Reserved
	X	38			Get/Set Country Information
	X	39			Create Subdirectory
	X	3A			Remove Subdirectory
	X	3B			Set Directory
	X	3C			Create/Truncate File (handle)
	X	3D			Open File (handle)
	X	3E			Close File (handle)
	X	3F			Read File or Device (handle)
	X	40			Write to File or Device (handle)
	X	41			Delete File
	X	42			Move File Pointer
	X	43			Get/Set File Attributes
	X	44		00	IOCTL: Get Device Information
	X			01	IOCTL: Set Device Information
	X			02	IOCTL: Character Device Read
	X			03	IOCTL: Character Device Write
	X			04	IOCTL: Block Driver Read
	X			05	IOCTL: Block Driver Write
	X			06	IOCTL: Get Input Status
	X			07	IOCTL: Get Output Status

BIOS	DOS	Interrupt Number	Memory	(AH)	(AL)	Description
	X	21	84	44	08	IOCTL: Block Device Removable?
	X				09	IOCTL: Block Device Local or Remote?
	X				0A	IOCTL: Handle Local or Remote?
	X				0B	IOCTL: Set Sharing Retry Count
	X				0C	IOCTL: Generic I/O for Handles
	X				0D	IOCTL: Generic I/O for Block Devices
	X				0E	IOCTL: Get Logical Drive Map
	X				0F	IOCTL: Set Logical Drive Map
	X			45		Duplicate Handle
	X			46		Force Duplicate Handle
	X			47		Get Current Directory
	X			48		Allocate Memory
	X			49		Release Memory
	X			4A		Modify Memory Allocation
	X			4B	00	Execute Program (EXEC)
	X				03	Load Overlay
	X			4C		Terminate With Return Code
	X			4D		Get Return Code
	X			4E		Search for First Match
	X			4F		Search for Next Match
	X			50		Reserved
	X			51		Reserved
	X			52		Reserved
	X			53		Reserved

BIOS	DOS	Interrupt Number	Memory	(AH)	(AL)	Description
	X			54		Get Verify Flag
	X			55		Reserved
	X			56		Rename File
	X			57	00	Get File Date and Time
					01	Set File Date and Time
	X			58		Reserved
	X			59		Get Extended Error Information
	X			5A		Create Temporary File
	X			5B		Create File
	X			5C		Set File Access
	X			5D		Reserved
	X			5E	00	Get Machine Name
	X				02	Set Printer Setup
	X				03	Get Printer Setup
	X			5F	02	Get Redirection List Entry
	X				03	Redirect Device
	X				04	Cancel Redirection
	X			60		Reserved
	X			61		Reserved
	X			62		Get PSP Address
	X			63	00	Get System Lead Byte Table
	X				01	Set Interim Console Flag
	X				02	Get Interim Console Flag
	X			64		Reserved

185

BIOS	DOS	Interrupt Number	Memory	(AH)	(AL)	Description
	X	21	84	65	01	Get Extended Country Information
	X			66	02	Get Global Code Page
	X			67		Set Global Code Page
	X			68		Set Handle Count
	X					Flush Buffer
	X			69		Reserved
	X			6A		Reserved
	X			6B		Reserved
	X			6C		Extended Open/Create
	X	22	88			Terminate Address
	X	23	8C			"Ctrl-C" Interrupt Vector
	X	24	90			Critical Error Vector
	X	25	94			Absolute Disk Read
	X	26	98			Absolute Disk Write
	X	27	9C			Terminate and Stay Resident
	X	28	A0			Idle Signal
	X	29	A4			TTY Output
	X	2A	A8			MS-Net Service
	X	2F	BC	01	00	Print Spool Installation Check
	X				01	Print Spool Submit File
	X				02	Print Spool Remove File
	X				03	Print Spool Remove All Files
	X				04	Print Spool Hold Queue/Get Status

BIOS	DOS	Interrupt Number	Memory	(AH)	(AL)	Description
	X				05	Print Spool Restart Queue
	X			B7	00	APPEND Installation Check
	X	30	C0			Long Jump Interface
	X	33	CC			Mouse Functions
	X	3F	FC			Overlay Interrupt
X		40	100			Hard Disk Chain
X		41	104			Hard Disk #1 Parameter Table Pointer
X		42	108			EGA Chain
X		43	10C			EGA Parameter Table Pointer
X		44	110			EGA Graphics Character Font
X		46	118			Hard Disk #2 Parameter Table Pointer
X		4A	128			AT Alarm Exit Address
X		50	140			AT Alarm Interrupt
X		51	144			Mouse Functions
	X(NET)	5A	168			Functions
	X(NET)	5B	16C			Boot Chain
	X(NET)	5C	170			NETBIOS Interface Entry
	X	67	19C	40		Get Extended Memory (EMM) Status
	X			41		Get Page Frame Segment
	X			42		Get Number Of Pages
	X			43		Get Handle/Allocate Memory
	X			44		Map Memory
	X			45		Release Handle and Memory
	X			46		Get Extended Memory (EMM) Version

BIOS	DOS	Interrupt Number	Memory	(AH)	(AL)	Description
	X			47		Save Mapping Context
	X			48		Restore Mapping Context
	X			49		Reserved
	X			4A		Reserved
	X			4B		Get Number Of EMM Handle
	X			4C		Get Pages Owned By Handle
	X			4D		Get Pages For All Handles
	X			4E	00	Get Page Mapping Registers
	X				01	Set Page Mapping Registers
	X				02	Get/Set Page Mapping Registers
	X				03	Get Size of Page Mapping Array
	X	67	19C	4F		Get/Set Partial Page Map
	X			50		Map/Unmap Multiple Handle Pages
	X			51		Reallocate Pages
	X			53		Get/Set Handle Name
	X			54		Get Handle Directory
	X			55		Alter Page Map and Jump
	X			56		Alter Page Map and Call
	X			57		Move/Exchange Memory Region
	X			58		Get Mappable Physical Address Array
	X			59		Get Expanded Memory Hardware Info
	X			5A		Allocate New Pages
	X			5B		Alternate Page Map Register Set
	X			5C		Prepare Expanded Memory Hardware

BIOS	DOS	Interrupt Number	Memory	(AH)	(AL)	Description
X	X	6D	1B4	5D		Enable/Disable OS/E Function Set VGA Service
X(AT)		70	1C0			IRQ8—Real-Time Clock
X(AT)		71	1C4			IRQ9—Redirected to IRQ2
X(AT)		72	1C8			IRQ10—Unassigned
X(AT)		73	1CC			IRQ11—Unassigned
X(AT)		74	1D0			IRQ12—Unassigned
X(AT)		75	1D4			IRQ13—80287 Coprocessor
X(AT)		76	1D8			IRQ14—AT Hard Disk
X(AT)		77	1DC			IRQ15—Unassigned
X		80–F0	200–3C0			BASIC
X		F1–FF	3C4–3FC			Not Used

DMA Channels

Channels 0–3 (DMA Number 1) are 8-bit channels (XT and AT)
Channels 4–7 (DMA Number 2) are 16-bit channels (AT only)

Channel	Usage
0	Memory Refresh
1	SDLC
2	Floppy Disk
3	Unassigned
4	Unassigned
5	Unassigned
6	Unassigned
7	Unassigned

8237 Direct Memory Access (DMA) Controller(s)

Controller 1: 8-bit (ports 000–00F)

Page Register	I/O Address
Channel 0 (AT)	087
Channel 1	083
Channel 2	081
Channel 3	082

Controller 2: 16-bit (AT Only—ports 0C0–0DF)

Page Register	I/O Address
Channel 5	08B
Channel 6	089
Channel 7	08A
Refresh (AT)	08F

Controller Registers:

Controller 1	Address 2	Command Codes
000	0C0	Channel 0/4 Base and Current Address
001	0C2	Channel 0/4 Base and Current Word Count
002	0C4	Channel 1/5 Base and Current Address
003	0C6	Channel 1/5 Base and Current Word Count

Controller 1	Address 2	Command Codes
004	0C8	Channel 2/6 Base and Current Address
005	0CA	Channel 2/6 Base and Current Word Count
006	0CC	Channel 3/7 Base and Current Address
007	0CE	Channel 3/7 Base and Current Word Count
008	0D0	Read Status; Write Command Register
009	0D2	Write Request Register
00A	0D4	Write Single Mask Register Bit
00B	0D6	Write Mode Register
00C	0D8	Clear Byte Pointer Flip-Flop
00D	0DA	Read Temporary Register; Write Master Clear
00E	0DC	Clear Mask Register
00F	0DE	Write All Mask Register Bits

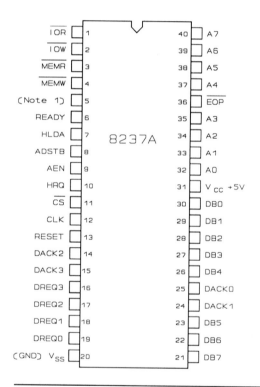

Pin Configuration.

Note: Pin 5 is an input that should always be at a logic high level. An internal pull-up resistor will establish a logic high when the pin is left floating. It is recommended that pin 5 be tied to V_{cc}.

22

8255 PIO (PC/XT)

Port A = 60   *Read Keyboard Scan Code or Power-On Diagnostic Outputs*

Port B = 61   *Write*

Bit 7   – Enable Keyboard/+ Clear Keyboard
Bit 6   – Hold Keyboard Clock Low
Bit 5   – Enable I/O Channel Check
Bit 4   – Enable RAM Parity Check
Bit 3   – Read High/+ Read Low Switches
Bit 2   Spare (often used for Turbo Mode)
Bit 1   + Speaker Data
Bit 0   + Timer 2 Gate Speaker

Port C = 62   *Read*

Bit 7   + RAM Parity Check
Bit 6   + I/O Channel Check
Bit 5   + Timer 2 Out
Bit 4   Spare
Bit 3   Switch Bit 4 or 8
Bit 2   Switch Bit 3 or 7
Bit 1   Switch Bit 2 or 6
Bit 0   Switch Bit 1 or 5

Control Port = 63

Normal Configuration Byte = 99 hexadecimal

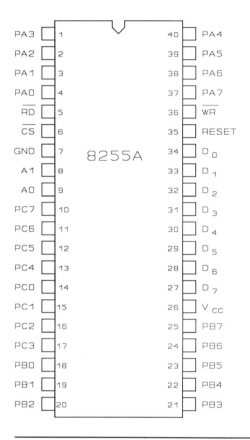

Pin Configuration.

23

AT 8255 Equivalent

The IBM AT uses an 8042 keyboard controller at ports 60h and 64h and an emulated read/write port at 61h to perform functions similar to those performed by the 8255 PIO.

Hex	Name		Description
60	Data		8042 Keyboard Controller Data Port
61	8255 Port B		Emulated Read/Write Port
	Bit 7	R	PC System Memory Parity Chcck
	Bit 6	R	CHK I/O Channel Check
	Bit 5	R	T20 Timer 2 Output
	Bit 4	R	RFD Refresh Detect
	Bit 3	R/W	EIC Enable I/O Channel Check
	Bit 2	R/W	ERP Enable Memory Parity Check
	Bit 1	R/W	SPK Speaker Data
	Bit 0	R/W	T2G Timer 2 Gate (speaker)
64	Control/Status 8042 Keyboard Controller		

Control Commands

20	Read Controller	
60	Write Controller	
AA	Self Test	
AB	Interface Test	

AC	Diagnostic Dump
AD	Disable Keyboard
AE	Enable Keyboard
C0	Read Discrete Input Port
D0	Read Discrete Output Port
D1	Write Discrete Output Port
E0	Read T0 and T1 Inputs
F0-FF	Pulse Discrete Output Port

Status Inputs

Bit 7	1 = Parity Error
Bit 6	1 = Receiver Time Out
Bit 5	1 = Transmitter Time Out
Bit 4	1 = Keyboard Inhibited
Bit 3	1 = Command; 0 = Data
Bit 2	1 = Reset OK; 0 = Power On
Bit 1	1 = Input Buffer Full
Bit 0	1 = Output Buffer Full

The AT keyboard controller also has a discrete input port and a discrete output port. These are accessed with the read/write port commands, as follows:

Discrete Input Port

Bit 7	Keyboard Inhibit Switch, 0 = Locked
Bit 6	Video Default, 0 = CGA; 1 = MDA
Bit 5	Manufacturing Jumper, 0 = Jumper; 1 = No Jumper
Bit 4	System RAM, 0 = 256K; 1 = 512K

Discrete Output Port

Bit 7	Keyboard Serial Data Out
Bit 6	Keyboard Serial Clock Out
Bit 5	Input Buffer Empty, 0 = Full; 1 = Empty
Bit 4	Output Buffer Full, 0 = Empty; 1 = Full
Bit 1	Gate A20
Bit 0	System Reset

Refer to Chapter 31 for additional details.

24

8259 Interrupt Controller

The 8259 programmable interrupt controller accesses its internal register set through two I/O ports. The 8259 is initialized by loading an up-to-4 byte configuration sequence. The 8259 then responds in its operation mode. Configuration bytes may vary due to hardware implementation. The port usage shown below is in the operation mode.

Interrupt Controller Number 1

Ports 20 and 21

Interrupts are positive-edge sense.

Port 20 is used to acknowledge and re-enable the 8259.

To send non-specific end-of-interrupt code
```
    mov     al,20h
    out     20h,al
```

Port 21 is used to set/clear the masking register.
A Mask Bit = 0 = > enable, 1 = > disable a specific IRQ

To read the Interrupt Mask Register
```
    in      al,21h          Bit 7-0 = IRQ 7-0
```
To write the Interrupt Mask Register
```
    mov     al,mask
    out     21h,al
```

Interrupt Controller Number 2 (AT Only)

Ports A0 and A1

Interrupts are positive-edge sense.

Port A0 is used to acknowledge and re-enable the 8259.

To send non-specific end-of-interrupt code
```
      mov       al,20h
      out       A0h,al
```

Port A1 is used to set/clear the masking register.
A Mask Bit = 0 = > enable, 1 = > disable a specific IRQ

To read the Interrupt Mask Register
```
      in        al,21h   Bit 7-0 = IRQ 15-8
```

To write the Interrupt Mask Register
```
      mov       al,mask
      out       A1h,al
```

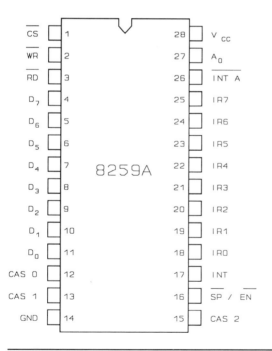

$\overline{CS}$ 1		28 V_{CC}
$\overline{WR}$ 2		27 A_0
$\overline{RD}$ 3		26 $\overline{INT\ A}$
D_7 4		25 IR7
D_6 5		24 IR6
D_5 6		23 IR5
D_4 7	8259A	22 IR4
D_3 8		21 IR3
D_2 9		20 IR2
D_1 10		19 IR1
D_0 11		18 IR0
CAS 0 12		17 INT
CAS 1 13		16 $\overline{SP}$ / $\overline{EN}$
GND 14		15 CAS 2

Pin Configuration.

25

8253/8254 Counter/Timer

The internal count registers of the 8253/8254 operate in a down-counter mode. If you are reading register counts for high-resolution timing routines, each count from counter 0 is equal to 1/1.19318 megahertz or 0.8380966 microseconds. The counter is reloaded after the count reaches zero approximately every 53 milliseconds.

Port	Section	Description
40	Counter 0	Real-Time Clock Tick Count = 0FFFFh Output to IRQ0 every 53 milliseconds (18.2 ticks per second)
41	Counter 1	DRAM Refresh Count = 0012h Output to DRQ0 (XT) Refresh Logic (AT) (Refresh approximately every 15 microseconds)
42	Counter 2	Speaker Oscillator Gated by Bit 0 of 8255 Port B

43   Control Register
                Bit 7, 6   Select Counter 0, 1, or 2
                Bit 5, 4   Latch LSB, MSB, LSB–MSB
                Bit 3, 2, 1   Mode
                  0— Interrupt on Count
                  1—One-Shot
                  2—Rate Generator
                  3—Square Wave Generator
                  4—Triggered Strobe (software)
                  5—Triggered Strobe (hardware)
                Bit 0   Binary/BCD Counting

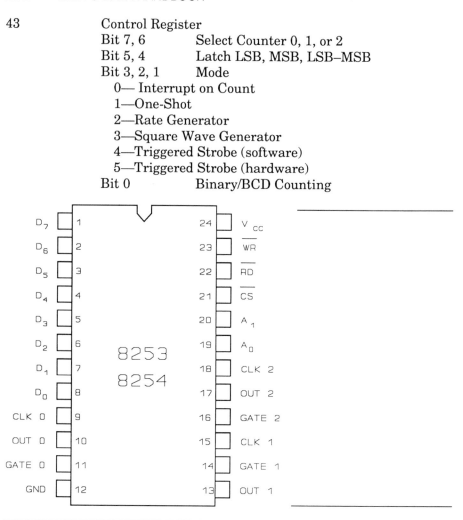

Pin Configuration.

26

8250 Serial Chip Notes

The XT/AT serial ports may be implemented with a variety of chips, all variations of the 8250 UART architecture. Currently, National Semiconductor produces seven versions of the part. Functionally, these parts appear to be the same. However, there are some differences between members of the 8250 family that may cause operational anomalies. The integrated circuits most commonly utilized are labeled:

INS8250	NMOS Device
INS8250-B	NMOS Device
INS8250A	XMOS Device
INS82C50A	CMOS Device
NS16450	XMOS Device
NS16C450	CMOS Device
NS16550A	XMOS Device

The INS8250 is the original version of the part. The INS8250 is the same as the INS8250-B but with faster CPU bus timing as compared with the INS8250-B. The INS8250-B is the slower of the two parts and is used in many popular 8088-based microcomputers. Both parts have relatively slow access cycle delays, requiring extra NOP's between CPU read/write cycles.

The early INS8250 had an "interrupt pending" glitch, which was corrected on later versions.

The INS8250A is a revision of the INS8250 using the more advanced XMOS process. The XMOS process yields closer threshold voltage control, more reliably implemented process topography, and finer control over the active area critical dimensions. It is used in many popular 8086-based microcomputers.

Some bugs in earlier parts that were previously avoided by BIOS coding were corrected in the INS8250A. Correcting these bugs possibly makes the INS8250A incompatible with some software packages. The scratch register, register number 7, was included on the INS8250A, the NS16450, the 16C450, and the 16550A versions.

The NS16450 is the faster-speed (CPU bus timing) version of the INS8250A. It is used by many popular 80286-based microcomputers.

The NS16550A is the newest member of the UART family. It powers-up in the NS16450 mode and is completely compatible with all software written for the NS16450. It has advanced features such as on-board FIFO's, a DMA interface, faster CPU bus timings, and a much higher maximum baud rate than the NS16450. The NS16550A should be used for all new non-CMOS designs, including those that were originally done with the NS16550. It is used in recent versions of popular 80286-based, 80386-based, and ROM-based microcomputers. Software written for the NS16550 is completely compatible with the NS16550A.

The NS16550 powers-up in the NS16450 mode and is completely compatible with all software written for the NS16450. The NS16550 has advanced features such as a DMA interface. The on-board FIFO's are essentially non-functional. This part was issued on a limited basis.

The INS82C50A is a CMOS version of the INS8250A. It functions identically and for most AC parameters has the same timing specifications as the INS8250A. It draws approximately 1/10 (10 milliamperes) of the maximum operating current of the INS8250A.

The NS16C450 is a CMOS version of the NS16450. It functions identically and for most AC parameters has the same timing specification as the NS16450. It draws approximately 1/12 (10 milliamperes) of the maximum operating current of the NS16450.

When selecting or replacing 8250 family integrated circuits, the preferred types are of the 16x50 series.

Note: The XMOS and CMOS UART's are not plug-in replacements for the INS8250/INS8250-B when used with ICU's that are in the popular edge-triggered configuration. However, there are easily implemented adjustments to the driving software or associated hardware that will allow these parts to be a plug-in replacement.

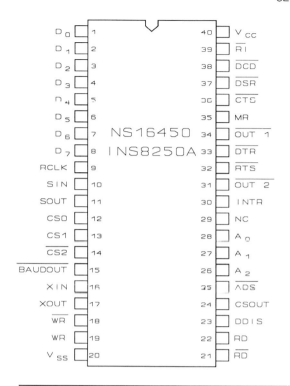

Pin Configuration.

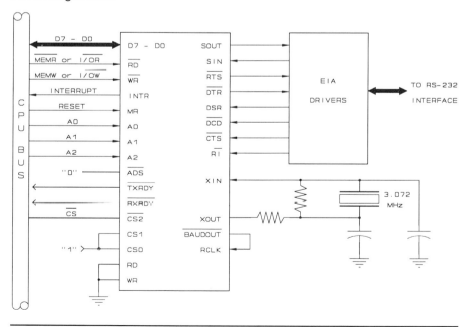

UART Connection Diagram.

27

8250 Register Descriptions

COM1

Register	Port	No.	Bit 7	Bit 6	Bit 5	Bit 4	Bit 3	Bit 2	Bit 1	Bit 0
DATA	3F8	0	Bit 7	Bit 6	Bit 5	Bit 4	Bit 3	Bit 2	Bit 1	Bit 0
DLL	3F8	0	Baud Rate Generator Least Significant Byte Divide Count (DLAB = 1)							
DLH	3F9	1	Baud Rate Generator Most Significant Byte Divide Count (DLAB = 1)							
IER	3F9	1	0	0	0	-	Modem Interrupt Enable	Receiver Line Interrupt Enable	Transmit Data Interrupt Enable	Receive Data Interrupt Enable
IIR	3FA	2	0	0	0	0	0	Active Interrupt Bit 1	Active Interrupt Bit 0	Interrupt Pending
LCR	3FB	3	DLAB Divisor Latch Bit	Set Break	Parity Mode Bit 2	Parity Mode Bit 1	Parity Mode Bit 0	Stop Bit Length	Character Length Bit 1	Character Length Bit 0
MCR	3FC	4	0	0	0	Loopback	-OUT2	0	-RTS	-DTR
LSR	3FD	5	0	TEMT	THRE	Break	Framing	Parity	Overrun	Receiver Ready
MSR	3FE	6	DCD	RI	DSR	CTS	DDCD	TERI	DDSR	DCTS
SCR	3FF	7	Scratch Pad Register							

COM2

Register	Port	No.	Bit 7	Bit 6	Bit 5	Bit 4	Bit 3	Bit 2	Bit 1	Bit 0
DATA	2F8	0	Bit 7	Bit 6	Bit 5	Bit 4	Bit 3	Bit 2	Bit 1	Bit 0
DLL	2F8	0	Baud Rate Generator Least Significant Byte Divide Count (DLAB = 1)							
DLH	2F9	1	Baud Rate Generator Most Significant Byte Divide Count (DLAB = 1)							
IER	2F9	1	0	0	0	-	Modem Interrupt Enable	Receiver Line Interrupt Enable	Transmit Data Interrupt Enable	Receive Data Interrupt Enable
IIR	2FA	2	0	0	0	0	0	Active Interrupt Bit 1	Active Interrupt Bit 0	Interrupt Pending
LCR	2FB	3	DLAB Divisor Latch Bit	Set Break	Parity Mode Bit 2	Parity Mode Bit 1	Parity Mode Bit 0	Stop Bit Length	Character Length Bit 1	Character Length Bit 0
MCR	2FC	4	0	0	0	Loopback	-OUT2	0	-RTS	-DTR
LSR	2FD	5	0	TEMT	THRE	Break	Framing	Parity	Overrun	Receiver Ready
MSR	2FE	6	DCD	RI	DSR	CTS	DDCD	TERI	DDSR	DCTS
SCR	2FF	7	Scratch Pad Register							

COM3

Register	Port	No.	Bit 7	Bit 6	Bit 5	Bit 4	Bit 3	Bit 2	Bit 1	Bit 0
DATA	3E8	0	Bit 7	Bit 6	Bit 5	Bit 4	Bit 3	Bit 2	Bit 1	Bit 0
DLL	3E8	0	Baud Rate Generator Least Significant Byte Divide Count (DLAB = 1)							
DLH	3E9	1	Baud Rate Generator Most Significant Byte Divide Count (DLAB = 1)							
IER	3E9	1	0	0	0	-	Modem Interrupt Enable	Receiver Line Interrupt Enable	Transmit Data Interrupt Enable	Receive Data Interrupt Enable
IIR	3EA	2	0	0	0	0	0	Active Interrupt Bit 1	Active Interrupt Bit 0	Interrupt Pending
LCR	3EB	3	DLAB Divisor Latch Bit	Set Break	Parity Mode Bit 2	Parity Mode Bit 1	Parity Mode Bit 0	Stop Bit Length	Character Length Bit 1	Character Length Bit 0
MCR	3EC	4	0	0	0	Loopback	-OUT2	0	-RTS	-DTR
LSR	3ED	5	0	TEMT	THRE	Break	Framing	Parity	Overrun	Receiver Ready
MSR	3EE	6	DCD	RI	DSR	CTS	DDCD	TERI	DDSR	DCTS
SCR	3EF	7	Scratch Pad Register							

COM4

Register	Port	No.	Bit 7	Bit 6	Bit 5	Bit 4	Bit 3	Bit 2	Bit 1	Bit 0
DATA	2E8	0	Bit 7	Bit 6	Bit 5	Bit 4	Bit 3	Bit 2	Bit 1	Bit 0
DLL	2E8	0	Baud Rate Generator Least Significant Byte Divide Count (DLAB = 1)							
DLH	2E9	1	Baud Rate Generator Most Significant Byte Divide Count (DLAB = 1)							
IER	2E9	1	0	0	0	-	Modem Interrupt Enable	Receiver Line Interrupt Enable	Transmit Data Interrupt Enable	Receive Data Interrupt Enable
IIR	2EA	2	0	0	0	0	0	Active Interrupt Bit 1	Active Interrupt Bit 0	Interrupt Pending
LCR	2EB	3	DLAB Divisor Latch Bit	Set Break	Parity Mode Bit 2	Parity Mode Bit 1	Parity Mode Bit 0	Stop Bit Length Bit 0	Character Length Bit 1	Character Length Bit 0
MCR	2EC	4	0	0	0	Locpback	-OUT2	0	-RTS	-DTR
LSR	2ED	5	0	TEMT	THRE	Break	Framing	Parity	Overrun	Receiver Ready
MSR	2EE	6	DCD	RI	DSR	CTS	DDCD	TERI	DDSR	DCTS
SCR	2EF	7	Scratch Fad Register							

28

Logical and Physical Devices

The logical names COM1, COM2, COM3, COM4, LPT1, LPT2, and LPT3 and their physical addresses on the I/O bus are often a source of confusion. A logical device such as "LPT1:" is not always found at the same address. As the port addresses are scanned by the execution of the BIOS code in a particular order, the first device found is always labeled number 1. The port addresses identified in this manner are stored in a device list.

Having a particular physical address does not ensure that a device will be assigned a particular device number.

The order in which the physical devices are scanned is:

COM Ports: 3F8, 2F8, 3E8, 2E8
LPT Ports: 3BC, 378, 278

Use DEBUG to inspect the port list.

dw40:0 7 = COM list
dw40:8 F = LPT list

The system BIOS on some PCs only enables COM1 and COM2. ADDCOM Software, P. O. Box 296, Candia, NH 03034, telephone (603) 483-5100, offers software to increase the possible number of serial ports from 2 to 4 for $24.95.

The ADDCOM software package consists of four programs, plus documentation. The package requires MS-DOS 3.3 or higher and the additional serial port hardware. The ports are enabled by ADDCOM.COM, which runs from your AUTOEXEC.BAT file. SWAP13.COM and SWAP24.COM permit application programs that support only COM1 and COM2 to actually access the COM3 and COM4 hardware when addressing COM1 and COM2. The fourth program is COMPORTS.EXE, a diagnostic utility that reports the addresses and status of the COM ports.

29

Using the User ROM

The Power-On Self Tests (POST) are described in Chapter 13. The occasion may arise when the designer of a PC adapter card desires to connect into the power-on initialization sequence. The BIOS provides a means for implementing this feature.

During the POST, the BIOS loads a set of default vectors into the appropriate BIOS interrupt addresses. The BIOS then executes code that scans the memory addresses from C8000 to F4000 in blocks of 2K searching for valid modules on the I/O bus. A valid module will have a 55h as the contents of byte 0, AAh as the contents of byte 1, and a length indicator as the contents of byte 2. A checksum (modulo hexadecimal 100) must be zero when calculated over the number of 512 byte blocks stored in the length indicator byte. The length indicator byte must not exceed FBh regardless of the length of the code. A sum of 00h must be forced starting with byte 0 up to whatever length is stored in byte 2. The actual code may be longer, but an error will be indicated if the length byte is larger than FBh.

If a module is found to be valid by passing the three tests listed above, the BIOS will execute a Far Call to the initialization code, which must start in byte 3. If it is desired to return control after the computer boots, at this point the boot vector is modified to point to the entry point of the user code. At the conclusion of the user initialization code a Far Return is executed so that the BIOS can complete the power-on routines. If the boot vector has been modified to point to the user entry point, the user will regain control when the computer boots.

If the user module has been coded correctly, it will begin with a word containing 55AAh and will have a checksum of 00h over the length indicator contained in byte 2. The length indicator is divisible by four.

30

PC/XT Keyboard
Scan Codes

Key Number	Scan Code	Base Case	Upper Case	CTRL	ALT
1	01	ESC	ESC	ESC	-
2	02	1	!	-	ext
3	03	2	@	NUL	ext
4	04	3	#	-	ext
5	05	4	$	-	ext
6	06	5	%	-	ext
7	07	6	<	RS	ext
8	08	7	&	-	ext
9	09	8	*	-	ext
10	0A	9	(	-	ext
11	0B	0	)	-	ext
12	0C	-	_	US	ext
13	0D	=	+	-	ext
14	0E	Backspace	Backspace	DEL	-
15	0F	TAB	Ext	-	-
16	10	q	Q	DC1	ext
17	11	w	W	ETB	ext
18	12	e	E	ENQ	ext
19	13	r	R	DC2	ext
20	14	t	T	DC4	ext
21	15	y	Y	EM	ext
22	16	u	U	NAK	ext
23	17	i	I	HT	ext
24	18	o	O	SI	ext
25	19	p	P	DLE	ext

Key Number	Scan Code	Base Case	Upper Case	CTRL	ALT
26	1A	[	{	ESC	-
27	1B	]	}	GS	-
28	1C	Enter	Enter	LF	-
29	1D	Ctrl	-	-	-
30	1E	a	A	SOH	ext
31	1F	s	S	DC3	ext
32	20	d	D	EOT	ext
33	21	f	F	ACK	ext
34	22	g	G	BEL	ext
35	23	h	H	BS	ext
36	24	j	J	LF	ext
37	25	k	K	VT	ext
38	26	l	L	FF	ext
39	27	;	:	-	-
40	28	'	"	-	-
41	29	`	~	-	-
42	2A	Left Shift	-	-	-
43	2B	\	|	FS	-
44	2C	z	Z	SUB	ext
45	2D	x	X	CAN	ext
46	2E	c	C	ETX	ext
47	2F	v	V	SYN	ext
48	30	b	B	STX	ext
49	31	n	N	SO	ext
50	32	m	M	CR	ext

Key Number	Scan Code	Base Case	Upper Case	CTRL	ALT
51	33	,	<	-	-
52	34	.	>	-	-
53	35	/	?	-	-
54	36	Right Shift	-	-	-
55	37	*	Print Screen	ext	-
56	38	Alt	-	-	-
57	39	Space	Space	Space	Space
58	3A	Caps Lock	-	-	-
59	3B	F1	ext	ext	ext
60	3C	F2	ext	ext	ext
61	3D	F3	ext	ext	ext
62	3E	F4	ext	ext	ext
63	3F	F5	ext	ext	ext
64	40	F6	ext	ext	ext
65	41	F7	ext	ext	ext
66	42	F8	ext	ext	ext
67	43	F9	ext	ext	ext
68	44	F10	ext	ext	ext
69	45	Number Lock	-	Pause	-
70	46	Scroll Lock	-	Break	-
71	47	Home	N/A	ext	-
72	48	Up	N/A	-	-
73	49	Page Up	N/A	ext	-
74	4A	Pad Minus	N/A	-	-
75	4B	Left	N/A	ext	-

Key Number	Scan Code	Base Case	Upper Case	CTRL	ALT
76	4C	Pad 5	N/A	-	-
77	4D	Right	N/A	ext	-
78	4E	Pad Plus	N/A	-	-
79	4F	End	N/A	ext	-
80	50	Down	N/A	ext	-
81	51	Page Down	N/A	ext	-
82	52	Insert	N/A	-	-
83	53	Delete	-	**	**

NOTES: 1) ext = extended (Returns a code of 00 followed by the Scan Code)
2) ** = CTRL-ALT-Del = Cold Boot

31

AT Keyboard

The keyboard is a low-profile, 84-key, detachable unit. The keyboard uses a bi-directional serial interface to carry signals between the keyboard and system unit.

The keyboard is able to detect all keys that are pressed, and their scan codes will be sent to the interface in correct sequence, regardless of the number of keys held down. Keystrokes entered while the interface is inhibited (when the keylock is on) will be lost. Keystrokes are stored only when the keyboard is not serviced by the system.

The keyboard has a 16-character, first-in/first-out (FIFO) buffer where data is stored until the interface is ready to receive it. A buffer-overrun condition will occur if more than sixteen codes are placed in the buffer before the first keyed data is sent. The seventeenth code will be replaced with the overrun code, 00, hexadecimal. (The 17th position is reserved for overrun codes.) If more keys are pressed before the system allows a keyboard output, the data will be lost. When the keyboard is allowed to send data, the characters in the buffer will be sent as in normal operation, and new data entered will be detected and sent.

All keys are classified as *make/break*, which means when a key is pressed, the keyboard sends a make code for that key to the keyboard controller. When the key is released, its break code is sent (the break code for a key is its make code preceded by F0, hexadecimal).

All keys are *typematic*. When a key is pressed and held down, the keyboard continues to send the make code for that key until the key is released. The rate at which the make code is sent is known as the *typematic rate*. When two or more keys are held down, only the last key pressed repeats at the typematic rate. Typematic operation stops when the last key pressed is released, even if other keys are still held down. When a key is pressed and held down while the interface is inhibited, only the first make code is stored in the buffer. This prevents buffer overflow as a result of typematic action.

The keyboard logic generates a power-on reset (POR) when power is applied to the keyboard. The POR lasts a minimum of 300 milliseconds and a maximum of 9 seconds. The keyboard may issue a false return during the first 200 milliseconds after the +5 volts DC is established at the 90% level. Therefore, the keyboard interface is disabled for this period.

Immediately following the POR, the keyboard executes a basic assurance test (BAT). This test consists of a checksum of all read-only memory (ROM), and a stuck-bit and addressing test of all random access memory (RAM) in the keyboard's microprocessor. The mode indicators—three light-emitting diodes (LED's) on the upper right-hand corner of the keyboard—are turned on then off, and must be observed to ensure they are operational. Execution of the BAT will take from 600 to 900 milliseconds. This is in addition to the time required for the POR. The BAT can also be started by a RESET command.

After the BAT, and when the interface is enabled ("clock" and "data" lines are set high), the keyboard sends a completion code to the interface — either AA, hexadecimal, for satisfactory completion or FC, hexadecimal (or any other code), for a failure. If the system issues a "RESEND" command, the keyboard sends the BAT completion code again. Otherwise, the keyboard sets the keys to typematic and make/break.

The keyboard cable connects to the system board through a 5-pin DIN connector described in Chapter 11, Section k. In addition, the system board has a test—input port for the keyboard. T0 is the keyboard clock (input) and T1 is the keyboard data (input).

The keyboard controller is a single-chip microcomputer (Intel 8042), located on the system board, that is programmed to support the IBM Personal Computer AT Keyboard serial interface. The keyboard controller receives serial data from the keyboard, checks the parity of the data, translates scan codes, and presents the data to the system as a byte of data in its output buffer. The controller will interrupt the system when data is placed in its output buffer.

The status register contains bits that indicate if an error was detected while receiving the data. Data may be sent to the keyboard by writing to the controller's input buffer. The byte of data will be sent from the system board to the keyboard, serially, with an odd parity bit inserted, automatically. The keyboard is required to acknowledge all data transmissions. No transmission should be sent to the keyboard until acknowledgment is received for the previous byte sent.

The keyboard sends data in a serial format using an 11-bit frame. The first bit is a start bit, and it is followed by eight data bits, an odd parity bit, and a stop bit. The data transmitted from the keyboard is synchronized to a clock supplied by the keyboard. At the end of a transmission the keyboard controller disables the interface until the system accepts the byte. If the byte of data is received by the system board with a parity error, a "RESEND" command is automatically sent to the keyboard. If the keyboard controller is unable to receive the data correctly, a hexadecimal "FF" is placed in the controller output buffer and the parity bit in the status register is set to "1", indicating a receive parity error.

The keyboard controller will also time a byte of data from the keyboard. If a keyboard transmission does not end within two milliseconds, a hexadecimal "FF" is placed in the keyboard controller's output buffer, and the receive time-out bit is set in the status register. No retries will be attempted on a receive time-out error.

Scan codes that are received from the keyboard are converted by the keyboard controller before they are placed into the controller's output buffer. The figure on the following page shows a keyboard layout with its key numbers.

Data is sent to the keyboard in the same serial format used to receive data from the keyboard. A parity bit is automatically inserted by the keyboard controller. If the keyboard does not start clocking the data out of the keyboard controller within 15 milliseconds, or complete that clocking within 2 milliseconds, a hexadecimal "FE" is placed in the keyboard controller's output buffer, and the transmit time-out error bit is set in the status register. The keyboard is required to respond to all transmissions. If the response contains a parity error, a hexadecimal "FE" is placed in the keyboard controller's output buffer, and the transmit time-out and parity error bits are set in the status register. The keyboard controller is programmed to set a time limit for the keyboard to respond. If 25 milliseconds are exceeded, the keyboard controller places a hexadecimal "FE" in its output buffer and sets the transmit and receive time-out error bits in the status register. No retries will be made by the keyboard controller for any transmission error.

The keyboard interface may be inhibited by a key-controlled hardware switch, although all transmissions to the keyboard will be allowed regardless of the state of the switch. The keyboard controller tests data received from the keyboard to determine if the byte received is a command response or a scan code. If the byte is a command response, it is placed in the keyboard controller's output buffer. If the byte is a scan code, it is ignored.

The keyboard controller communicates with the system through a status register, an output buffer, and an input buffer. The following figure is a block diagram of the keyboard interface.

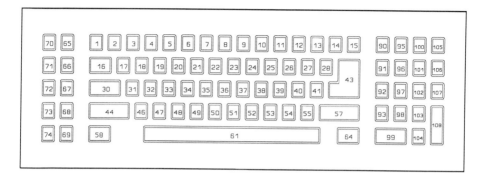

Keyboard Layout—84-key.

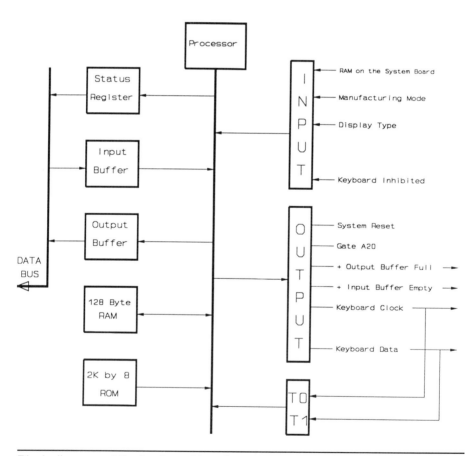

Block diagram of the keyboard interface.

Scan Code Translation Table

Key	Keyboard Scan Code	System Scan Code	Key	Keyboard Scan Code	System Scan Code
90	00	FF	44	12	2A
2	76	01	14	5D	2B
3	16	02	46	1A	2C
4	1E	03	47	22	2D
5	26	04	48	21	2E
6	25	05	49	2A	2F
7	2E	06	50	32	30
8	36	07	51	31	31
9	3D	08	52	3A	32
10	3E	09	53	41	33
11	46	0A	54	49	34
12	45	0B	55	4A	35
13	4E	0C	57	59	36
15	55	0D	106	7C	37
16	66	0E	58	11	38
17	0D	0F	61	29	39
18	15	10	64	58	3A
19	1D	11	70	05	3B
20	24	12	65	06	3C
21	2D	13	71	04	3D
22	2C	14	66	0C	3E
23	35	15	72	03	3F
24	3C	16	67	0B	40
	43	17	73	02 or 83	41

Key	Keyboard Scan Code	System Scan Code	Key	Keyboard Scan Code	System Scan Code
25	44	18	68	0A	42
26	4D	19	74	01	43
27	54	1A	69	09	44
28	5B	1B	95	77	45
43	5A	1C	100	7E	46
30	14	1D	91	6C	47
31	1C	1E	96	75	48
32	1B	1F	101	7D	49
33	23	20	107	7B	4A
34	2B	21	92	6B	4B
35	34	22	97	73	4C
36	33	23	102	74	4D
37	3B	24	108	79	4E
38	42	25	93	69	4F
39	4B	26	98	72	50
40	4C	27	103	7A	51
41	52	28	99	70	52
1	0E	29	104	71	53
			105	7F or 84	54

The following Scan Codes are reserved:

Keyboard Scan Codes	System Scan Codes	Keyboard Scan Codes	System Scan Codes
60	55	40	6B
61	56	48	6C
78	57	50	6D
07	58	57	6E
0F	59	6F	6F
17	5A	13	70
1F	5B	19	71
27	5C	39	72
2F	5D	51	73
37	5E	53	74
3F	5F	5C	75
47	60	5F	76
4F	61	62	77
56	62	63	78
5E	63	64	79
08	64	65	7A
10	65	67	7B
18	66	68	7C
20	67	6A	7D
28	68	6D	7E
30	69	6E	7F
38	6A		

STATUS REGISTER

The keyboard status register is an 8-bit read-only register at I/O address 64, hexadecimal. It contains information about the state of the keyboard controller (Intel microcomputer 8042) and interface. It may be read at any time.

Status Register Bit Definition

Bit 0   Output Buffer Full—A "0" in this bit indicates that the keyboard controller's output buffer contains no data. A "1" in this bit indicates that the controller has placed data into its output but the system has not yet read the data. When the system reads the output buffer (I/O address 60, hexadecimal), this bit will change back to a "0".

Bit 1   Input Buffer Full—A "0" in this bit indicates that the keyboard controller's input buffer I/O address 60 or 64, hexadecimal) is empty. A "1" in this bit indicates that data has been written into the buffer but the controller has not read the data. When the controller reads the input buffer, this bit will change back to a "0".

Bit 2   System Flag—This bit may be set to a "0" or a "1" by writing to the system's flag bit in the keyboard controller's command byte. It is set to "0" after a power on reset.

Bit 3   Command/Data—The keyboard controller's input buffer may be addressed as either I/O address 60 or 64, hexadecimal. Address 60, hexadecimal, is defined as the data port, and address 64, hexadecimal, is defined as the command port. Writing to address 64, hexadecimal, sets this bit to a "1"; writing to address 60, hexadecimal, sets this bit to a "0". The controller uses this bit to determine whether the byte in its input buffer should be interpreted as a command byte or a data byte.

Bit 4   Inhibit Switch—This bit is updated whenever data is placed in the keyboard controller's output buffer. It reflects the state of the keyboard-inhibit switch. A "0" in this bit indicates that the keyboard is inhibited.

Bit 5   Transmit Time-Out—A "1" in this bit indicates that a transmission started by the keyboard controller was not properly completed. If the transmit byte was not clocked out within the specified time limit, this will be the only error. If the transmitted byte was clocked out but a response was not received within the programmed time limit, the transmit time-out and receive time-out error bits are set to "1" (On). If the transmit byte was clocked out but the response was received with a parity error, the transmit time-out and parity error bits are set to "1" (On).

Bit 6   Receive Time-Out—A "1" in this bit indicates that a transmission was started by the keyboard but did not finish within the programmed receive time-out delay.

Bit 7   Parity Error—A "0" in this bit indicates that the last byte of data received from the keyboard has odd parity. A "1" in this bit indicates that the last byte has even parity. The keyboard should send with odd parity.

OUTPUT BUFFER

The output buffer is an 8-bit read-only register at I/O address 60, hexadecimal. The keyboard controller uses the output buffer to send scan codes received from the keyboard, and data bytes requested by commands to the system. The output buffer should be read only when the output buffer's full bit in the status register is a "1".

INPUT BUFFER

The input buffer is an 8-bit write-only register at I/O address 60 or 64, hexadecimal. Writing to address 60, hexadecimal, sets a flag that indicates a data write; writing to address 64, hexadecimal, sets a flag that indicates a command write. Data written to I/O address 60, hexadecimal, is sent to the keyboard unless the keyboard controller is expecting a data byte following a controller command. Data should be written to the controller's input buffer only if the input buffer's full bit in the status register is a "0". The following are valid keyboard controller commands:

Commands (I/O address 64, hexadecimal)

20   Read Keyboard Controller's Command Byte—The controller sends its current command byte to its output buffer.

60   Write Keyboard Controller's Command Byte—The next byte of data written to I/O address 60, hexadecimal, is placed in the controller's command byte. Bit definitions of the command byte are as follows:

Bit 7   Reserved—Should be written to a "0".

Bit 6   IBM Personal Computer Compatibility Mode—Writing a "1" to this bit causes the controller to convert the scan codes received from the keyboard to those used by the IBM Personal Computer. This includes converting a two-byte break sequence to the one-byte IBM Personal Computer format.

Bit 5   IBM Personal Computer Mode—Writing a "1" to this bit programs the keyboard to support the IBM Personal Computer keyboard interface. In this mode the controller does not check parity or convert scan codes.

Bit 4   Disable Keyboard—Writing a "1" to this bit disables the keyboard interface by driving the "clock" line low. Data is not sent or received.

Bit 3 Inhibit Override—Writing a "1" to this bit disables the keyboard inhibit function.

Bit 2 System Flag—The value written to this bit disables the keyboard inhibit function.

Bit 1 Reserved—Should be written to a "0".

Bit 0 Enable Output-Buffer-Full Interrupt—Writing a "1" to this bit causes the controller to generate an interrupt when it places data into its output buffer.

AA Self-Test—This commands the controller to test the keyboard clock and data lines. A 55, hexadecimal, is placed in the output buffer if no errors are detected.

AB Interface Test—This commands the controller to test the keyboard clock and data lines. The test result is placed in the output buffer, as follows:

00 No error detected.

01 The "keyboard clock" line is stuck low.

02 The "keyboard clock" line is stuck high.

03 The "keyboard data" line is stuck low.

04 The "keyboard data" line is stuck high.

AC Diagnostic Dump—Sends 16 bytes of the controller's RAM, the current state of the input port, the current state of the output port, and the controller's program status word to the system. All items are sent in scan-code format.

AD Disable Keyboard Feature—This command sets bit 4 of the controller's command byte. This disables the keyboard interface by driving the clock line low. Data will not be sent or received.

AE Enable Keyboard Interface—This command clears bit 4 of the command byte, which releases the keyboard interface.

C0 Read Input Port—This commands the controller to read its input port and place the data in its output buffer. This command should be used only if the output buffer is empty.

D0 Read Output Port—This command causes the controller to read its output port and place the data in its output buffer. This command should be issued only if the output buffer is empty.

D1 Write Output Port—The next byte of data written to I/O address 60, hexadecimal, is placed in the controller's output port.

Note: Bit 0 of the controller's output port is connected to System Reset. This bit should not be written low.

E0   Read Test Inputs—This command causes the controller to read its T0 and T1 inputs. This data is placed in the output buffer. Data bit "0" represents T0, and data bit "1" represents T1.

F0-FF   Pulse Output Port—Bits 0 through 3 of the controller's output port may be pulsed low for approximately 6 microseconds. Bits 0 through 3 of this command indicate which bits are to be pulsed. A "0" indicates that the bit should be pulsed, and a "1" indicates the bit should not be modified.

Note: Bit 0 of the controller's output port is connected to System Reset. Pulsing this bit resets the microprocessor.

I/O PORTS

The keyboard controller has two 8-bit I/O ports and two test inputs. One of the ports is assigned for input and the other for output. The controller uses the test inputs to read the state of the keyboard's "clock" line and the keyboard's "data" line.

Input Port Bit Definition

Bit 0   Undefined
Bit 1   Undefined
Bit 2   Undefined
Bit 3   Undefined
Bit 4   RAM on the System Board
                 "0" = Disable 2nd 256 Kbyte of System Board RAM
                 "1" = Enable 2nd 256 Kbyte of System Board RAM
Bit 5   Manufacturing Jumper
                 "0" = Manufacturing Jumper installed
                 "1" = Manufacturing Jumper not installed
Bit 6   Display Type Switch
                 "0" = Primary display attached to Color/Graphics adapter
                 "1" = Primary display attached to Monochrome adapter
Bit 7   Keyboard Inhibit Switch
                 "0" = Keyboard inhibited
                 "1" = Keyboard not inhibited

Output Port Bit Definitions

Bit 0	System Reset
Bit 1	Gate A20
Bit 2	Undefined
Bit 3	Undefined
Bit 4	Output Buffer Full
Bit 5	Input Buffer Empty
Bit 6	Keyboard Clock (output)
Bit 7	Keyboard Data (output)

Test-Input Port Bit Definitions

T0	Keyboard Clock (input)
T1	Keyboard Data (input)

32

AT 84-Key Keyboard Scan Codes

Key Number	Scan Code	Base Case	Upper Case	CTRL	ALT
1	29	`	~	-	-
2	02	1	!	-	ext
3	03	2	@	NUL	ext
4	04	3	#	-	ext
5	05	4	$	-	ext
6	06	5	%	-	ext
7	07	6	<	RS	ext
8	08	7	&	-	ext
9	09	8	*	-	ext
10	0A	9	(	-	ext
11	0B	0	)	-	ext
12	0C	-	_	US	ext
13	0D	=	+	-	ext
14	2B	\	|	FS	-
15	0E	Backspace	Backspace	DEL	-
16	0F	TAB	Ext	-	-
17	10	q	Q	DC1	ext
18	11	w	W	ETB	ext
19	12	e	E	ENQ	ext
20	13	r	R	DC2	ext
21	14	t	T	DC4	ext
22	15	y	Y	EM	ext
23	16	u	U	NAK	ext
24	17	i	I	HT	ext
25	18	o	O	SI	ext
26	19	p	P	DLE	ext

Key Number	Scan Code	Base Case	Upper Case	CTRL	ALT
27	1A	[	{	ESC	-
28	1B	]	}	GS	-
30	1D	Ctrl	-	-	-
31	1E	a	A	SOH	ext
32	1F	s	S	DC3	ext
33	20	d	D	EOT	ext
34	21	f	F	ACK	ext
35	22	g	G	BEL	ext
36	23	h	H	BS	ext
37	24	j	J	LF	ext
38	25	k	K	VT	ext
39	26	l	L	FF	ext
40	27	;:	:;	-	-
41	28	'	"	-	-
43	1C	Enter	Enter	LF	-
44	2A	Left Shift	-	-	-
46	2C	z	Z	SUB	ext
47	2D	x	X	CAN	ext
48	2E	c	C	ETX	ext
49	2F	v	V	SYN	ext
50	30	b	B	STX	ext
51	31	n	N	SO	ext
52	32	m	M	CR	ext
53	33	,	<	-	-
54	34	.	>	-	-
55	35	/	?	-	-

Key Number	Scan Code	Base Case	Upper Case	CTRL	ALT
57	36	Right Shift	-	-	-
58	38	Alt	-	-	-
61	39	Space	Space	Space	Space
64	3A	Caps Lock	-	-	-
65	3C	F2	ext	ext	ext
66	3E	F4	ext	ext	ext
67	40	F6	ext	ext	ext
68	42	F8	ext	ext	ext
69	44	F10	ext	ext	ext
70	3B	F1	ext	ext	ext
71	3D	F3	ext	ext	ext
72	3F	F5	ext	ext	ext
73	41	F7	ext	ext	ext
74	43	F9	ext	ext	ext
75	52	Insert	-	-	-
90	01	Esc	Esc	Esc	-
91	47	Home	N/A	ext	-
92	4B	Left Arrow	N/A	ext	-
93	4F	End	N/A	ext	-
95	45	Number Lock	-	Pause	-
96	48	Up Arrow	N/A	-	-
97	4C	Pad 5	N/A	-	-
98	50	Down Arrow	N/A	ext	-
99	52	Insert	N/A	-	-
100	46	Scroll Lock	-	break	-
101	49	Page Up	N/A	ext	-

Key Number	Scan Code	Base Case	Upper Case	CTRL	ALT
102	4D	Right Arrow	N/A	ext	-
103	51	Page Down	N/A	ext	-
104	53	Delete	-	**	**
105	54	Sys Req	-	-	-
106	37	Pad *	Print Screen	-	-
107	4A	Pad –	N/A	-	-
108	4E	Pad +	N/A	-	-

NOTES: 1) ext = extended (Returns a code of 00 followed by the Scan Code)
2) CTRL-ALT-Del = Warm Boot

33

AT 101-Key Keyboard Scan Codes

Key Number	Scan Code	Base Case	Upper Case	CTRL	ALT
1	29	`	~	-	-
2	02	1	!	-	ext
3	03	2	@	NUL	ext
4	04	3	#	-	ext
5	05	4	$	-	ext
6	06	5	%	-	ext
7	07	6	<	RS	ext
8	08	7	&	-	ext
9	09	8	*	-	ext
10	0A	9	(	-	ext
11	0B	0	)	-	ext
12	0C	-	_	US	ext
13	0D	=	+	-	ext
15	0E	Backspace	Backspace	DEL	-
16	0F	TAB	Ext	-	-
17	10	q	Q	DC1	ext
18	11	w	W	ETB	ext
19	12	e	E	ENQ	ext
20	13	r	R	DC2	ext
21	14	t	T	DC4	ext
22	15	y	Y	EM	ext
23	16	u	U	NAK	ext
24	17	i	I	HT	ext
25	18	o	O	SI	ext
26	19	p	P	DLE	ext
27	1A	[	{	ESC	ext
28	1B	]	}	GS	-

Key Number	Scan Code	Base Case	Upper Case	CTRL	ALT
29	2B	\	|	FS	-
30	3A	Caps Lock	-	-	-
31	1E	a	A	SOH	ext
32	1F	s	S	DC3	ext
33	20	d	D	EOT	ext
34	21	f	F	ACK	ext
35	22	g	G	BEL	ext
36	23	h	H	BS	ext
37	24	j	J	LF	ext
38	25	k	K	VT	ext
39	26	l	L	FF	ext
40	27	;	:	-	-
41	28	'	"	-	-
43	1C	Enter	Enter	LF	-
44	2A	Left Shift	-	-	-
46	2C	z	Z	SUB	ext
47	2D	x	X	CAN	ext
48	2E	c	C	ETX	ext
49	2F	v	V	SYN	ext
50	30	b	B	STX	ext
51	31	n	N	SO	ext
52	32	m	M	CR	ext
53	33	,	<	-	-
54	34	.	>	-	-
55	35	/	?	-	-
57	36	Right Shift	-	-	-
58	1D	Left Ctrl	-	-	-

Key Number	Scan Code	Base Case	Upper Case	CTRL	ALT
60	38	Left Alt	-	-	-
61	39	Space	Space	Space	Space
62	E0, 38	Right Alt	-	-	-
64	E0, 1D	Right Ctrl	-	-	-
75	E0, 52	Insert	-	-	-
76	E0, 53	Delete	-	-	-
79	E0, 4B	Left Arrow	-	-	-
80	E0, 47	Home	-	-	-
81	E0, 4F	End	-	-	-
83	E0, 48	Up Arrow	-	-	-
84	E0, 50	Down Arrow	-	-	-
85	E0, 49	Page Up	-	-	-
86	E0, 51	Page Down	-	-	-
89	E0, 4D	Right Arrow	-	-	-
90	45	Number Lock	-	-	-
91	47	Pad 7	Home	-	-
92	4B	Pad 4	Left Arrow	-	-
93	4F	Pad 1	End	-	-
95	E0, 35	Pad /	Pad /	-	-
96	48	Pad 8	Up Arrow	-	-
97	4C	Pad 5	-	-	-
98	50	Pad 2	Down Arrow	-	-
99	52	Pad 0	Insert	-	-
100	E0, 37	Pad *	Pad *	-	-
101	49	Pad 9	Page Up	-	-
102	4D	Pad 6	Right Arrow	-	-
103	51	Pad 3	Page Down	-	-

Key Number	Scan Code	Base Case	Upper Case	CTRL	ALT
104	53	Pad .	Delete	-	-
105	4A	Pad −	Pad −	-	-
106	4E	Pad +	Pad +	-	-
108	E0, 1C	Pad Enter	Pad Enter	-	-
110	01	ESC	ESC	-	-
112	3B	F1	ext	ext	ext
113	3C	F2	ext	ext	ext
114	3D	F3	ext	ext	ext
115	3E	F4	ext	ext	ext
116	3F	F5	ext	ext	ext
117	40	F6	ext	ext	ext
118	41	F7	ext	ext	ext
119	42	F8	ext	ext	ext
120	43	F9	ext	ext	ext
121	44	F10	ext	ext	ext
122	D9	F11	ext	ext	ext
123	DA	F12	ext	ext	ext
124	2A, 37	Print Screen	-	-	-
125	46	Screen Lock	-	-	-
126	1D, E0, 45, E0, C5, 9D			Pause-Break	Pause-Break

NOTES: 1) ext = extended (Returns a code of 00 followed by the Scan Code)
2) CTRL-ALT-Del = Warm Boot
3) Pause-Break = CTRL and Number Lock combination

34.

ASCII (American Standard Code for Information Interchange) Control Codes

The American Standard Code For Information Interchange (ASCII) is the code used today for all microprocessors, computer peripherals, and data communication equipment. It is also the code generated by most keyboards and teletypes. Often, an additional bit (b_8) is incorporated as an (even or odd) parity bit. As a historical note, IBM used EBCDIC (Extended Binary Coded Decimal For Information Interchange) on their mainframes, and ASCII was promulgated by AT & T.

With 7 bits available, there are $2^7 = 128$ possible codes available. These may be grouped into four sets of 32 characters each and, depending on the system complexity, one may or may not use all four of these 32-character groups.

The two middle groups, 2 and 3, make up the subset that includes the uppercase alphabet, the numbers, and some frequently used punctuation symbols. The numbers are represented in BCD (Binary Coded Decimal) in bits b_4 to b_1 with bits b_7, b_6, and $b_5 = 011$. Groups 2 and 3 may be transmitted as a 6-bit code and reconstituted into 7 bits by forming b_7 as the complement (the inverse) of b_6.

The first group, 1, contains the machine commands or control functions for support circuitry, which always have b_6 and $b_7 = 0$. See Chapter 35 to see how they are displayed on the screen and printed on some printers. Group 1 characters are generated on the keyboard by a combination of the CTRL key (indicated by ^) and the corresponding Group 3 characters.

The last group, 4, contains the lowercase alphabet and some infrequently used punctuation symbols. The characters contained in Group 4 always have b_6 and $b_7 = 1$.

The Machine Commands or Control Functions

NUL	Null	DLE	Data Link Escape
SOH	Start Of Heading	DC1	Device Control 1
STX	Start Of Text	DC2	Device Control 2
ETX	End Of Text	DC3	Device Control 3
EOT	End Of Transmission	DC4	Device Control 4
ENQ	Enquiry	NAK	Negative Acknowledge
ACK	Acknowledge	SYN	Synchronous Idle
BEL	Bell	ETB	End Of Transmission Block
BS	Backspace	CAN	Cancel
HT	Horizontal Tab	EM	End Of Medium
LF	Line Feed	SUB	Substitute
VT	Vertical Tab	ESC	Escape
FF	Form Feed	FS	File Separator
CR	Carriage Return	GS	Group Separator
SO	Shift Out	RS	Record Separator
SI	Shift In	US	Unit Separator

Bit	$b_7\rightarrow$	0	0	0	0	1	1	1	1
Numbers	$b_6\rightarrow$	0	0	1	1	0	0	1	1
	$b_5\rightarrow$	0	1	0	1	0	1	0	1
$b_4\,b_3\,b_2\,b_1$ $\downarrow\downarrow\downarrow\downarrow$		0	1	2	3	4	5	6	7
0 0 0 0	0	NUL	DLE	SP	0	@	P	´	p
0 0 0 1	1	SOH	DC1	!	1	A	Q	a	q
0 0 1 0	2	STX	DC2	"	2	B	R	b	r
0 0 1 1	3	ETX	DC3	£	3	C	S	c	s
0 1 0 0	4	EOT	DC4	$	4	D	T	d	t
0 1 0 1	5	ENQ	NAK	%	5	E	U	e	u
0 1 1 0	6	ACK	SYN	&	6	F	V	f	v
0 1 1 1	7	BEL	ETB	'	7	G	W	g	w
1 0 0 0	8	BS	CAN	(	8	H	X	h	x
1 0 0 1	9	HT	EM	)	9	I	Y	i	y
1 0 1 0	10	LF	SUB	*	:	J	Z	j	z
1 0 1 1	11	VT	ESC	+	;	K	[	k	{
1 1 0 0	12	FF	FS	,	<	L	\	l	‖
1 1 0 1	13	CR	GS	-	=	M	]	m	}
1 1 1 0	14	SO	RS	.	>	N	^	n	~
1 1 1 1	15	SI	US	/	?	O	_	o	DEL
GROUP		1		2		3		4	

35

IBM Extended Character Set With Screen Codes

Each character that is displayed on the monitor screen is represented inside the computer as a number, referred to as its ASCII (American Standard Code For Information Interchange) code. The letter "A" is ASCII 65, "B" is ASCII 66, and "a" is ASCII 97.

The original ASCII code consisted of 128 characters (0–127) and it was extended to 256 characters (128–255) with the advent of the IBM PC. The original 128 characters included those found on an English-language typewriter: uppercase and lowercase letters, digits, and punctuation. Added to the original set are many foreign characters, mathematical symbols, and line-drawing characters.

Hexadecimal	Decimal	Screen	Control	Keyboard
00h	0		NUL	^@
01h	1	☺	SOH	^A
02h	2	☻	STX	^B
03h	3	♥	ETX	^C
04h	4	♦	EOT	^D
05h	5	♣	ENQ	^E
06h	6	♠	ACK	^F
07h	7	•	BEL	^G
08h	8	◘	BS	^H
09h	9	○	HT	^I
0Ah	10	◙	LF	^J
0Bh	11	♂	VT	^K
0Ch	12	♀	FF	^L
0Dh	13	♪	CR	^M
0Eh	14	♫	SO	^N
0Fh	15	☼	SI	^O
10h	16	►	DLE	^P
11h	17	◄	DC1	^Q
12h	18	↕	DC2	^R
13h	19	‼	DC3	^S
14h	20	¶	DC4	^T
15h	21	§	NAK	^U
16h	22	▬	SYN	^V
17h	23	↨	ETB	^W
18h	24	↑	CAN	^X
19h	25	↓	EM	^Y
1Ah	26	→	SUB	^Z
1Bh	27	←	ESC	^[
1Ch	28	∟	FS	^\
1Dh	29	↔	GS	^]
1Eh	30	▲	RS	^^
1Fh	31	▼	US	^_
20h	32			

Hexadecimal	Decimal	Screen	Hexadecimal	Decimal	Screen
21h	33	!	47h	71	G
22h	34	"	48h	72	H
23h	35	#	49h	73	I
24h	36	$	4Ah	74	J
25h	37	%	4Bh	75	K
26h	38	&	4Ch	76	L
27h	39	'	4Dh	77	M
28h	40	(	4Eh	78	N
29h	41	)	4Fh	79	O
2Ah	42	*	50h	80	P
2Bh	43	+	51h	81	Q
2Ch	44	,	52h	82	R
2Dh	45	-	53h	83	S
2Eh	46	.	54h	84	T
2Fh	47	/	55h	85	U
30h	48	0	56h	86	V
31h	49	1	57h	87	W
32h	50	2	58h	88	X
33h	51	3	59h	89	Y
34h	52	4	5Ah	90	Z
35h	53	5	5Bh	91	[
36h	54	6	5Ch	92	\
37h	55	7	5Dh	93	]
38h	56	8	5Eh	94	^
39h	57	9	5Fh	95	_
3Ah	58	:	60h	96	`
3Bh	59	;	61h	97	a
3Ch	60	<	62h	98	b
3Dh	61	=	63h	99	c
3Eh	62	>	64h	100	d
3Fh	63	?	65h	101	e
40h	64	@	66h	102	f
41h	65	A	67h	103	g
42h	66	B	68h	104	h
43h	67	C	69h	105	i
44h	68	D	6Ah	106	j
45h	69	E	6Bh	107	k
46h	70	F	6Ch	108	l

Hexadecimal	Decimal	Screen	Hexadecimal	Decimal	Screen
6Dh	109	m	93h	147	ô
6Eh	110	n	94h	148	ö
6Fh	111	o	95h	149	ò
70h	112	p	96h	150	û
71h	113	q	97h	151	ù
72h	114	r	98h	152	ÿ
73h	115	s	99h	153	Ö
74h	116	t	9Ah	154	Ü
75h	117	u	9Bh	155	¢
76h	118	v	9Ch	156	£
77h	119	w	9Dh	157	¥
78h	120	x	9Eh	158	₧
79h	121	y	9Fh	159	ƒ
7Ah	122	z	A0h	160	á
7Bh	123	{	A1h	161	í
7Ch	124	|	A2h	162	ó
7Dh	125	}	A3h	163	ú
7Eh	126	~	A4h	164	ñ
7Fh	127	⌂	A5h	165	Ñ
80h	128	Ç	A6h	166	ª
81h	129	ü	A7h	167	º
82h	130	é	A8h	168	¿
83h	131	â	A9h	169	⌐
84h	132	ä	AAh	170	¬
85h	133	à	ABh	171	½
86h	134	å	ACh	172	¼
87h	135	ç	ADh	173	¡
88h	136	ê	AEh	174	«
89h	137	ë	AFh	175	»
8Ah	138	è	B0h	176	░
8Bh	139	ï	B1h	177	▒
8Ch	140	î	B2h	178	▓
8Dh	141	ì	B3h	179	│
8Eh	142	Ä	B4h	180	┤
8Fh	143	Å	B5h	181	╡
90h	144	É	B6h	182	╢
91h	145	æ	B7h	183	╖
92h	146	Æ	B8h	184	╕

Hexadecimal	Decimal	Screen	Hexadecimal	Decimal	Screen
B9h	185	╣	DDh	221	▌
BAh	186	║	DEh	222	▐
BBh	187	╗	DFh	223	▀
BCh	188	╝	E0h	224	α
BDh	189	╜	E1h	225	ß
BEh	190	╛	E2h	226	Γ
BFh	191	┐	E3h	227	π
C0h	192	└	E4h	228	Σ
C1h	193	┴	E5h	229	σ
C2h	194	┬	E6h	230	µ
C3h	195	├	E7h	231	ι
C4h	196	─	E8h	232	Φ
C5h	197	┼	E9h	233	Θ
C6h	198	╞	EAh	234	Ω
C7h	199	╟	EBh	235	δ
C8h	200	╚	ECh	236	∞
C9h	201	╔	EDh	237	φ
CAh	202	╩	EEh	238	ε
CBh	203	╦	EFh	239	∩
CCh	204	╠	F0h	240	≡
CDh	205	═	F1h	241	±
CEh	206	╬	F2h	242	≥
CFh	207	╧	F3h	243	≤
D0h	208	╨	F4h	244	⌠
D1h	209	╤	F5h	245	⌡
D2h	210	╥	F6h	246	÷
D3h	211	╙	F7h	247	≈
D4h	212	╘	F8h	248	°
D5h	213	╒	F9h	249	·
D6h	214	╓	FAh	250	·
D7h	215	╫	FBh	251	√
D8h	216	╪	FCh	252	ⁿ
D9h	217	┘	FDh	253	²
DAh	218	┌	FEh	254	■
DBh	219	█	FFh	255	
DCh	220	▄			

SORT SEQUENCE FOR ASCII CHARACTERS IN THE EXTENDED CHARACTER SET

ASCII Value		SORT Value		
Decimal	Hexadecimal	Decimal	Hexadecimal	Character
128	80	67	43	C
129	81	85	55	U
130	82	69	45	E
131	83	65	41	A
132	84	65	41	A
133	85	65	41	A
134	86	65	41	A
135	87	67	43	C
136	88	69	45	E
137	89	69	45	E
138	8A	69	45	E
139	8B	73	49	I
140	8C	73	49	I
141	8D	73	49	I
142	8E	65	41	A
143	8F	65	41	A
144	90	69	45	E
145	91	65	41	A
146	92	65	41	A
147	93	79	4F	O
148	94	79	4F	O
149	95	79	4F	O
150	96	85	55	U
151	97	85	55	U
152	98	89	59	Y
153	99	79	4F	O
154	9A	85	55	U
155	9B	36	24	$
156	9C	36	24	$
157	9D	36	24	$
158	9E	36	24	$
159	9F	36	24	$
160	A0	65	41	A
161	A1	73	49	I
162	A2	79	4F	O
163	A3	85	55	U
164	A4	78	4E	N
165	A5	78	4E	N

ASCII Value		SORT Value		
Decimal	Hexadecimal	Decimal	Hexadecimal	Character
166	A6	166	A6	ª
167	A7	167	A7	º
168	A8	63	3F	?
169	A9	169	A9	⌐
170	AA	170	AA	¬
171	AB	171	AB	½
172	AC	172	AC	¼
173	AD	33	21	!
174	AE	34	22	"
175	AF	35	23	#
225	E1	83	53	S

36

Data Transfer Links and Networks

IBM has developed several products to facilitate information interchange between IBM PC series computers and its office automation equipment such as the IBM DisplayWriter series of dedicated word processors, the IBM 6670 Information Distributor, the IBM 5520 Administrative System, and the IBM Office System 6.

The simplest is the DisplayWriter/Personal Computer Attachment Convenience Kit, which connects IBM PC series computers to the IBM DisplayWriter word processing system. A program, designed for use with IBM's DisplayWrite series of personal computer word processing software, is the more expensive IBM Personal Computer DisplayComm Binary Synchronous Communications Program. This program permits document exchange with the IBM DisplayWriter, the 6670 Information Distributor, the Office System 6, and IBM mainframes equipped with special software.

Another product available from IBM is the IBM 5520/Personal Computer Attachment Program, which exchanges information between IBM PC series computers and the IBM 5520 Administrative System.

Document Control Architecture (DCA) is a protocol that governs a standard format for documents. DCA deals with such factors as typeface, typestyle, and paragraph format. Software that supports this standard has been developed for both the IBM PC series computers and the Apple Macintosh.

Today, advances in both hardware and software lets you obtain the best of both worlds by combining IBM PC and Apple Macintosh systems. Documents may be created on an IBM PC with a word processing program and sent to an Apple Macintosh for formatting, laser printing, and/or

Comparison Of Serial Asynchronous Standards

Specification	EIA-232D	Standard EIA-423A	EIA-422A	RS-485
Mode Of Operation	Single-Ended	Single-Ended	Differential	Differential
Number of Transmitters Allowed On One Line	1	1	1	32
Number of Receivers Allowed On One Line	1	10	10	32
Maximum Cable Length	Load Dependent	4,000 ft.	4,000 ft.	4,000 ft.
Maximum Data Rate (in bits/second)	20,000	100,000	10,000,000	10,000,000
Maximum Transmitter Volts Output	±25 V	±6 V	-0.25 V	-7 V
Transmitter Output Level, Loaded	±5 V	±3.6 V	±2 V	±1.5 V
Transmitter Output Level, Unloaded	±15 V	±6 V	±5 V	±5 V
Transmitter Load Impedance (in ohms)	3,000–7,000	450	100	54
Slew Rate	< 30 V/μsec.	–	–	–
Voltage Range Of Receiver Input	±15 V	±12 V	±7 V	-7 →12 V
Sensitivity Of Receiver Input	±3 V	±200 mV	±200 mV	±200 mV
Resistance Of Receiver Input (in ohms)	3,000–7,000	4,000 min.	4,000 min.	12,000 min.

typesetting. One Macintosh can collect documents from several IBM PC series computers and integrate the assembled documents into a single body of text, which may be combined with graphics and other design elements to create a publication. Documents may be moved quickly and accurately between various computers using Ethernet, AppleTalk, and IBM's networks. Software such as TOPS from Sitka Corp., 950 Marina Village Parkway, Alameda, CA 94501, telephone (415) 769-9669, facilitate the sharing of data between the Apple Macintosh and the IBM PC.

Dataviz, Incorporated, 16 Winfield Street, Norwalk, CT 06855, telephone (203) 866-4944, sells MacLink, a communication program that links IBM PC series computers and the Apple Macintosh by a direct cable connection or modems. Using DCA, the two-way translators retain paragraphs, margins, and typestyles, and convert text to its new format. It sells for $125, plus $30 for an eight-foot interface cable.

Tangent Technologies, 5720 Peachtree Parkway, Suite 100, Norcross, GA 30092, telephone (404) 662-0366, sells PC MacBridge, a hardware/software combination that connects the IBM PC with the Apple LaserWriter. The hardware is a short card that fits into the bus of a PC or AT and connects to the AppleTalk connector and cable. The software is called Apple Bus Link Access Protocol and it puts your PC on the network. The software can be used to send mail and files to Macintoshes and the LaserScript software will convert files into PostScript, which is the language that the Apple LaserWriter requires. It sells for $650.

Dayna Communications, Inc., 50 South Main Street, Salt Lake City, UT 84144, telephone (800) 531-0600, offers MacCharlie Plus, a software and hardware product that lets the Apple Macintosh use IBM PC series software, connect to mainframe computers, and connect to Apple or IBM networks. The basic coprocessing workstation includes a single disk drive, 256K of RAM, ten function keys, Apple's Switcher program, and MS-DOS and GW-BASIC software. A second disk drive, memory upgrades to 640K, an expansion chassis with slots for up to six IBM PC-compatible cards, and a hard drive may be added. Macintosh and IBM application programs can run simultaneously on this system, and Apple's Switcher program provides quick access to all of them. The basic MacCharlie Plus sells for $1,295.

A *local area network* (LAN) is a term that refers to any two or more computers connected by some sort of link (cable, fiber optics, RF, etc.). The LAN not only facilitates communication between computers but allows the computers connected to it to share common resources such as printers, disks, and even modems. Each device connected to a network is called a node. The sharing of hardware resources saves money by dividing resource costs among several users.

LANs are available with a variety of performance specifications ranging from low-speed networks that use RS-232 serial communications to high-speed varieties such as Ethernet and FDDI. Other networks available are AppleTalk, Omninet, TOPS, Novell NetWare, and IBM's token ring network.

AppleTalk is among the least expensive networks available for the IBM PC. It is slow by network standards, but it is much faster than the highest-speed modems. AppleTalk boards for the IBM PC are available from Tangent Technologies which offers the PC McBridge, and Centram Systems West, which makes an IBM PC AppleTalk board in combination with its TOPS network software. It is not necessary to have a Macintosh connected to the network when you are using AppleTalk. With TOPS software any disk drive, whether it is a hard drive or a floppy disk drive, connected to any computer hooked up to the AppleTalk network can share files with any IBM series computer or other computer such as an Apple Macintosh or a DEC VAX connected to the system. File access and exchange are easy with TOPS, and the files move from one workstation to another without delay. TOPS solves the problem of machine incompatibility by translating requests from individual machines into universal requests that TOPS software recognizes. TOPS can link up to 254 devices, with a recommended maximum of 32 users per network, and allows a linkage of more than 65,000 networks. The PC-only version of TOPS runs up to 800,000 bits per second, almost four times the 230,000 bits per second of AppleTalk. LaserLink utility software provides a channel from the IBM PC to the Apple LaserWriter using the TOPS network adapter. Anything you can print on an IBM graphics-capable printer you can also generate on the LaserWriter. A TOPS Macintosh node sells for $149; a TOPS IBM PC network adapter, software, and manuals sell for $349; the LaserLink utility software (providing a channel from the IBM PC to the Apple LaserWriter) sells for $325.

A TOPS network that combines Mac's and PC's allows files created on a Mac to be stored on a PC's hard disk—or vice versa. It also allows you to access any published file from any computer on the network, regardless of the types of computers involved. To a PC on the network, a remote volume (group of files) that has been "published" through TOPS is used as a PC drive (e.g., drive E:). This means that even when a PC accesses a volume that is stored on a Mac, it looks and acts just like a local PC drive. To the Mac user, a file created on a PC looks like a generic *document* icon: that is, an icon of a piece of paper with no design. Files created by a Mac and stored on a PC appear to the Mac as regular Mac icons filled in with a representative design. The Mac applications can access data stored on other Mac drives or on disks in PC drives. PC "volumes" will appear on the Mac screen as disk icons, just as if they were on the internal floppy drive of the Mac.

Ethernet is a high-speed network, originally developed by Xerox, DEC, and Intel working together, that transmits information at up to 10 Megabits per second. It is certainly the most popular network configuration with a great many suppliers and is expected to remain so for the foreseeable future. The predominant supplier of Ethernet adapter boards, cabling, and network software is 3Com Corporation. 3Com's Ethernet system allows connection of as many as 1024 devices. Using 3Com's 3Server Ethernet fileserver, a group of IBM PC's can share files on a common hard disk. A version of the 3Server lets you partition the hard disk and create a separate volume for Macintosh users, with software that converts documents from the PC volume to the Macintosh volume. A network node can cost as little as $125.00 on an Ethernet network.

When a network component sends a message on the Ethernet, that message is broadcast to every other network component. Each Ethernet interface card on the network examines the address information contained in the message. Only the addressee accepts the message, and all other interface cards ignore the message. When two or more network components attempt to broadcast simultaneously on an Ethernet network, a collision is said to occur. The collision is detected by the senders, a random delay is instituted by each sender, and the messages are transmitted again. As traffic increases more collisions occur, but overall the transmission efficiency of Ethernet is very high.

Thick Ethernet, the original configuration, is a bus topology. The doubly shielded coaxial cable is installed in the area to be covered by the network. Network components are attached to the cable via electro-mechanical taps, which route the signal to a transceiver and then to an interface card.

Thin Ethernet is a bus topology. The network geography is laid out so that coaxial cable is used for interconnecting one network component to the next. There is no central network hub. Thin Ethernet requires that each network component (like a workstation) have an interface card and a "T" connector, which facilitates the connection of the coaxial cable to the network interface card. Each end of the coaxial cable is terminated in a 75 ohm terminating resistor. Thin Ethernet is used mainly for smaller networks (of about 10 network components) that are located in a single room or in a single department.

10Base-T Ethernet is a star topology. The network geography is laid out so that all network components are connected to a central hub using unshielded twisted pair wire, like telephone hook-up wire. 10Base-T Ethernet requires that each network component (like a workstation) have an interface card and an available port on the 10Base-T hub. All network communication is routed through the 10Base-T hub.

The main differences between Thick Ethernet, Thin Ethernet, and 10Base-T Ethernet are initial hardware cost, installation cost, distance supported, number of terminals supported, maintenance requirements, built-in diagnostic capability, and ease of adding network components. There is no difference in performance between any of the interconnect methods. The main design disadvantage of Ethernet is that if the interconnecting cable is severed, the network crashes. Ethernets may be extended via repeaters, may be connected to fiber optic cables or RF links via bridges, and may be connected to other types of networks via gateways.

Omninet, from Corvus Systems, 160 Great Oak Boulevard, San Jose, CA 95119, telephone (408) 281-4100, transmits information at about one Megabit per second and provides for connection of up to 64 devices to the network. This network also allows for intermixing IBM PC's and Apple Macintoshes in the same network. Although each operating system requires a separate partition and a separate volume on the hard disk (i.e., a diskserver configuration), text files may be transferred between volumes, and systems that share a common operating system have fileserver access to their volume on the hard disk.

The IBM PC Network, developed for IBM by Sytek, operates at two Megabits per second. IBM suggests that you use an IBM PC AT as your fileserver, although you don't have to.

An alternative to IBM's PC Network is the NetWare series of LAN products from Novell, Inc., 1610 Berryessa Road, San Jose, CA 95133, telephone (408) 729-6700. The first version is Advanced NetWare, which provides an MS-DOS network operating system that accommodates multiple fileservers, bridges, and gateways and is capable of supporting large internetworking schemes. The second version, SFT NetWare 286 (System Fault Tolerance), has all the main features of Advanced NetWare plus disk backup, media correction capabilities, file and record locking, independent user, group, and directory access controls with eight levels of access rights assignable to each, and other options. Both of these software systems can use all three of Novell's network hardware systems: G-Net, ARCNET, and ProNET. G-Net is a baseband CSMA/CD (ANSI/IEEE Standard 802.3, entitled "Carrier Sense Multiple Access with Collision Detection") network (like Ethernet) that operates at 1.43 Megabits per second and allows up to 50 devices to be interconnected over a distance of up to 7,000 feet. ARCNET is a token-passing network that operates at speeds up to 2.5 Megabits per second. ProNET is a high-speed token passing network that operates at speeds up to 9.94 Megabits per second.

Novell NetWare runs on over 80 brands of networks, provides a standard software interface, and includes spooled access to shared network printers. The installation of NetWare is completely menu-driven and NetWare is fully compatible with IBM NetBIOS, enabling it to work with a variety of multi-user applications that run with the IBM PC Network and Token Ring. NetWare operating systems may be upgraded from the simplest ELS NetWare Level I to the most complex SFT NetWare, which even has facilities to provide duplicate hard disk channels and hard disk mirroring. Prices range from $500.00 for Novell ELS Level I (v2.12) to $5,000.00 for Novell 386 Netware (v3.0). Certified interconnect cards are about $100.00 for 8-bit cards and $175.00 for 16-bit interconnect cards.

37

Line and Box Drawing on the Monitor and Printer

IBM has included as a portion of its Extended Character Set (see Chapter 35) a set of codes (179–223) for drawing both lines and boxes on the monitor and the printer.

To enter these characters into the computer, depress the ALT key simultaneously with entering the decimal character code on the numeric keypad. (Do not use the base case numbers across the top of the keyboard.)

Single Line Box:

218	196	196	194	196	196	191
┌	─	─	┬	─	─	┐
179			179			179
│			│			│
195	196	196	197	196	196	180
├	─	─	┼	─	─	┤
179			179			179
│			│			│
192	196	196	193	196	196	217
└	─	─	┴	─	─	┘

Double Line Box:

201	205	205	203	205	205	187
╔	═	═	╦	═	═	╗
186			186			186
║			║			║
204	205	205	206	205	205	185
╠	═	═	╬	═	═	╣
186			186			186
║			║			║
200	205	205	202	205	205	188
╚	═	═	╩	═	═	╝

Single Line (horizontal only) Box:

214	196	196	210	196	196	183
⌐	─	─	⊤	─	─	⌐

186			186			186
‖			‖			‖

199	196	196	215	196	196	182
‖─	─	─	‖	─	─	─‖

186			186			186
‖			‖			‖

211	196	196	208	196	196	189
⌐	─	─	⊥	─	─	⌐

Single Line (vertical only) Box:

213	205	205	209	205	205	184
╒	═	═	╤	═	═	╕

179			179			179

198	205	205	216	205	205	181
╞	─	═	╪	═	═	╡

179			179			179

212	205	205	207	205	205	190
╘	═	═	╧	═	═	╛

38

XT I/O Card
Dimensions

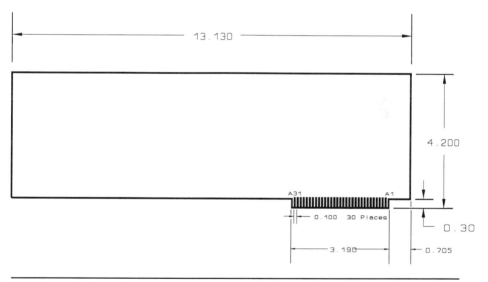

XT I/O card dimensions.

The following card edge connectors for the IBM PC and XT style bus pattern are manufactured by SOURIAU and are available from Active Electronics (see Appendix A).

267

Dual 31 position (62 pins), P. C. Mount
SOURIAU P/N 245-062-520-201
Active P/N 20014
Spacing 0.100" × 0.200"
Price $5.57

Dual 31 position (62 pins), P. C. Mount
SOURIAU P/N PB31DNS1D
Active P/N INDUS
Spacing 0.100" × 0.200"
Price $2.45

The following bus-specific (IBM PC and XT style bus pattern) prototyping boards are manufactured by VECTOR and are available from Active Electronics (see Appendix A).

Circuit Pad-Per-Hole

Size	4.210" wide × 13.235" long; holes 0.042" dia.
Capacity	91 DIP
Material	Epoxy Glass, 2 oz. copper
Extender Number	3690-22
VECTOR P/N	4613-3
Active P/N	56106
Price	$60.35

Circuit 3 Hole Solder Pad

Size	4.210" wide × 13.235" long; holes 0.042" dia.
Capacity	44 DIP
Material	Epoxy Glass
Extender Number	3690-22
VECTOR P/N	4613
Active P/N	56102
Price	$60.35

Circuit Peripheral Bus

Size	4.210" wide × 13.235" long; holes 0.042" dia.
Capacity	84 DIP
Material	Epoxy Glass
Extender Number	3690-22
VECTOR P/N	4613-1
Active P/N	56092
Price	$44.64

Circuit Voltage Plane

Size	4.210" wide × 13.235" long; holes 0.042" dia.
Capacity	55 DIP
Material	Epoxy Glass
Extender Number	3690-22
VECTOR P/N	4613-2
Active P/N	56105
Price	$60.35

39

AT I/O Card Dimensions

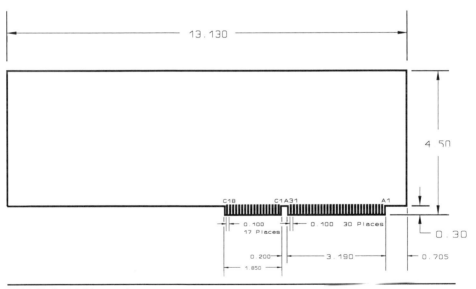

AT I/O Card Dimensions

The following card edge connectors for the IBM AT style bus pattern are manufactured by SOURIAU and are available from Active Electronics (see Appendix A).

Dual 31 position (62 pins), P. C. Mount
SOURIAU P/N 245-062-520-201
Active P/N 20014
Spacing 0.100" × 0.200"
Price $5.57

Dual 18 position (36 pins), P. C. Mount
SOURIAU P/N PB18DNS1D
Active P/N INDUS
Spacing 0.100" × 0.200"
Price $1.49

Dual 31 position (62 pins), P. C. Mount
SOURIAU P/N PB31DNS1D
Active P/N INDUS
Spacing 0.100" × 0.200"
Price $2.45

The following bus-specific (IBM AT style bus pattern) prototyping boards are manufactured by VECTOR and are available from Active Electronics (see Appendix A).

Circuit Pad-Per-Hole

Size	4.800" wide × 13.250" long; holes 0.042" dia.
Capacity	96 DIP
Material	Epoxy Glass, 2 oz. copper
Extender Number	3690-26
VECTOR P/N	4617-3
Active P/N	56107
Price	$60.35

Circuit 3 Hole Solder Pad

Size	4.800" wide × 13.250" long; holes 0.042" dia.
Capacity	39 DIP
Material	Epoxy Glass
Extender Number	3690-26
VECTOR P/N	4617
Active P/N	56103
Price	$60.35

Circuit Peripheral Bus

Size	4.800" wide × 13.250" long; holes 0.042" dia.
Capacity	108 DIP

Material	Epoxy Glass, 2 oz. copper
Extender Number	3690-26
VECTOR P/N	4617-1
Active P/N	56104
Price	$44.64

Circuit Voltage / Ground

Size	4.800" wide × 13.250" long; holes 0.055" dia.
Capacity	130 DIP
Material	Epoxy Glass, 2 oz. copper
Extender Number	3690-26
VECTOR P/N	4617-4
Active P/N	56156
Price	$60.35

Card Bracket Position

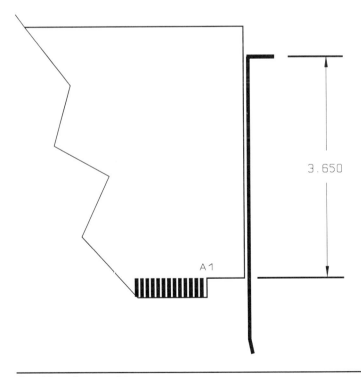

Card bracket position.

Switch Settings on the PC and XT

	Switch 1	
Number of Drives	**Section 7**	**Section 8**
One	On	On
Two	Off	On
Three	On	Off
Four	Off	Off

	Switch 1	
Monitor Type	**Section 5**	**Section 6**
EGA	On	On
CGA 40 × 25	Off	On
CGA 80 × 25	On	Off
MDA or Both	Off	Off

	Switch 1 Section 2
8087 Mathematics Coprocessor	
Present	On
Absent	Off

Memory On System Board

PC	XT	Switch 1	
		Section 3	Section 4
16K	64K	On	On
32K	128K	Off	On
48K	192K	On	Off
64K	256K	Off	Off

Memory On Expansion Bus (PC)

	Switch 2			
	Section 1	Section 2	Section 3	Section 4
96K	Off	On	On	On
128K	On	Off	On	On
160K	Off	Off	On	On
192K	On	On	Off	On
224K	Off	On	Off	On
256K	On	Off	Off	On
288K	Off	Off	Off	On
320K	On	On	On	Off
352K	Off	On	On	Off
384K	On	Off	On	Off
416K	Off	Off	On	Off
448K	On	On	Off	Off
480K	Off	On	Off	Off
512K	On	Off	Off	Off
544K	Off	Off	Off	Off

42

Video

Virtually everything you do with your PC requires the use of a video monitor. A discussion of some of the key features that determine performance and price follows:

1. RESOLUTION—The higher the resolution of a video display, the sharper and crisper the screen image will appear. Resolution is measured by the number of horizontal and vertical pixels (dots) displayed. For example, 640 × 480 resolution has 640 dots across the screen and 480 dots down the screen and produces a sharper picture when compared to a monitor with a lower resolution. Another factor that affects the crispness of the display is the dot pitch (pixel size). The smaller the dot pitch (less than 0.31 mm) the crisper the image.

2. COLOR—Monochrome monitors display images in a single color on a dark background. They are generally available in green, amber, or white. Monochrome monitors offer outstanding resolution for the price. Color monitors vary greatly in resolution as well as in the number of colors available. These variations depend on the specific video standard utilized.

3. VIDEO BOARDS—The vital link between the monitor and the PC is the video board, which translates the computer bits and bytes into an image on the monitor's screen. Because the monitor can only display what is built into the video board's capability, it is essential that the proper monitor/board combination be selected to get the most out of your monitor. Consideration during the selection process should be

given to the requirements of your future applications and for general flexibility.

4. MDA VIDEO STANDARD—IBM's Monochrome Display Adapter is capable of displaying a resolution of 720×350. This is a text-only (no graphics) standard.

5. HERCULES VIDEO STANDARD—Monochrome adapter capable of high resolution (720×348) text and graphics.

6. CGA VIDEO STANDARD—IBM's Color Graphics Adapter produces text and graphics in two modes; choose four colors from a palette of 16 with 320×200 resolution, or two colors with 640×200 resolution.

7. EGA VIDEO STANDARD—IBM's Enhanced Graphics Adapter produces sharp text and graphics in 16 colors from a palette of 64 colors with 640×350 resolution.

8. MCGA VIDEO STANDARD—IBM's Multi-Color Graphics Array is an adapter built into the IBM PS/2 Model 30. It produces sharp text and graphics in several modes and 256 colors from a palette of 256,000 colors with 320×200 resolution. Two-color display has 640×480 resolution. MCGA also offers 320×200 resolution with 64 shades of gray.

9. VGA VIDEO STANDARD—Video Graphics Array is IBM's newest adapter, built into the IBM PS/2 Models 50, 60, and 80. In addition to CGA, EGA, and MCGA modes, VGA also displays text and graphics in 16 colors with 640×480 resolution, and monochrome text with 720×400 resolution.

10. XGA VIDEO STANDARD—When IBM introduced its new 486-based PS/2's it also unveiled a new specification for high-resolution video, called XGA (for Extended Graphics Array). The XGA provides a resolution of $1,024 \times 768$ and a high-performance VGA mode. The XGA is optimized for use with graphical environments. In its present configuration XGA is confined to the Micro Channel Architecture (MCA), and like the 8514/A it is interlaced. However, like the 8514/A, the XGA specifications reveal potential support for noninterlaced modes. Whether in the motherboard version used in the PS/2 Model 90 or the card version used in the PS/2 Model 95, the XGA offers a 32-bit interface. In addition, the XGA can act as a regular 16-bit VGA board. The 256-color 640×480 mode is equivalent to VGA resolution, but with more colors. Similarly, the $1,024 \times 768$ mode is equivalent to 8514/A resolution. Also included are a 132-column text mode that is of little interest to *Microsoft Windows* users and a 640×480 deep-color mode that can show 65,536 colors at one time. XGA is not directly hardware-compatible with 8514/A. Instead of being good at drawing lines like the 8514/A, XGA is meant to move blocks of bits, similar to what is found in the contents of a window.

11. MULTISCANNING MONITORS—Multiscanning monitors are not tied to a particular video standard. On the contrary, they have the ability to display a wide range of common video standards so that you can change video boards without having to buy a new monitor. The resolution is therefore dependent on that which is produced by the video board.

12. AUTOSWITCHING VIDEO BOARD—A video board that can adapt itself to different types of monitors.

Note: Do not use a monitor with an incompatible video board. Permanent damage to the monitor and/or the video board could result.

The DOS service routines, memory, and I/O ports may be utilized by the video display adapters to do many interesting and useful things. As a clarification it is noted that ports 3B4/3D4 (in hexadecimal) can actually be accessed through ports 3X0, 3X2, 3X4, or 3X6 (replacing X with B for monochrome and with D for color). Similarly, port 3X5 can actually be accessed via ports 3X1, 3X3, 3X5, or 3X7. This is why these other ports are not used. Of all the video ports in the adapter, only 3X5 and 3XA can be read; all others are write-only.

In respect to the 6845 registers, only C–11 (in hexadecimal) may be read (through 3X5). Registers C–F should contain half the offset from the beginning of the display buffer rather than the full amount. The cursor location registers (E–F) should be the same as the page start registers (C–D) plus the number of positions into the page.

MDA Board:

3B4	6845 Address Register
3B5	6845 Data Register
3B8	Control Register-Write
	Bit 5—Disable/Enable Blink
	Bit 3—Disable/Enable Video
	Bit 0—High Resolution Mode
3BA	Status Register-Read
	Bit 7—Vertical Synchronization
	Bit 3—Video
	Bit 0—Horizontal Synchronization

Buffer at B0000

EGA Board:

3C0	ATC Index Register
3C2	Input Status Register 0
3C4	TS Index Register

3C5		TS Data Register
3CA		Graphics Position Register 2
3CC		Graphics Position Register 1
3CE		GDC Index Register
3CF		GDC Data Register
3B4	3D4	CRTC Index Register
3B5	3D5	CRTC Data Register
3BA	3DA	Input Status Register 1

Buffer at A0000

CGA Board:

3D4	6845 Address Register
3D5	6845 Data Register
3D8	Control Register-Write
	Bit 5—Background Intensity/Blink Selector
	Bit 4—Disable/Enable 640 × 200 Black and White Mode
	Bit 3—Disable/Enable Video
	Bit 2—Color/Black and White Mode
	Bit 1—Text/Graphics Mode
	Bit 0—40 × 25/80 × 25 Mode (characters × lines)
3D9	Color Select Register-Write
	Bit 7—Not used
	Bit 6—Not used
	Bit 5—Active Color Set (320 × 200)
	Bit 4—Intensified Alternate Color Set (Graphics Mode)
	Background Colors (Alphanumeric Mode)
	Bit 3—Selects Intensified:
	Border Color (40 × 25)
	Background Color (320 × 200)
	Foreground Color (640 × 200)
	Bit 2—Selects Red:
	Border Color (40 × 25)
	Background Color (320 × 200)
	Foreground Color (640 × 200)
	Bit 1—Selects Green:
	Border Color (40 × 25)
	Background Color (320 × 200)
	Foreground Color (640 × 200)
	Bit 0—Selects Blue:
	Border Color (40 × 25)
	Background Color (320 × 200)
	Foreground Color (640 × 200)

3DA   Status Register-Read
Bit 3—Vertical Synchronization
Bit 2—Light Pen Switch
Bit 1—Light Pen Trigger Armed
Bit 0—Display Enabled
Buffer at B8000

VGA Board:

3C0	RW		Address Register
3C0	W		Attribute Register
3C1	R		Attribute Register
3C2	R		Input Status Register 0
3C2	W		Miscellaneous Output
3C3	RW		Video Subsystem Enable
3C4	RW		Address Register
3C5	RW		Sequence Register
3C6	RW		PEL Mask Register
3C7	RW		PEL Address Read Mode
3C7	R		DAC State Register
3C8	RW		PEL Address Write Mode
3C9	RW		PEL Data Register
3CA	R		Feature Control Register
3CC	R		Miscellaneous Output
3CE	RW		Address Register
3CF	RW		Graphics Register
3B4	3D4	W	CRTC Index Register
3B5	3D5	RW	CRTC Data Register
3BA	3DA	R	Input Status Register 1
3BA	3DA	W	Feature Control Register

Buffer at A0000

PROGRAMMING THE 6845 VIDEO CONTROLLER I. C. FOR DIFFERENT MODES

To set up the 6845, the address register, 3X4, is loaded with the register number and the values in the following table are written to 3X5. Each column represents a different mode. Care should be used when experimenting with the first ten 6845 registers because incorrect values in these registers can damage the display adapter or the monitor.

Column Data: A: 40 × 25 Color—Text
                   B: 80 × 25 Color—Text
                   C: 320 × 400/640 × 200 Mode For Color Board
                   D: 80 × 25 Monochrome—Text
                   E: 80 × 25 Monochrome—Hercules Graphics

Register Number	Register Name	A	B	C	D	E
0	Horiz Total Characters −1	38	71	38	61	36
1	Horiz Displayed/Line	28	50	28	50	2D
2	Horiz Sync Position	2D	5A	2D	52	2F
3	Horiz Sync Width	0A	0A	0A	0F	07
4	Vertical Total Lines −1	1F	1F	7F	19	5B
5	Vertical Total Adjusted	06	06	06	06	00
6	Vertical Displayed Rows	19	19	64	19	57
7	Vertical Sync Position	1C	1C	70	19	57
8	Interlace Mode	02	02	02	02	02
9	Maximum Scan Line Address	07	07	01	0D	03
10	Cursor Starting Line	06	06	06	0B	00
11	Cursor Ending Line	07	07	07	0C	00
12	Memory Start Address (H)	00	00	00	00	00
13	Memory Start Address (L)	00	00	00	00	00
14	Cursor Address (H)	00	00	00	00	00
15	Cursor Address (L)	00	00	00	00	00
16	Light Pen (H)	00	00	00	00	00
17	Light Pen (L)	00	00	00	00	00

43

DOS Commands

This section lists the MS-DOS commands and gives the syntax and switches for each. The commands that do not work over a network are CHKDSK, DSKCOMP, DISKCOPY, FDISK, FORMAT, LABEL, RECOVER, SUBST, and SYS.

a. Internal Commands

BREAK: Sets Ctrl-C check.

BREAK [ON] or BREAK [OFF]

CHCP: Displays or changes the current code page for the command processor, COMMAND.COM.

CHCP [nnn]

CHDIR: Changes a directory to a different path; displays the working directory.

CD: CHDIR [path] or CD [path] or CD..

CLS: Clears the terminal screen.

CLS

COPY: Copies one or more files (source) to another disk (destination). This command also appends files and copies files on the same disk.

	COPY [drive:]pathname[/A][/B] [drive:][pathname][/V][/A][/B] or COPY pathname + pathname ... (to append files)
CTTY:	Lets you change the device from which you issue commands.
	CTTY device
DATE:	Enters or changes the date known to the system.
	DATE [mm-dd-yy] or DATE [mm/dd/yy] or DATE [mm.dd.yy]
DEL:	Deletes all files specified by the drive and pathname.
ERASE:	DEL [drive:][path]filename or ERASE [drive:][path]filename
DIR:	Lists the files in a directory.
	DIR [drive:][path][filename][/P][/W]
EXIT:	Exits the COMMAND.COM program (the command processor) and returns to a previous level, if one exists.
	EXIT
FASTOPEN:	Decreases the amount of time needed to open frequently used files and directories.
	FASTOPEN [drive:[=nnn][...]][/X]
MKDIR:	Makes a new directory.
MD:	MKDIR [drive:][path]new-directory or
	MD [drive:][path]new-directory
PATH:	Lets you tell MS-DOS which directories to search for external commands—after it searches your working directory.
	PATH [drive:][path][;[drive:][path]...] or PATH ;
PROMPT:	Changes the MS-DOS command prompt.
	PROMPT [[text][$character]...] characters=$,t,d,p,v,n,g,l,b,-,s,e
REN:	Changes the name of a file.

RENAME:	REN [drive:][path]oldname newname or
	RENAME [drive:][path]oldname newname
RMDIR:	Removes a directory from a multilevel directory structure.
RD:	RMDIR [drive:][path]directory-name or
	RD [drive:][path]directory-name
RUN:	Run a program.
	[drive:]filename[parameters]
SET:	Sets one string of characters in the environment equal to another string for later use in programs.
	SET [string=[string]]
TIME:	Displays and sets the time.
	TIME [hours:minutes[:seconds[:hundredths]]]
TYPE:	Displays the contents of a text file on the screen.
	TYPE [drive:][path]filename
VER:	Prints the MS-DOS version number.
	VER
VERIFY:	Turns the verify switch on or off when writing to a disk.
	VERIFY [ON] or VERIFY [OFF]
VOL:	Displays the disk volume label or volume ID, if it exists.
	VOL [drive:]

b. External Commands

APPEND:	Sets a search path for data files.
	APPEND ; or APPEND [/X][/E] or
	APPEND [drive:]path[;[drive:][path]...] or
	APPEND [[path][/X[:ON]] or APPEND [[path] [/X[:OFF]]
ASSIGN:	Tells MS-DOS to direct all requests from one drive to another.
	ASSIGN [x=y] [...]

ATTRIB: Displays or changes the attributes of selected
                        files in a directory.

                        ATTRIB [[+ or –]R][[+ or –]A]] [drive:]
                        pathname[/S]

BACKUP: Backs up one or more files from one disk
                        (source—drive 1) to another
                        (destination—drive 2).

                        BACKUP [drive 1:][path][filename] [drive 2:][/S]
                        [/M][/A][/F]

                        [/D:mm-dd-yy][/T:hh:mm]
                        [/L:[[drive:][path]filename]]

CHKDSK: Scans the disk in the specified drive and checks it
                        for errors.

                        CHKDSK [drive:][path][filename][/F][/V]

COMMAND: Starts the command processor.

DOSSHELL: COMMAND [drive:][path][cttydev][/E:nnnnn]
                        [/P][/C string]

COMP: Compares the contents of a file or a group of files
                        with another file or group of files to verify that
                        they are identical.

                        COMP [drive:][path][filename[.ext]]
                        [drive:][path][filename[.ext]]

CRTDUMP: Enables the printing of the video screen, gener-
                        ated by either the Color Graphics Board (CGB),
                        or the Advanced Graphics Board (AGB) on an
                        NEC Pinwriter P5, P6, P7, or P5XL.

                        CRTDUMP [printer type][/manual mode][/R]
                        [/B][/NO]

DISKCOMP: Compares the contents of the diskette in the first-
                        specified drive to the contents of the diskette in
                        the second-specified drive. Used after DISKCOPY
                        to ensure that the two diskettes are identical.

                        DISKCOMP [drive1:][drive2:][/1][/8]

DISKCOPY: Copies all the files on the source drive to a
                        destination drive. The diskettes must be in

separate drives unless your computer has a single diskette drive. Drives must agree in density.

DISKCOPY [drive1:][drive2:][/1]

EXE2BIN: Converts .EXE (executable) files to binary format.

EXE2BIN [drive:]pathname1 [drive:]pathname2

FDISK: Configures hard disk for MS-DOS.

FDISK

FILE COMPARE: Compares the contents of two files, or two sets of files and lists the differences.

FC [/A][/C][/L][/LBn][/N][/T][/W][/nnnn][drive:] pathname1
[drive:]pathname2 (for ASCII files)

FC [/B][/nnnnn][drive:]pathname1
[drive:]pathname2 (for binary files)

FIND: Searches for a specific string of text in a file or files.

FIND [/V][/C][/N] "string" [[drive:][path]filename] [[drive:][path]filename]....

FORMAT: Formats the disk in the specified drive to accept MS-DOS files.

FORMAT drive:[/1][/4][/8][/N:xx][/T:yy][/V][/S] [/B][f:size]

GRAFTABL: Enables an extended character set to be displayed when using display adapters in graphics mode.

GRAFTABL [437 | 850 | 860 | 863 | 865] | /STA[TUS] | [?]

GRAPHICS: Lets you print a graphics display screen on a printer when you are using a color or graphics monitor adapter.

GRAPHICS [printer][profile][/R][/B][/LCD][/C] [/F][/P=port] [/printbox:id]

INSTALL: INSTALL = [drive:][path]filename

JOIN: Joins a disk drive to a specific path.

	JOIN [[drive1:][/D][drive2:path]]
KEYB:	Loads a keyboard program.
	KEYB [xx[,[yyy],[[drive:][path]filename]]]
LABEL:	Creates, changes, or deletes a volume label on a disk.
	LABEL [drive:][volume label]
MEM:	MEM [/program][/debug]
MODE:	Sets printer options, color graphics board options, asynchronous communication adapter options, and sets or displays code pages for parallel printers or console screen device.
	MODE LPTn[:]=COMm[:][80 I 132(cols)] [,[[RETRY= [E I B I R] I [LINES=[6 I 8]] [,P]
	MODE LPTn[:][chars][,[lines][,P]]
	MODE [40 I 80 I BW40 I BW80 I CO40 I CO80 I MONO][25 I 43 I 50 I R I L][,T(test)]n
	MODE display[,shift[,T]]
	MODE COMm[:]baud,[parity],[databits], [stopbits],[P]
	MODE CON[COLS=m][LINES=n][RATE=r][DELAY=d]
	MODE device CP[PREP=((cplist)filename)][SELECT=CP] [/STATUS]
	PREPARE=[[yyy][drive:][path]filename]
MORE:	Sends output to console one screen at a time.
	MORE < source (or source I MORE)
NLSFUNC:	Loads country-specific information.
	NLSFUNC [[drive:][path]filename]
PRINT:	Prints a text file on a line printer while you are processing other MS-DOS commands (usually called background printing.)
	PRINT [/D:device][/B:size][/U:value1][/M:value2]

	[/S:time-slice] [/Q:qsize][[drive:] [pathname]filename][/T][/C][/P]...
RECOVER:	Recovers a file or disk containing bad sectors.
	RECOVER [drive:] or RECOVER [drive:][path]filename
REPLACE:	Selectively adds or replaces files on a destination disk with files from a source disk. When replacing, the source and destination files must have the same name.
	REPLACE [drive:][path]filename[.ext] [drive:][path][/A][/P][/R]
	[/S][/W][/D]
RESTORE:	Restores files that were backed up using the backup program.
	RESTORE drive1:[drive2:][pathname][/S][/P] [/B:date][/A:date]
	[/E:time][/L:time][/M][/N]
RETRACT:	Moves the heads on all installed Hard Disk units to a safe, non-data landing zone.
	RETRACT or PARK
SELECT:	Creates a version of DOS on the destination diskette with the keyboard layout, date, and time format of your choice.
	SELECT [[A:	B:] D:[path]] xxx yy
	SELECT [[drive1:]drive2:[path]] country keyboard
SHARE:	Installs file sharing and locking.
	SHARE [/F:space][/L:locks]
SORT:	Reads input, sorts the data, then writes the sorted data to your terminal screen, to a file, or to another device. (Alphabetical sort filter).
	SORT [drive:][pathname][/R][/+column]
SUBSTITUTE:	Substitutes a path with a drive letter.
	SUBST [drive1:][/D]	[[drive2:]path]]

SYSTEM: Transfers MS-DOS system files from the disk in
                       the default drive to the disk in the destination
                       drive.

                       SYS drive:

TREE: Displays all the directory paths found on the
                       specified drive, and optionally lists the files in
                       each directory.

                       TREE [drive:][/F]

TURBO: Sets the processor speed to high speed or low
                       speed.

                       TURBO [+ I −]

XCOPY: Selectively copies groups of files that can include
                       subdirectories.

                       XCOPY
                       [drive:][path]filename[.ext][drive:][path][filename[.ext]]

                       [/A][/D][/E][/M][/P][/S][/V][/W] or

                       XCOPY source[destination][/A][/drive:mm-dd-
                       yy][/E][/M][/P] [/S][/V][/W]

c. EDLIN Commands

START: Invokes EDLIN.

                       EDLIN [drive:][path]filename[/B]

END: Ends editing, saves work, and returns to MS-
                       DOS.

                       E

QUIT: Quits the editing, does not save any editing
                       changes, and exits to MS-DOS.

                       Q

APPEND: Adds a specified number of lines from your disk
                       to the file being edited in memory.

                       [n]A

COPY: Copies a range of lines to a specified line number,
                       and when used with the *count* option, copies this
                       range as many times as you want.

	[line],[line],line[,count]C
DELETE:	Deletes a specified range of lines in a file.
	[line][,line]D
EDIT:	Edits a line of text.
	[line]
INSERT:	Inserts text immediately before the specified line.
	[line]I (Ctrl-Brk when done)
LIST:	Lists a range of lines, including the two lines specified.
	[line][,line]L
MOVE:	Moves a range of text to the specified line.
	[line],+line,line M
PAGE:	Displays a file, one page (23 lines) at a time.
	[line][,line]P
REPLACE:	Replaces all occurrences of a string of text in a range with a different string of test.
	[line][,line][?]R *text1* **Ctrl-Z** *text2*
SEARCH:	Searches a range of lines for a string of text.
	[line][,line][?]S *text*
TRANSFER:	Inserts, at a specified line number, the contents of another file into the file you are currently editing.
	[line]T [drive:]filename
WRITE:	Writes a specific number of lines to a disk.
	[n]W
F1:	Copies one character from the template to the current line.
F2:	Copies multiple characters up to a given character.
F3:	Copies the template to the current line.
DEL:	Skips over one character in the template.

F4:	Skips multiple characters in the template up to the specified character.
ESC:	Quits input and clears the current line.
INS:	Enters insert mode or replace mode.
F5:	Creates a new template.

d. DEBUG Commands

START:	Invokes DEBUG.
	DEBUG[drive:][path][filename][parm1][parm2]
END:	Terminates DEBUG and returns to MS-DOS.
	Q
ASSEMBLE:	Assembles 8086/8087/8088 mnemonics directly into memory.
	A[address]
COMPARE:	Compares the portion of memory specified by a range to a portion of the same size beginning at the specified address.
	C range address
DUMP:	Displays the contents of the specified range of memory.
	D[range] or D[address]
ENTER:	Enters byte values into memory at the specified address.
	E address [list]
FILL:	Fills the address in the specified range with the values in the specified list.
	F range list
GO:	Executes the program currently in memory. When optional addresses are set, execution stops at the first address encountered (break point) and the registers, flags, and decoded instructions are displayed.
	G [= address [addresses]] or G [= address] [break0][...break9]

HEX:	Performs hexadecimal arithmetic (addition and subtraction) on the two specified numbers.
	H value value
INPUT:	Inputs and displays one byte from the specified port.
	I port
LOAD:	Loads a file into memory.
	L [address[drive: sector number, number of sectors]]
MOVE:	Moves the block of memory specified by range to the location starting at the specified address.
	M range address
NAME:	Sets file names.
	N filename [filename parameter....]
OUTPUT:	Sends the specified byte to the output port specified by value.
	O port byte
PROCEED:	Continues from this address.
	P [= address][number]
QUIT:	Terminates the DEBUG utility.
	Q
REGISTER:	Displays the contents of one or more CPU registers.
	R [F] I [register name]
SEARCH:	Searches the specified range for the specified list of bytes.
	S range list
TRACE:	Executes one instruction and displays the contents of all registers, flags, and the decoded instruction.
	T [= address][number of steps]
UNASSEMBLE:	Dissassembles bytes and displays the source

statements that correspond to them, with addresses and byte values.

U [address] or U [range]

WRITE: Writes the file being debugged to a disk file.

W [address [drive: sector number, number of sectors]]

e. BATCH Commands

CALL: Calls one batch file from another without ending itself.

CALL [drive:][path] batchfile [argument]

ECHO: Turns the batch file echo feature on or off, or displays the current setting.

ECHO [ON] or ECHO [OFF] or ECHO [message]

FOR: Performs a command for a set of files.

FOR [%] %variable IN (set) DO command

GOTO: Processes commands starting with the line after the specified label.

GOTO label

IF: Performs a command if a condition is met.

IF [not] errorlevel number command or

IF [not] string1 == string2 command or

IF [not] EXIST filename command

PAUSE: Pauses during the processing of a batch.

PAUSE [comment]

REM: During execution of a batch file, REM displays remarks that are on the same line as the REM command in that batch file.

REM [comment]

SHIFT: Lets you change the position of replaceable parameters in batch file processing.

SHIFT

f. LIBRARY (LIB) Commands

The Library (LIB) Program requests responses to the following prompts:

Library Name	OldLibrary name (a semicolon (;) immediately after the name causes LIB to perform a consistency check on the OldLibrary).

Operations

	"blank"	No operation
	−	Delete module from OldLibrary
	+	Add module to OldLibrary
	−+	Replace module in OldLibrary
	*	Copy module to object module or Output Library
	−*	Copy module and delete from OldLibrary

List File	Name of optional cross reference list file.
Output Library	NewLibrary name (only if argument in Operations field).

g. DOS Keystrokes

F1:	Copies one character from the template to the current line.
F2:	Copies multiple characters up to a given character.
F3:	Copies the template to the current line.
DEL:	Skips over one character in the template.
F4:	Skips multiple characters in the template up to the specified character.
ESC:	Quits input and clears the current line.
INS:	Enters insert mode or replace mode.
F5:	Creates a new template.
F6:	Puts a Ctrl-Z (1Ah) end-of-file character in the new template.
Ctrl-C:	Aborts the current command.
Ctrl-H:	Removes the last character from a command line

	and erases that character from the terminal screen.
Ctrl-J	Inserts a physical end-of-line, but does not empty the command line. Use the LINEFEED key to extend the current logical line beyond the physical limits of the terminal screen.
Ctrl-N	Causes echoing of output to a lineprinter.
Ctrl-P	Causes terminal output to a lineprinter.
Ctrl-S	Suspends output display on the screen. Press Ctrl-S again to resume.
Ctrl-X	Cancels the current line, empties the command line, and then outputs a backslash (\), Return, and LINEFEED. Ctrl-X does not affect the template used by the special editing commands.
Ctrl-Alt-Del	Warm boot.
Ctrl-NumLock	Stop Scroll.
Any Key	Resume Scroll.
Shift-PrtSc	Print Screen (Screen dump).
Ctrl-PrtSc	Continuous Print Screen
Ctrl-Enter	Next Line (without carriage return)
ESC	Cancel Line.
Ctrl-Break	End Operation.

Keystroke characters and symbols may be entered from the keyboard by holding down ALT, entering the decimal character code *on the numeric keyboard* (numerals 0–9), then releasing ALT. The symbol corresponding to the code will appear on the screen. This is the manner in which the symbolic character codes greater than 127 decimal (7Fh) which are used for the special symbols are entered. (See Chapter 35.)

h. CONFIG.SYS Commands

BREAK:	Sets Ctrl-C check.
	BREAK = ON	OFF
BUFFERS:	Sets the number of sector buffers
	BUFFERS = nn

COUNTRY: Allows for international time, date, and currency.

                       COUNTRY = nnn[,yyy][,[drive:]filename]

DEVICE: Installs the device driver in the system.

                       DEVICE = [drive:][path]filename[options]

                       DEVICE = [drive:][path]ANSI.SYS[/X][/L][/K]

                       DEVICE = [drive:][path]DISPLAY.SYS CON =
                       ([LCD | EGA],hwcp,n)

                       DEVICE = [drive:][path]DRIVER.SYS /D:ddd
                       [/T:ttt][/S:ss][/H:hh][/C][/N][/F:f]....

                       DEVICE = [drive:][path]PRINTER.SYS LPTn[:] =
                       ([4201 | 4208 | 5202],hwcp,n)

                       DEVICE = [drive:][path]VDISK.SYS
                       [text][bbb][text][sss][text][ddd][/E][;m]

                       DEVICE = [drive:][path]XMAEM.SYS....

                       DEVICE = [drive:][path]XMA2EMS.SYS....

DRIVPARM: Defines parameters for block devices.

                       DRIVPARM = /D:n[/C][/F:n][/H:n][/N][/S:n][T:n]

FCBS: Specifies the number of File Control Blocks
                       (FCBs) that can be open concurrently.

                       FCBS = m,p

FILES: Sets the number of open files that can access
                       certain MS-DOS system calls.

                       FILES = n

LASTDRIVE: Sets the maximum number of drives you may
                       access.

                       LASTDRIVE = drive

SHELL: Begins execution of the shell from a specific file
                       (usually COMMAND.COM)

                       SHELL = [drive:][path]filename[options]

STACKS: Supports the dynamic use of data stacks.

                       STACKS = number,size

SWITCHES: SWITCHES = /K

44

DOS and BASIC
Versions

File Sizes of DOS

DOS Level	3.3	3.2	3.1	3.0	2.1	2.0	1.1	1.0
IBMBIO.COM	22,100	16,369	9,564	8,964	4,736	4,608	1,920	1,920
IBMDOS.COM	30,159	28,477	27,760	27,920	17,024	17,152	6,400	6,400
COMMAND.COM	25,307	23,791	23,210	22,042	17,792	17,664	4,959	3,231
Total	77,566	68,637	60,534	58,926	39,552	39,424	13,279	11,551

Approximate DOS Memory Usage

DOS Level	3.3	3.2	3.1	3.0	2.1	2.0	1.1	1.0
				36K	24K	24K	12K	

File Sizes of BASIC

DOS Level	3.3	3.2	3.1	3.0	2.1	2.0	1.1	1.0
BASIC				17,024	16,256	16,256	11,392	
BASICA				26,880	26,112	25,984	16,768	
GWBASIC	80,592							

Source: IBM Corporation, Boca Raton, Florida 33432

45

IBM Machine Identification

Programs may be written for machine-specific features, but they must test for specific machine type. Location 0FFFF:0E contains the machine identification.

Hex	Machine Identification	Date	Sub Mod	Revision
0FF	IBM Personal Computer			
0FE	IBM Personal Computer XT			
0FD	IBM PC jr.			
0FC	IBM Personal Computer AT	6/10/85	00	01
0FC	IBM Personal Computer AT	11/15/85	01	00
0FC	IBM Personal Computer XT286	4/21/86	02	00
0FB	IBM Personal Computer XT	1/10/86	00	01
0FB	IBM Personal Computer XT	5/9/86	00	02
0F9	IBM PC Convertible	9/13/85	00	00
0FA	IBM PS/2 Model 25	6/27/87	01	00
0FA	IBM PS/2 Model 30	9/2/86	00	00
0FC	IBM PS/2 Model 50	2/13/87	04	00
0FC	IBM PS/2 Model 60	2/13/87	05	00
0F8	IBM PS/2 Model 80	3/30/87	00	00
0F8	IBM PS/2 Model 80	10/7/87	01	00

46

Mathematics Coprocessor Data Types and Miscellaneous Constants

Data Type	Bits	Significant Digits (Decimal)	Aproximate Range (Decimal)
Word Integer	16	4	$-32{,}768 \leq X \leq +32{,}767$
Short Integer	32	9	$-2 \times 10^9 \leq X \leq +2 \times 10^9$
Long Integer	64	19	$-9 \times 10^{18} \leq X \leq +9 \times 10^{18}$
Packed Decimal	80	18	$-99...99 \leq X \leq +99...99$ (18 Digits)
Short Real (Single Precision)	32	6–7	$8.43 \times 10^{-37} \leq X \leq 3.37 \times 10^{+38}$
Long Real (Double Precision)	64	15–16	$4.19 \times 10^{-307} \leq X \leq 1.67 \times 10^{+308}$
Temporary Real	80	19	$3.4 \times 10^{-4932} \leq X \leq 1.2 \times 10^{+4932}$

MISCELLANEOUS CONSTANTS

$\pi =$	3.14159	26535	89793	23846	26433	83279	50288	41971	69399	37510
$\log_e \pi =$	1.14472	98858	49400	17414	34273	51353	05871	16972	94812	91531
$\log_{10} \pi =$	0.49714	98726	94133	85435	12682	88290	89887	36516	78324	38044
$e =$	2.71828	18284	59045	23536	02874	71352	66249	77572	47093	69995
$\log_{10} e =$	0.43429	44819	03251	82765	11289	18916	60508	22943	97005	80366
$\pi^e =$	22.45915	77183	61045	47342	71522					
$e^\pi =$	23.14069	26327	79269	00572	90864					
$\sqrt{2} =$	1.41421	35623	73095	04880	16887	24209	69807	85696	71875	37694
$\sqrt[3]{2} =$	1.25992	10498	94873	16476	72106	07278	22835	05702	51464	70150
$\log_e 2 =$	0.69314	71805	59945	30941	72321	21458	17656	80755	00134	36025
$\log_{10} 2 =$	0.30102	99956	63981	19521	37388	94724	49302	67681	89881	46210
$\sqrt{3} =$	1.73205	08075	68877	29352	74463	41505	87236	69428	05253	81038
$\sqrt[3]{3} =$	1.44224	95703	07408	38232	16383	10780	10958	83918	69253	49935
$\log_e 3 =$	1.09861	22886	68109	69139	52452	36922	52570	46474	90557	82274
$\log_{10} 3 =$	0.47712	12547	19662	43729	50279	03255	11530	92001	28864	19069

$$
\begin{aligned}
1 \text{ Radian} &= 57.\ 29577\ 95131 \text{ Degrees} \\
&= 3437.\ 74677\ 07849 \text{ Minutes} \\
&= 206264.\ 80625 \text{ Seconds} \\
&= 57° \ 17' \ 44".80625 \\
1 \text{ Mil} &= 0.00098175 \text{ Radians} = 0.05625° = 3.375' - 202.5" \\
1 \text{ Degree} &= 17.777778 \text{ Mils} \\
1 \text{ Centimeter} &= 0.393701 \text{ Inch} = 0.0328084 \text{ Foot} \\
1 \text{ Liter} &= 0.264179 \text{ Gallon} = 1.056718 \text{ Quarts} \\
1 \text{ Kilogram} &= 2.2046226 \text{ Pounds (Avoirdupois)}
\end{aligned}
$$

CONSTANTS IN OCTAL

$$
\begin{aligned}
\pi &= 3.11037 \quad 552421_8 \\
\pi^{-1} &= 0.24276 \quad 301556_8 \\[6pt]
\sqrt{\pi} &= 1.61337 \quad 611067_8 \\
\log_e \pi &= 1.11206 \quad 404435_8 \\
\log_2 \pi &= 1.51544 \quad 163223_8 \\[6pt]
\sqrt{10} &= 3.12305 \quad 407267_8 \\
e &= 2.55760 \quad 521305_8 \\
e^{-1} &= 0.27426 \quad 530661_8 \\[6pt]
\sqrt{e} &= 1.51411 \quad 230704_8 \\
\log_{10} e &= 0.33626 \quad 754251_8 \\
\log_2 e &= 1.34252 \quad 166245_8 \\
\log_2 10 &= 3.24464 \quad 741136_8 \\[6pt]
\gamma &= 0.44742 \quad 147707_8 \\
\log_e \gamma &= -0.43127 \quad 233602_8 \\
\log_2 \gamma &= -0.62573 \quad 030645_8 \\[6pt]
\sqrt{2} &= 1.32404 \quad 746320_8 \\
\log_e 2 &= 0.54271 \quad 027760_8 \\
\log_e 10 &= 2.23273 \quad 067355_8
\end{aligned}
$$

MATHEMATICAL NOTATION

	Mathematical Power	Name
10^{18} or	1,000,000,000,000,000,000	one quintillion
10^{15} or	1,000,000,000,000,000	one quadrillion
10^{12} or	1,000,000,000,000	one trillion
10^{9} or	1,000,000,000	one billion
10^{6} or	1,000,000	one million
10^{3} or	1,000	one thousand
10^{2} or	100	one hundred
10^{1} or	10	ten
10^{0} or	1	one
10^{-1} or	0.1	one tenth
10^{-2} or	0.01	one hundredth
10^{-3} or	0.001	one thousandth
10^{-6} or	0.000 001	one millionth
10^{-9} or	0.000 000 001	one billionth
10^{-12} or	0.000 000 000 001	one trillionth
10^{-15} or	0.000 000 000 000 001	one quadrillionth
10^{-18} or	0.000 000 000 000 000 001	one quintillionth

METRIC INTERRELATIONSHIPS

Conversions from a multiple or submultiple to the basic units of meters, liters, or grams can be done using the table. For example, to convert from kilometers to meters, multiply by 1,000 (9.26 kilometers equals 9,260 meters) or to convert from meters to kilometers, multiply by 0.001 (9,260 meters equals 9.26 kilometers).

Prefix	Symbol	Length, Weight, Capacity	Area	Volume
exa	E	10^{18}	10^{36}	10^{54}
peta	P	10^{15}	10^{30}	10^{45}
tera	T	10^{12}	10^{24}	10^{36}
giga	G	10^{9}	10^{18}	10^{27}
mega	M	10^{6}	10^{12}	10^{18}
hectokilo	hk	10^{5}	10^{10}	10^{15}
myria	ma	10^{4}	10^{8}	10^{12}
kilo	k	10^{3}	10^{6}	10^{9}
hecto	h	10^{2}	10^{4}	10^{6}

Prefix	Symbol	Length, Weight, Capacity	Area	Volume
deka	da	10^1	10^2	10^3
basic unit		1 meter, 1 gram, 1 liter	1 meter^2	1 meter^3
deci	d	10^{-1}	10^{-2}	10^{-3}
centi	c	10^{-2}	10^{-4}	10^{-6}
milli	m	10^{-3}	10^{-6}	10^{-9}
decimilli	dm	10^{-4}	10^{-8}	10^{-12}
centimilli	cm	10^{-5}	10^{-10}	10^{-15}
micro	u	10^{-6}	10^{-12}	10^{-18}
nano	n	10^{-9}	10^{-18}	10^{-27}
pico	p	10^{-12}	10^{-24}	10^{-36}
femto	f	10^{-15}	10^{-30}	10^{-45}
atto	a	10^{-18}	10^{-36}	10^{-54}

POSITIVE POWERS OF 2

n	2^n	
0	1	
1	2	
2	4	
3	8	
4	16	
5	32	
6	64	
7	128	
8	256	
9	512	
10	1024	
11	2048	
12	4096	
13	8192	
14	16384	
15	32768	
16	65536	
17	13107	2
18	26214	4
19	52428	8

n	2^n			
20	10485	76		
21	20971	52		
22	41943	04		
23	83886	08		
24	16777	216		
25	33554	432		
26	67108	864		
27	13421	7728		
28	26843	5456		
29	53687	0912		
30	10737	41824		
31	21474	83648		
32	42949	67296		
33	85899	34592		
34	17179	86918	4	
35	34359	73836	8	
36	68719	47673	6	
37	13743	89534	72	
38	27487	79069	44	
39	54975	58138	88	
40	10995	11627	776	
41	21990	23255	552	
42	43980	46511	104	
43	87960	93022	208	
44	17592	18604	4416	
45	35184	37208	8832	
46	70368	74417	7664	
47	14073	74883	55328	
48	28147	49767	10656	
49	56294	99534	21312	
50	11258	99906	84262	4
51	22517	99813	68524	8
52	45035	99627	37049	6
53	90071	99254	74099	2
54	18014	39850	94819	84
55	36028	79701	89639	68
56	72057	59403	79279	36
57	14411	51880	75855	872
58	28823	03761	51711	744
59	57646	07523	03423	488

n	2^n						
60	11529	21504	60684	6976			
61	23058	43009	21369	3952			
62	46116	86018	42738	7904			
63	92233	72036	85477	5808			
64	18446	74407	37095	51616			
65	36893	48814	74191	03232			
66	73786	97629	48382	06464			
67	14757	39525	89676	41292	8		
68	29514	79051	79352	82585	6		
69	59029	58103	58705	65171	2		
70	11805	91620	71741	13034	24		
71	23611	83241	43482	26068	48		
72	47223	66482	86964	52136	96		
73	94447	32965	73929	04273	92		
74	18889	46593	14785	80854	784		
75	37778	93186	29571	61709	568		
76	75557	86372	59143	23419	136		
77	15111	57274	51828	64683	8272		
78	30223	14549	03657	29367	6544		
79	60446	29098	07314	58735	3088		
80	12089	25819	61462	91747	06176		
81	24178	51639	22925	83494	12352		
82	48357	03278	45851	66988	24704		
83	96714	06556	91703	33976	49408		
84	19342	81311	38340	66795	29881	6	
85	38685	62622	76681	33590	59763	2	
86	77371	25245	53362	67181	19526	4	
87	15474	25049	10672	53436	23905	28	
88	30948	50098	21345	06872	47810	56	
89	61897	00196	42690	13744	95621	12	
90	12379	40039	28538	02748	99124	224	
91	24758	80078	57076	05497	98248	448	
92	49517	60157	14152	10995	96496	896	
93	99035	20314	28304	21991	92993	792	
94	19807	04062	85660	84398	38598	7584	
95	39614	08125	71321	68796	77197	5168	
96	79228	16251	42643	37593	54395	0336	
97	15845	63250	28528	67518	70879	00672	
98	31691	26500	57057	35037	41758	01344	
99	63382	53001	14114	70074	83516	02688	
100	12676	50600	22822	94014	96703	20537	6
101	25353	01200	45645	88029	93406	41075	2

NEGATIVE POWERS OF 2

n	2^{-n}
0	1.0
1	0.5
2	0.25
3	0.125
4	0.0625
5	0.0312 5
6	0.0156 25
7	0.0078 125
8	0.0039 0625
9	0.0019 53125
10	0.0009 76562 5
11	0.0004 88281 25
12	0.0002 44140 625
13	0.0001 22070 3125
14	0.0000 61035 15625
15	0.0000 30517 57812 5
16	0.0000 15258 78906 25
17	0.0000 07629 39453 125
18	0.0000 03814 69726 5625
19	0.0000 01907 34863 28125
20	0.0000 00953 67431 64062 5
21	0.0000 00476 83715 82031 25
22	0.0000 00238 41857 91015 625
23	0.0000 00119 20928 95507 8125
24	0.0000 00059 60464 47753 90625
25	0.0000 00029 80232 23876 95312 5
26	0.0000 00014 90116 11938 47656 25
27	0.0000 00007 45058 05969 23828 125
28	0.0000 00003 72529 02984 61914 0625
29	0.0000 00001 86264 51492 30957 03125
30	0.0000 00000 93132 25746 15478 51562 5
31	0.0000 00000 46566 12873 07739 25781 25
32	0.0000 00000 23283 06436 53869 62890 625
33	0.0000 00000 11641 53218 26934 81445 3125
34	0.0000 00000 05820 76609 13467 40722 65625
35	0.0000 00000 02910 38304 56733 70361 32812 5
36	0.0000 00000 01455 19152 28366 85180 66406 25

n	2^{-n}
37	0.0000 00000 00727 59576 14183 42590 33203 125
38	0.0000 00000 00363 79788 07091 71295 16601 5625
39	0.0000 00000 00181 89894 03545 85647 58300 78125
40	0.0000 00000 00090 94947 01772 92823 79150 39062 5
41	0.0000 00000 00045 47473 50886 46411 89575 19531 25
42	0.0000 00000 00022 73736 75443 23205 94787 59765 625
43	0.0000 00000 00011 36868 37721 61602 97393 79882 8125
44	0.0000 00000 00005 68434 18860 80801 48696 89941 40625
45	0.0000 00000 00002 84217 09430 40400 74348 44970 70312 5
46	0.0000 00000 00001 42108 54715 20200 37174 22485 35156 25
47	0.0000 00000 00000 71054 27357 60100 18587 11242 67578 125
48	0.0000 00000 00000 35527 13678 80050 09293 55621 33789 0625
49	0.0000 00000 00000 17763 56839 40025 04646 77810 66894 53125
50	0.0000 00000 00000 08881 78419 70012 52323 38905 33447 26562 5

Source: Standard Mathematical Tables
The Chemical Rubber Co. Cleveland, OH 44128

47

Octal (Base 8) and Hexadecimal (Base 16) Arithmetic

In our ordinary system of writing numbers, the value of any digit depends on its position in the number with reference to the radix point. This is known as the positional notation of number systems.

The positional system in most common use is the base (or radix) 10 system (the decimal system). Base 10 means that the system has 10 admissible marks, 0–9. Base 2 means that the system has 2 admissible marks, 0–1. The base 10 system is the one in which most people can compute easily. The value of a digit (or single number) in any position is ten times the value of the same digit one position to the right, or one-tenth the value of the same digit one position to the left. Thus, for a base 10 number:

$$642.371_{10} = 6 \times 10^2 + 4 \times 10^1 + 2 \times 10^0 + 3 \times 10^{-1} + 7 \times 10^{-2} + 1 \times 10^{-3}$$

or
$$
\begin{array}{r}
600.000 \\
40.000 \\
2.000 \\
.300 \\
.070 \\
.001 \\
\hline
642.371
\end{array}
$$

There is no reason why a number other than 10 (decimal) cannot be used as the base (or radix). Bases of 2 (binary), 8 (octal), and 16 (hexadecimal) are commonly used in working with computers. Base 3 (trinary) and base 9 (noval) are not commonly used. When the base in use is not clear from the context, it is usually indicated as a subscript following the number. For example,

$$347._8 = 3 \times 8^2 + 4 \times 8^1 + 7 \times 8^0 = 192_{10} + 32_{10} + 7_{10} = 231_{10}$$

$$1011.101_2 = 1 \times 2^3 + 0 \times 2^2 + 1 \times 2^1 + 1 \times 2^0 + 1 \times 2^{-1} + 0 \times 2^{-2} + 1 \times 2^{-3} =$$

$$
\begin{array}{r}
8.000 \\
2.000 \\
1.000 \\
.500 \\
\underline{.125} \\
11.625_{10}
\end{array}
$$

In general, a number in positional notation may be written:

$$\ldots\ldots + A_8B^8 + A_7B^7 + A_6B^6 + A_5B^5 + A_4B^4 + A_3B^3 + A_2B^2 + A_1B^1 + A_0B^0. + A_{-1}B^{-1} + A_{-2}B^{-2} + A_{-3}B^{-3} + A_{-4}B^{-4} + A_{-5}B^{-5} + A_{-6}B^{-6} + A_{-7}B^{-7} + A_{-8}B^{-8} + \ldots\ldots\ldots$$

where   A is the multiplier,
         B is the base to be raised to its positional power,
         and the radix point follows the B^0 term.

To convert a number *from any base to base 10* the procedure is as indicated in the examples above, that is,

1. Write down the number.
2. Multiply each digit by its corresponding positional value using base 10 arithmetic.
3. Add all the base 10 products to obtain the base 10 conversion.

To convert a number *from base 10 into another base*

1. Separate the number at the decimal point, and operate on each half individually.
2. For the integer half (the part to the left of the decimal point), divide the number by the new base, getting an integer quotient and a remainder.
3. Using the quotient from the division is step 2 in place of the original number, repeat steps 2 and 3 until the quotient becomes 0. For example:

$$301.811_{10} = ?_8$$

$$
\begin{array}{lll}
301 \div 8 = 37 & \text{remainder} & 5 \\
37 \div 8 = 4 & \text{remainder} & 5 \\
4 \div 8 = 0 & \text{remainder} & 4
\end{array}
$$

therefore $301._{10} = 455._8$

4. For the fractional part (the part to the right of the decimal point), multiply the decimal number by the new base.
5. Record the integral portion of the product as the first digit of the fractional part of the number in the new base.
6. Using the fractional part of the product in step 5 in place of the original number, repeat steps 4, 5, and 6 until the product becomes an integer (the fractional part becomes zero) or the desired number of places have been computed.

$$
\begin{array}{r}
.811 \\
8 \\
\hline
6.488 \\
8 \\
\hline
3.904 \\
8 \\
\hline
7.232 \\
8 \\
\hline
1.856 \\
8 \\
\hline
6.848
\end{array}
$$

therefore $0.811_{10} = 0.63716...._8$

and $301.811_{10} = 455.63716......_8$

To convert from one base to another, neither of which is 10, the easiest procedure is usually to convert to base 10 and then to the desired base. There are two exceptions to this:

1. If computational facility is available in either of the bases, it may be utilized instead of base 10, and the appropriate one of the above methods applied.
2. If the two bases are different powers of the same number, the conversion may be done digit by digit to the base that is the common root of both bases. The conversion is then made from the common root to the other base. For example:

$$356.721_8 = ?_{16}$$

First convert octal to binary by inspection.

$$= 011\ 101\ 110\ .\ 111\ 010\ 001_2$$

Next convert binary to hexadecimal by sectioning off groups of 4 both left and right from the radix point.

$$= 0\ 1110\ 1110\ .\ 1110\ 1000\ 1000_2$$
$$= EE.E88_{16}$$

The following tables are supplied to assist in conversion of hexadecimal to decimal.

Integer Conversion Of Hexadecimal To Decimal

Multiply	F^7	F^6	F^5	F^4	F^3	F^2	F^1	F^0
0x	0	0	0	0	0	0	0	0
1x	268,435,456	16,777,216	1,048,576	65,536	4,096	256	16	1
2x	536,870,912	33,554,432	2,097,152	131,072	8,192	512	32	2
3x	805,306,368	50,331,648	3,145,728	196,608	12,288	768	48	3
4x	1,073,741,824	67,108,864	4,194,304	262,144	16,384	1,024	64	4
5x	1,342,177,280	83,886,080	5,242,880	327,680	20,480	1,280	80	5
6x	1,610,612,736	100,663,296	6,291,456	393,216	24,576	1,536	96	6
7x	1,879,048,192	117,440,512	7,340,032	458,752	28,672	1,792	112	7
8x	2,147,483,648	134,217,728	8,388,608	524,288	32,768	2,048	128	8
9x	2,415,919,104	150,994,944	9,437,184	589,824	36,864	2,304	144	9
Ax	2,684,354,560	167,772,160	10,485,760	655,360	40,960	2,560	160	10
Bx	2,952,790,016	184,549,376	11,534,336	720,896	45,056	2,816	176	11
Cx	3,221,225,472	201,326,592	12,582,912	786,432	49,152	3,072	192	12
Dx	3,489,660,928	218,103,808	13,631,488	851,968	53,248	3,328	208	13
Ex	3,758,096,384	234,881,024	14,680,064	917,504	57,344	3,584	224	14
Fx	4,026,531,840	251,658,240	15,728,640	983,040	61,440	3,840	240	15

$1 \times F^8 = 4{,}294{,}967{,}296$

$1 \times F^9 = 68{,}719{,}476{,}736$

$1 \times F^{10} = 1{,}099{,}511{,}627{,}776$

$1 \times F^{11} = 17{,}592{,}186{,}044{,}416$

$1 \times F^{12} = 281{,}474{,}976{,}710{,}656$

$1 \times F^{13} = 4{,}503{,}599{,}627{,}370{,}496$

$1 \times F^{14} = 72{,}057{,}594{,}037{,}927{,}936$

$1 \times F^{15} = 1{,}152{,}921{,}504{,}606{,}846{,}976$

Fractional Conversion of Hexadecimal to Decimal

Hex	Decimal	Hex	Decimal	Hex	Decimal	Hex	Decimal
.0	.0000 0000	.00	.0000 0000	.000	.0000 0000 0000	.0000	.0000 0000 0000 0000
.1	.0625 0000	.01	.0039 0625	.001	.0002 4414 0625	.0001	.0000 1525 8789 0625
.2	.1250 0000	.02	.0078 1250	.002	.0004 8828 1250	.0002	.0000 3051 7578 1250
.3	.1875 0000	.03	.0117 1875	.003	.0007 3242 1875	.0003	.0000 4577 6367 1875
.4	.2500 0000	.04	.0156 2500	.004	.0009 7656 2500	.0004	.0000 6103 5156 2500
.5	.3125 0000	.05	.0195 3125	.005	.0012 2070 3125	.0005	.0000 7629 3945 3125
.6	.3750 0000	.06	.0234 3750	.006	.0014 6484 3750	.0006	.0000 9155 2734 3750
.7	.4375 0000	.07	.0273 4375	.007	.0017 0898 4375	.0007	.0001 0681 1523 4375
.8	.5000 0000	.08	.0312 5000	.008	.0019 5312 5000	.0008	.0001 2207 0312 5000
.9	.5625 0000	.09	.0351 5625	.009	.0021 9726 5625	.0009	.0001 3732 9101 5625
.A	.6250 0000	.0A	.0390 6250	.00A	.0024 4140 6250	.000A	.0001 5258 7890 6250
.B	.6875 0000	.0B	.0429 6875	.00B	.0026 8554 6875	.000B	.0001 6784 6679 6875
.C	.7500 0000	.0C	.0468 7500	.00C	.0029 2968 7500	.000C	.0001 8310 5468 7500
.D	.8125 0000	.0D	.0507 8125	.00D	.0031 7382 8125	.000D	.0001 9836 4257 8125
.E	.8750 0000	.0E	.0546 8750	.00E	.0034 1796 8750	.000E	.0002 1362 3046 8750
.F	.9375 0000	.0F	.0585 9375	.00F	.0036 6210 9375	.000F	.0002 2888 1835 9375

Hexadecimal Addition (Horizontal Plus Vertical)

+	1	2	3	4	5	6	7	8	9	A	B	C	D	E	F
1	2	3	4	5	6	7	8	9	A	B	C	D	E	F	10
2	3	4	5	6	7	8	9	A	B	C	D	E	F	10	11
3	4	5	6	7	8	9	A	B	C	D	E	F	10	11	12
4	5	6	7	8	9	A	B	C	D	E	F	10	11	12	13
5	6	7	8	9	A	B	C	D	E	F	10	11	12	13	14
6	7	8	9	A	B	C	D	E	F	10	11	12	13	14	15
7	8	9	A	B	C	D	E	F	10	11	12	13	14	15	16
8	9	A	B	C	D	E	F	10	11	12	13	14	15	16	17
9	A	B	C	D	E	F	10	11	12	13	14	15	16	17	18
A	B	C	D	E	F	10	11	12	13	14	15	16	17	18	19
B	C	D	E	F	10	11	12	13	14	15	16	17	18	19	1A
C	D	E	F	10	11	12	13	14	15	16	17	18	19	1A	1B
D	E	F	10	11	12	13	14	15	16	17	18	19	1A	1B	1C
E	F	10	11	12	13	14	15	16	17	18	19	1A	1B	1C	1D
F	10	11	12	13	14	15	16	17	18	19	1A	1B	1C	1D	1E

Hexadecimal Subtraction (Horizontal Minus Vertical)

–	1	2	3	4	5	6	7	8	9	A	B	C	D	E	F
1	0	1	2	3	4	5	6	7	8	9	A	B	C	D	E
2	F	0	1	2	3	4	5	6	7	8	9	A	B	C	D
3	E	F	0	1	2	3	4	5	6	7	8	9	A	B	C
4	D	E	F	0	1	2	3	4	5	6	7	8	9	A	B
5	C	D	E	F	0	1	2	3	4	5	6	7	8	9	A
6	B	C	D	E	F	0	1	2	3	4	5	6	7	8	9
7	A	B	C	D	E	F	0	1	2	3	4	5	6	7	8
8	9	A	B	C	D	E	F	0	1	2	3	4	5	6	7
9	8	9	A	B	C	D	E	F	0	1	2	3	4	5	6
A	7	8	9	A	B	C	D	E	F	0	1	2	3	4	5
B	6	7	8	9	A	B	C	D	E	F	0	1	2	3	4
C	5	6	7	8	9	A	B	C	D	E	F	0	1	2	3
D	4	5	6	7	8	9	A	B	C	D	E	F	0	1	2
E	3	4	5	6	7	8	9	A	B	C	D	E	F	0	1
F	2	3	4	5	6	7	8	9	A	B	C	D	E	F	0

Hexadecimal Multiplication (Horizontal Times Vertical)

×	1	2	3	4	5	6	7	8	9	A	B	C	D	E	F
1	1	2	3	4	5	6	7	8	9	A	B	C	D	E	F
2	2	4	6	8	A	C	E	10	12	14	16	18	1A	1C	1E
3	3	6	9	C	F	12	15	18	1B	1E	21	24	27	2A	2D
4	4	8	C	10	14	18	1C	20	24	28	2C	30	34	38	3C
5	5	A	F	14	19	1E	23	28	2D	32	37	3C	41	46	4B
6	6	C	12	18	1E	24	2A	30	36	3C	42	48	4E	54	5A
7	7	E	15	1C	23	2A	31	38	3F	46	4D	54	5B	62	69
8	8	10	18	20	28	30	38	40	48	50	58	60	68	70	78
9	9	12	1B	24	2D	36	3F	48	51	5A	63	6C	75	7E	87
A	A	14	1E	28	32	3C	46	50	5A	64	6E	78	82	8C	96
B	B	16	21	2C	37	42	4D	58	63	6E	79	84	8F	9A	A5
C	C	18	24	30	3C	48	54	60	6C	78	84	90	9C	A8	B4
D	D	1A	27	34	41	4E	5B	68	75	82	8F	9C	A9	B6	C3
E	E	1C	2A	38	46	54	62	70	7E	8C	9A	A8	B6	C4	D2
F	F	1E	2D	3C	4B	5A	69	78	87	96	A5	B4	C3	D2	E1

POWERS OF 10 (10^n and 10^{-n}) IN OCTAL

10^n	n	10^{-n}
1_8	0	$1.000\ 000\ 000\ 000\ 000_8$
12_8	1	$0.063\ 146\ 314\ 631\ 463_8$
144_8	2	$0.005\ 075\ 341\ 217\ 270_8$
$1\ 750_8$	3	$0.000\ 406\ 111\ 564\ 570_8$
$23\ 420_8$	4	$0.000\ 032\ 155\ 613\ 530_8$
$303\ 240_8$	5	$0.000\ 002\ 476\ 132\ 610_8$
$3\ 641\ 100_8$	6	$0.000\ 000\ 015\ 327\ 745_8$
$46\ 113\ 200_8$	7	$0.000\ 000\ 015\ 327\ 745_8$
$575\ 360\ 400_8$	8	$0.000\ 000\ 001\ 257\ 143_8$
$7\ 346\ 545\ 000_8$	9	$0.000\ 000\ 000\ 104\ 560_8$
$112\ 402\ 762\ 000_8$	10	$0.000\ 000\ 000\ 006\ 676_8$
$1\ 351\ 035\ 564\ 000_8$	11	$0.000\ 000\ 000\ 000\ 537_8$
$16\ 432\ 451\ 210\ 000_8$	12	$0.000\ 000\ 000\ 000\ 043_8$
$221\ 441\ 634\ 520\ 000_8$	13	$0.000\ 000\ 000\ 000\ 003_8$
$2\ 657\ 142\ 036\ 440\ 000_8$	14	$0.000\ 000\ 000\ 000\ 000_8$
$34\ 327\ 724\ 461\ 500\ 000_8$	15	$0.000\ 000\ 000\ 000\ 000_8$
$434\ 157\ 115\ 760\ 200\ 000_8$	16	$0.000\ 000\ 000\ 000\ 000_8$
$5\ 432\ 127\ 413\ 542\ 400\ 000_8$	17	$0.000\ 000\ 000\ 000\ 000_8$
$67\ 405\ 553\ 164\ 731\ 000\ 000_8$	18	$0.000\ 000\ 000\ 000\ 000_8$

OCTAL ADDITION (Horizontal Plus Vertical)

+	1	2	3	4	5	6	7
1	2	3	4	5	6	7	10
2	3	4	5	6	7	10	11
3	4	5	6	7	10	11	12
4	5	6	7	10	11	12	13
5	6	7	10	11	12	13	14
6	7	10	11	12	13	14	15
7	10	11	12	13	14	15	16

OCTAL SUBTRACTION (Horizontal Minus Vertical)

−	1	2	3	4	5	6	7
1	0	1	2	3	4	5	6
2	7	0	1	2	3	4	5
3	6	7	0	1	2	3	4
4	5	6	7	0	1	2	3
5	4	5	6	7	0	1	2
6	3	4	5	6	7	0	1
7	2	3	4	5	6	7	0

OCTAL MULTIPLICATION (Horizontal Times Vertical)

×	1	2	3	4	5	6	7
1	1	2	3	4	5	6	7
2	2	4	6	10	12	14	16
3	3	6	11	14	17	22	25
4	4	10	14	20	24	30	34
5	5	12	17	24	31	36	43
6	6	14	22	30	36	44	52
7	7	16	25	34	43	52	61

48

Electrostatic-Sensitive Devices (ESDS) and Radio Frequency Interference (RFI)

Computers contain electrostatic sensitive devices. Proper device handling procedures must be followed. Additional information to that supplied here is available by referring to DOD-HBK-263 and DOD-STD-1686.

ESDS components and circuit cards are shipped in special antistatic/conductive shipping containers. Ensure that all required precautions are taken before opening the containers. Retain the containers for future use when shipping ESDS components. All antistatic/conductive containers are identified with a warning label alerting the handler to the fact that the contents are ESDS-sensitive. It is noted that individual components are not generally identified as being ESDS, except by markings on the packaging.

When handling ESDS assemblies or devices, the handler must wear a static control wrist strap connected to his or her skin. The wrist strap must be connected, through a 1 megohm resistor, to either an antistatic/conductive tabletop or to the equipment chassis ground. Most wrist straps have the 1 megohm resistor built in. The antistatic tabletop must be connected to ground through a 1 megohm to 10 megohm resistor.

The handlers must neutralize static buildup by placing their hands on the antistatic/conductive tabletop or ground for several seconds before handling ESDS circuit cards or components.

Handle ESDS components by the case or body whenever possible, and minimize touching of the leads.

Do not use air blasts or aerosol sprays on ESDS circuit cards or components. Keep all common plastics and clothing away from ESDS devices. All soldering irons, test equipment, and electrical chassis must be grounded. Grounded power cords must be plugged in, even if the equipment is turned off. Solder suckers must be of the antistatic type. Brushes must be of natural bristle.

Ensure that all ESDS devices are properly packaged in antistatic/conductive covering when in storage or transit.

Computer equipment can generate, use, and radiate radio frequency energy and, if not installed and used in accordance with the manufacturer's instructions, may cause interference to radio communications. In general, most equipment has been tested and found to comply with the limits for a Class A computing device pursuant to Subpart J of Part 15 of the FCC Rules, which are designed to provide reasonable protection against such interference when operated in a commercial environment.

Operation of computer equipment in a residential area may cause interference in which case the user, at his own expense, will be required to take whatever measures may be required to correct the interference. The manufacturer of the computer, in general, is not responsible for any interference caused by unauthorized modifications to the equipment.

In today's environmentally conscious world a great deal of concern has been generated regarding the safety of computer monitors or, as they are otherwise called, VDT's (Video Display Terminals).

Environmental Computer Supplies, 1001 Louisiana Avenue, Suite 407, Corpus Christi, TX 78404, telephone 1-(800) 521-3289, FAX (512) 852-8542, offers the NoRad Shield for $109.00 for placement in front of your monitor.

The NoRad Shield blocks 99.99% of VDT electromagnetic radiation emitted from your monitor.

The NoRad Shield improves the viewing of the monitor by dramatically increasing the perceived contrast, eliminates glare and reflections, and facilitates the use of high-resolution displays. In addition, it eliminates the entire range of through-screen E-field (electric) radiation to frequencies beyond 1 gigahertz and eliminates H-field (magnetic) radiation at frequencies above 30 kilohertz while simultaneously eliminating the static field.

Vendor Information— Where to Go If You Need a Part

Occasionally you will require a tool, a piece of test equipment, or simply a part to repair a system or to finish a prototype. You would like the item off the shelf with a minimum of additional service charges and hassle. Some of these vendors have self-service stores and others can offer expertise and advice to get you up and running quickly. Many offer catalogs to assist in your component selection. Others have telemarketing departments with 800 (toll free) numbers. The listing of a vendor is not to be considered as an endorsement of its product or services but merely as an indication of where to start your search.

1. Active Electronics, 133 Flanders Road, Westborough, MA 01581
    1 (800) 677-8899; FAX (514) 697-5112

    Retail Stores:

    2010 Duane Avenue, Santa Clara, CA 95054
    (408) 727-4550; FAX (408) 727-1114

    941 Busse Road, Elk Grove, IL 60007
    (708) 593-6655; FAX (708) 593-6799

    1530 Caton Centre Drive, Suite F, Baltimore, MD 21227
    (301) 536-5400; FAX (301) 536-5406

    133 Flanders Road, Westborough, MA 01581
    (508) 366-8899; FAX (508) 366-1195

    11 Cummings Park, Woburn, MA 01801
    (617) 932-4616; FAX (617) 933-8884

1393 Wheaton, Suite 100, Troy, MI 48083
(313) 689-8000; FAX (313) 689-8716

107 Gaither Drive, Mount Laurel, NJ 08054
(609) 273-2700; FAX (609) 273-1848

3340 Veterans Memorial Highway, Bohemia, NY 11716
(516) 471-5400; FAX (516) 471-5410

13107 Northup Way, 20th Street N. E., Bellevue, WA 98005
(206) 881-8191; FAX (206) 883-6820

237 Hymus Boulevard, Point Claire, Quebec, Canada H9R5C7
(514) 630-7410; FAX (514) 697-8112

2. Digi-Key Corporation, 701 Brooks Avenue, P. O. Box 677, Thief River Falls,
   MN 56701-0677
   1 (800) 344-4539; FAX (218) 681-3380

3. Mouser Electronics, 2401 Highway 287 North, P. O. Box 699, Mansfield, TX
   76063
   1 (800) 346-6873; FAX (817) 483-0931

4. Newark Electronics, 4801 N. Ravenswood Avenue, Chicago, IL 60640-4496
   (312) 784-5100; FAX (312) 784-3107

5. Radio Shack, 500 One Tandy Center, Fort Worth, TX 76102
   (over 7,000 retail locations—consult your local phone book)

6. Sager Electronics, 60 Research Road, Hingham, MA 02043
   1 (800) 541-9371; FAX (617) 740-2559

7. Upgrades Etc. Incorporated, 15251 N. E. 90th Street, Redmond, WA 98052
   1 (800) 541-1942; TECH SUPPORT (206) 882-3634; FAX (206) 881-8294
   Source for ROM BIOS upgrades with all the latest features.

8. MegaHaus Hard Drives, 1110 NASA Road, Suite 306, Houston, TX 77058
   1 (800) 426-0560; TECH SUPPORT (713) 333-1910; FAX (713) 333-3024
   Source for Hard Drive upgrades and Hard Drive On A Card.

9. Data Storage Marketing, Inc., 111 Canfield Ave., #A-11, Randolph, NJ
   07869
   1 (800) 424-2203; (201) 927-5050
   Source for Hard Drives, Floppy Drives, and Controllers.

10. New England Electronics & Technology Corp., 225 Stedman Street, Bldg. 9,
    Lowell, MA 01853, (508) 454-9192; FAX (508) 454-9319
    Source for Hard Drives, Floppy Drives, Optical Drives, Tape Drives, and
    Controllers.

11. MicroTel Components, 17401 Irvine Blvd., Suite M, Tustin, CA 92680
    1 (800) 676-4276; TECH SUPPORT (714) 730-3484; FAX (714) 730-4071
    Source for Memory Upgrades.

12. Hard Drives International, 1912 West Fourth Street, Tempe, AZ 85281
    1 (800) 733-0889; (602) 350-1128; FAX (602) 350-1880
    Source for all types of Drives and Memory Upgrades.

13. I. C. Express, 15140 Valley Boulevard, City Of Industry, CA 91744
    1 (800) 877-8188; TECH SUPPORT (818) 369-2688; FAX (818) 369-1236
    Source for Memory Upgrades.

14. D-C-Drives, 1110 NASA One, Suite 304, Nassau Bay, TX 77058
    1 (800) 872-6007; TECH SUPPORT (713) 333-9602; FAX (713) 333-3024
    Source for Hard Drives, Floppies, and Controllers.

15. JB Technologies, Inc. 5105 Maureen Lane, Moorpark, CA 93021
    (805) 529-0908; FAX (805) 529-7712
    Source for Disk Drive Sales and Repairs.

16. ELKCO Corporation, 2 Hawthorne Street, North Grafton, MA 01536
    1 (800) 243-5526; (508) 839-2111; FAX (508) 839-7753
    Source for Memory Upgrades and Math Coprocessors.

17. Powerplus, 4932 Sharp Street, Dallas, TX 75247
    1 (800) 878-5530; TECH SUPPORT (214) 631-2550; FAX (214) 631-8697
    Source for Accessories, Cables, Data Switches, Cleaning Kits, etc.

18. Commercial & Industrial Design Co., Inc., 1711 Langley Avenue, Irvine,
    CA 92714
    (714) 261-5524; FAX (714) 261-6861
    Source for Drive Mounting Hardware and Installation Kits.

19. Altex Electronics, Inc., 11342 IH-35 North, San Antonio, TX 78233
    1 (800) 531-5369; FAX (512) 344-2985
    Source for Cases, Cables, Switch Boxes, Network Cards, Battery Backup, etc.

Reference
Documents

1. Microprocessor and Peripheral Handbook
    Intel Corporation, Literature Distribution, Mail Stop SC6-714
    3065 Bowers Avenue, Santa Clara, CA 95051, (800) 548-4725
    210844.001

2. Microsystem Components Handbook (2 volumes)
    Intel Corporation, Literature Distribution, Mail Stop SC6-714
    3065 Bowers Avenue, Santa Clara, CA 95051, (800) 548-4725
    230843.002, 1987, $25.00

3. CHMOS Handbook
    Intel Corporation, Literature Distribution, Mail Stop SC6-714
    3065 Bowers Avenue, Santa Clara, CA 95051, (800) 548-4725
    290005.001, $12.00

4. Introduction To The iAPX 286
    Intel Corporation, Literature Distribution, Mail Stop SC6-714
    3065 Bowers Avenue, Santa Clara, CA 95051, (800) 548-4725
    210308.001

5. iAPX Operating Systems Writer's Guide
    Intel Corporation, Literature Distribution, Mail Stop SC6-714
    3065 Bowers Avenue, Santa Clara, CA 95051, (800) 548-4725
    121960.001

6. iAPX 286 Programmer's Reference Manual
    Intel Corporation, Literature Distribution, Mail Stop SC6-714
    3065 Bowers Avenue, Santa Clara, CA 95051, (800) 548-4725
    210498.001

7. iAPX 286 Hardware Reference Manual
    Intel Corporation, Literature Distribution, Mail Stop SC6-714
    3065 Bowers Avenue, Santa Clara, CA 95051, (800) 548-4825
    210760.001

8. Numeric Processor Extension Data Sheet
    Intel Corporation, Literature Distribution, Mail Stop SC6-714
    3065 Bowers Avenue, Santa Clara, CA 95051, (800) 548-4725
    210920

9. 80287 Support Library Reference Manual
    Intel Corporation, Literature Distribution, Mail Stop SC6-714
    3065 Bowers Avenue, Santa Clara, CA 95051, (800) 548-4725
    122129

10. Guide To Operations for the IBM Personal Computer XT
    IBM Corporation, P.O. Box 1328-S, Boca Raton, FL 33432
    6137861

11. BASIC for the IBM Personal Computer
    IBM Corporation, P.O. Box 1328-S, Boca Raton, FL 33432

12. Disk Operating System (DOS) Version 3.10, Reference, Programming
    Family
    IBM Corporation, P.O. Box 1328-S, Boca Raton, FL 33432
    6138519

13. Disk Operating System (DOS) Version 3.30, User's Guide, Programming
    Family
    IBM Corporation, P.O. Box 1328-S, Boca Raton, FL 33432
    80X0933

14. Disk Operating System (DOS) Version 3.30, Quick Reference Card, Pro-
    gramming Family
    IBM Corporation, P.O. Box 1328-S, Boca Raton, FL 33432
    80X0683

15. Disk Operating System (DOS) Version 3.30, Reference, Programming
    Family
    IBM Corporation, P.O. Box 1328-S, Boca Raton, FL 33432
    00F9593
    80X0667, April 1987

16. IBM DOS Technical Reference
    IBM Corporation, P.O. Box 1328-S, Boca Raton, FL 33432
    80X0945, April 1987

17. Hardware Maintenance and Service for the IBM Personal Computer XT
    (2 volumes)
    IBM Corporation, P.O. Box 1328-S, Boca Raton, FL 33432
    Volume 1 6137841, April 1984
    Volume 2 6137846, April 1984

18. MACRO Assembler for the IBM Personal Computer
    IBM Corporation, P.O. Box 1328-S, Boca Raton, FL 33432

19. Technical Reference, Options and Adapters (Revised Edition) (2 volumes)
    IBM Corporation, P.O. Box 1328-S, Boca Raton, FL 33432
    Volume 1 6137804, April 1984
    Volume 2 6137806, April 1984

20. Personal Computer Hardware Reference Library, Technical Reference
    IBM Corporation, P.O. Box 1328-S, Boca Raton, FL 33432

PC1	6025008, July 1982	
PC	6025005, April 1983	
XT	6936808, April 1983 (2.02 Sticker)	
XT	6280089, March 1986	
Jr	1502293, November 1983	
PC2	6322507, April 1984	
AT	1502494,	1984
AT	6280099, March 1986 (Revised)	
All	6322509, April 1984 (Options and Adapters, Volumes 1 and 2)	

21. Personal System/2 and Personal Computer BIOS Interface Technical
    Reference
    IBM Corporation, P.O. Box 1328-S, Boca Raton, FL 33432
    84X1514, April 1987

22. Personal System/2 Model 30 Technical Reference
    IBM Corporation, P.O. Box 1328-S, Boca Raton, FL 33432
    68X2201, January 1987

23. Personal System/2 Models 50 and 60 Technical Reference
    IBM Corporation, P.O. Box 1328-S, Boca Raton, FL 33432
    68X2224, April 1987

24. Technical Reference, PC Network
    IBM Corporation, P.O. Box 1328-S, Boca Raton, FL 33432
    6322916, September 1984

25. Personal System/2 Hardware Interface (Micro Channel) Technical Reference
    IBM Corporation, P. O. Box 1328-S, Boca Raton, FL 33432
    S68X2330
    S15F2160, Supplement

26. IBM BIOS Technical Reference
    IBM Corporation, P. O. Box 1328-S, Boca Raton, FL 33432
    S68X2341
    S15F2161, Supplement

27. Micro Channel Architecture Bus Master Release 1.0
    IBM Corporation, P. O. Box 1328-S, Boca Raton, FL 33432
    GG243477

28.   IBM Personal Systems Technical Journal
      IBM Corporation, P. O. Box 1328-S, Boca Raton, FL 33432
      G3255004

29.   Hardware Adapter Catalogue
      IBM Corporation, P. O. Box 1328-S, Boca Raton, FL 33432
      G3602824

30.   Communications and Networking for the IBM PC and Compatibles
      Larry Jordan and Bruce Churchill
      A Brady Book, Prentice-Hall Press,
      New York, NY, 1987, ISBN 0-89303-634-X

31.   Assembler For The IBM/PC and PC-XT
      Peter Abel
      Reston Publishing Company, a Prentice-Hall Company
      Reston, VA 22090 1983, 416 pp., ISBN 0-8359-0153-X (Pbk)
      ISBN 0-8359-0110-6 (Case)

32.   MS-DOS Encyclopaedia
      Ray Duncan and William Gates
      Microsoft Press
      Redmond, WA 98073-9717, 1989, ISBN 1-55615-174-8

33.   Compute!'s Mapping the IBM PC and PCjr
      Russ Davies
      Compute! Publications, Inc., one of the ABC Publishing Companies
      Greensboro, NC 27403, 1985, 336 pp., ISBN 0-942386-92-2

34.   Assembly Programming and the 8086 Microprocessor
      Douglas S. Jones
      Oxford University Press
      New York, NY, 1988, ISBN 0-19-853742-5 (Pbk)
      ISBN 0-19-853743-3 (Case)

35.   The 8086 Book
      Russel Rector and George Alexy
      Osborne/McGraw-Hill
      Berkeley, CA 94710, 1980, ISBN 0-931988-29-2

36.   Peter Norton's Assembly Language Book For The IBM PC
      Peter Norton
      A Brady Book, Prentice-Hall Press
      New York, NY, 1986, ISBN 0-13-661901-0

Computer and Electronics Periodicals

1. COMPUTER SYSTEMS NEWS, CMP Publications, Inc., 600 Community Drive, Manhasset, NY 11030-3875, (516) 562-5000, Newsweekly for Systems Integration (ISSN #0164-9981). Controlled Circulation. $69.95/year to others.

2. ELECTRONIC NEWS, Chilton Co. a Capital Cities/ABC Publishing Co., Diversified Publishing Group, 825 Seventh Avenue, New York, NY 10019, (215) 630-0951, Newsweekly Business Newspaper for Electronics Industry (ISSN #0013-4937). $45.00/year.

3. ELECTRONIC ENGINEERING TIMES, CMP Publications, Inc., 600 Community Drive, Manhasset, NY 11030-3875, (516) 562-5000, Newsweekly For Engineers and Technical Management (ISSN #0192-1541). Controlled Circulation. $90.00/year to others.

4. EDN, Cahners Publishing Co., A Division Of Reed Publishing, USA, 275 Washington Street, Newton, MA 02158-1630, (303) 388-4511, Weekly Magazine Of Electronic Technology For Engineers and Engineering Managers (ISSN #0012-7515). Controlled Circulation. $105.00/year to others.

5. ECN, ELECTRONIC COMPONENT NEWS, Chilton Co., a Capital Cities/ABC Publishing Co., Diversified Publishing Group, 825 Seventh Avenue, New York, NY 10019—Chilton Way, Radnor, PA 19089, (215) 964-4347, Monthly Equipment, Subsystems, Components, Software (ISSN #0193-614X). Controlled Circulation. $50.00/year to others.

6. PC SOURCES, Coastal Associates Publishing, Division Of Ziff-Davis Publishing Company, One Park Avenue, New York, NY 10016, (212) 503-3800, Monthly What to Buy and Where to Buy It (ISSN #1052-6579). $16.97/year.

7. COMPUTERWORLD, DG Communications, Inc., 375 Cochituate Road, Box 9171, Framingham, MA 01701-9171, (617) 879-0700, Newsweekly for the Computer Community (ISSN #0010-4841). $44.00/year.

8. SHOP BY MAIL DIRECTORY FOR PERSONAL COMPUTER USERS, Pilot Books, 103 Cooper Street, Babylon, NY 11702, (516) 422-2225, Lists of Suppliers of Systems, Peripherals, and Accessories. $3.95.

9. COMPUTER SHOPPER, Coastal Associates Publishing, Division Of Ziff-Davis Publishing Company, One Park Avenue, New York, NY 10016, (407) 269-3211, Computer Magazine for Direct Buyers (ISSN #0886-0556). $29.97/year.

10. LAN TECHNOLOGY, M & T Publishing, Inc., Subsidiary Of Markt & Technik, 501 Galveston Drive, Redwood City, CA 94063, (415) 366-3600, Local Area Networks for the Personal Computer System Integrator (ISSN #8750-9482). $25.00/year.

11. INFOWORLD, CW Communications, Inc., Subsidiary Of Popular Computing Inc., 1060 Marsh Road, Suite C-200, Menlo Park, CA 94025, (415) 328-4602, The Personal Computing Weekly (ISSN #0199-6649). $31.00/year.

12. COMPUTE!, Compute Publications, Subsidiary Of American Broadcasting Companies, Inc., 324 W. Wendover Avenue, Suite 200, Box 5406, Greensboro, NC 27408, (919) 275-9809, Personal Computers, at Home, at Work, and in the School (ISSN #0194-357X). $9.97/year.

13. BYTE, McGraw-Hill Information Services Co., One Phoenix Mill Lane, Peterborough, NH 03458, (603) 924-9281, Broad-Based Microcomputer Monthly Magazine Emphasizing Technical Information, Applications, and Products (ISSN #0360-5280). $22.95/year.

14. EVERYTHING BOOK FOR IBM, Tenex Computer Express, Box 6578, South Bend, IN 45645, (219) 259-7051, Quarterly.

15. PC COMPUTING, Ziff-Davis Publishing Co., Computer Publications Division, One Park Avenue, New York, NY 10017, (212) 503-5100, Monthly Computer Applications For Personal Computer Users. $19.94/year.

16. PC MAGAZINE, THE INDEPENDENT GUIDE TO IBM-STANDARD PERSONAL COMPUTING, Ziff-Davis Publishing Co., Computer Publications Division, One Park Avenue, New York, NY 10016, (212) 503-5100, Biweekly Reviews of Hardware and Software (ISSN #0888-8507). $44.97/year.

17. PC RESOURCE, IDG Communications, Subsidiary Of Popular Computing, Inc., 80 Elm Street, Peterborough, NH 03458, (800) 441-4403, Practical Guide to MS-DOS Computing. $24.97/year.

18. PC WEEK, Ziff-Davis Publishing Co., 800 Boylston Street, Boston, MA 02199-8102, (617) 375- 4100, The National Weekly Newspaper of IBM Standard Microcomputing (ISSN #0740-1604). Controlled Circulation. $160.00/year to others.

19. PC WORLD, PCW Communications, Inc., 501 Second Street, Suite 600, San Francisco, CA 94107, (415) 861-3861, The Monthly Comprehensive Guide to IBM PCs and Compatibles (ISSN #0737-8939). $29.90/year.

20. PERSONAL COMPUTING, VNU Business Publications, Inc., Ten Holland Drive, Hasbrouck Heights, NJ 07640, (201) 393-6000, Hardware and Software Reviews for Executives Who Use Computers (ISSN #0192-5490). $18.00/year.

21. USED COMPUTER GUIDE, Trade Broker, Inc., Re 3, Box 638B, Colville, WA 99114-9525, The Quarterly Microcomputer Bluebook (ISSN #0742-6089). $32.50/year.

22. CD-ROM REVIEW, IDG Communications, Subsidiary Of Popular Computing, Inc., 80 Elm Street, Peterborough, NH 03458, The Monthly Magazine of Optical Publishing (ISSN #0891-3188). $35.00/year.

23. COMPUTER GRAPHICS WORLD, Penn Will Publishing Company, 1421 South Sheridan, Tulsa, OK 74101, Monthly Features Related To Computer Graphics, Desktop Publishing, and Computer-Assisted Design (ISSN #0271-4159). $30.00/year.

Suppliers of Computers

The following list of suppliers of computers is by no means complete nor is it meant to be a recommendation of one supplier in preference to another.

Some suppliers offer systems that seem to be identical to that of other suppliers. Occasionally computers that have different brand names are actually manufactured by a single supplier and yet their prices vary widely. This is by no means a unique situation as demonstrated by the fact that many years ago manufacturers of vacuum tubes divided up the types of tubes to be made. Agreements were implemented that some types were produced by one manufacturer while other types were produced by a different manufacturer. At the end of the production line the tubes were branded to order and boxed accordingly. A similar situation exists in the manufacture of some computer systems.

The job of the purchaser of a computer system is to make his selection based on a careful evaluation of a variety of factors. These factors include price, of course, the data sheet specifications (ask for it in writing just like the phone company), recommendations of the numerous available publications that have performed detailed evaluations (refer to Appendix C), the comments of acquaintances who have made purchases, whether there is a period just after the purchase in which a money-back guarantee evaluation is offered, whether the vendor can deliver in a timely fashion, if the documentation relates exactly to the items you have purchased and whether the documentation is adequate, what level of installation or setup is required of you, the purchaser, (i.e., is it a kit or a computer system?), what the local Better Business Bureau has to say about the vendor, the terms of the warranty, how repairs are to be made and whether the system has to be returned to the manufacturer (in Tibet?) (in the original carton, which is the current home of your cat or dog?), who pays the shipping?, whether the vendor comes to your home or office to make a repair, will the vendor be around when you need him?, if you register the system will the vendor keep you informed of recalls or upgrades, does the vendor have telephone support? (800 number? during business hours? 24 hours a day? phone answered by machine, android, or human?), and will replacement parts be available for what you hope to be the life of the computer system?

Remember, the computer system you are purchasing is five to ten times the price of your home refrigerator. Is it your expectation that it will have equal reliability? Should it be more reliable? Less reliable? How often do we really see the Maytag repairman?

As a minimum, try to get advice from a reasonable sampling of both salespeople and your peers. You should prepare a short document that summarizes the uses and special characteristics of the system you are purchasing, and whether or not you are a first-time buyer. Do you want the system for everyday use, for computer games, spreadsheets, word processing, graphics, CAD-CAM, database, scientific calculations, software development, and so on? Do you require special features such as cache, large hard-disk drives, super-speed mathematics coprocessors, high resolution or many colored graphics, animation, CD-ROM, laser printers, extended or expanded memory, a lock in front, removable hard drives, or a tilt-swivel monitor? Evaluate your needs carefully and discuss them with the prospective vendors.

In addition, look at a picture of the system to evaluate its ergonomics and see how the system fits in with your application. (Is the system packaged in a tower case when there is no room for it below the desk?) Try to realistically estimate the amount of hand-holding you require. If the hand-holding requirements are small, mail-order possibly is for you.

Buy what you need. Try hard not to buy too little or too much computer. Either way it will cost you money in the end. You must have a mathematics coprocessor if you are going to run AutoCAD, but you don't need a 486 to run WordPerfect. Keep your expansion options open, but remember that every year we improve our position on the price/performance curve. Memory, whether RAM or disk, gets less expensive every year and the CPU power continually increases.

PC MARKET SHARES FOR 1990

The following list shows market shares of the leading PC manufacturers in the $83.1 billion worldwide PC market.

IBM	15.3%
Apple	10.6%
NEC	6.9%
Compaq	6.6%
Toshiba	3.0%
Hewlett-Packard	1.8%
Tandy	1.6%

The following companies have a market share of less than 1.5% each.

Commodore
Packard Bell
Zenith
Epson
AST
Hyundai
Dell
Wyse
CompuAdd
Everex
AT&T
Unisys
Grid
Acer
Tandon
NCR
Wang
Panasonic
Digital (DEC)

Source: Dataquest, Inc. San Jose, CA 95131

This represents about 2/3 of the total shipments. The remaining 1/3 of the shipments may be attributed to other manufacturers.

WHERE TO BUY YOUR NEW COMPUTER

Name and Address	Telephone	
	Sales	**Service**
ABTECH, Inc. 1431 North Potrero Ave., South El Monte, CA 91733	(800) 992-1928 (818) 575-1007	(818) 575-8307
Acma Computers, Inc. 177 Fourier Ave., Fremont, CA 94539	(800) 456-1818 (415) 623-1212	(800) 456-8898
Altec Technology Corp. 18555 E. Gale St., City Of Industry, CA 91748	(800) 255-9971 (818) 912-8688	(800) 255-9968
Altex Electronics, Inc. 11342 1H-35 North, San Antonio, TX 78233	(800) 531-5369	(512) 349-8795
American Computer Source 15136 East Valley Blvd., Suite D, City Of Industry, CA 91744	(800) 368-3681	(800) 368-3681
American Research Corp. 1101 Monterey Pass Road, Monterey Park, CA 91754	(800) 346-3272 (800) 423-3877	(213) 269-1174
Anderson International Corp. 45 Campus Drive, Edison, NJ 08837	(908) 417-0552	(908) 417-0552
APlus Computer Inc. 398 Lemon Creek Drive, Unit H, Walnut, CA 91789	(800) 443-5373	(714) 594-1112
Ares Microdevelopment 24762 Crestview Court, Farmington Hills, MI 48335	(800) 322-3200	(313) 473-0808
Asean Computer Technologies, Inc. 971 Fairway Drive, Walnut, CA 91789	(714) 598-2828	(714) 598-5498
Associates Mega Sub-Systems, Inc. 4801 Little John Street, Unit A, Baldwin Park, CA 91706	(818) 814-8851	(818) 814-8851
A-Tech Computer 7150 Beverly Blvd., Los Angeles, CA 90036	(213) 930-2823	(213) 930-2823
A-Tronic Computer 15703 East Valley Blvd., City Of Industry, CA 91744	(818) 333-0193	(818) 333-0193

Name and Address	Telephone	
	Sales	Service
Austin Computer Systems 10300 Metric Blvd., Austin, TX 78758	(800) 331-1701 (512) 339-3500	(512) 752-4171
Automated Computer Technology Corp. 2307 Spencer Highway, Pasadena, TX 77504	(800) 521-9237 (713) 946-0731	(800) 521-9237
Best Computer, Inc. 9480 Telstar Ave., #3, El Monte, CA 91731	(800) 634-7920 (818) 452-1700	(818) 452-1700
Binary Technology, Inc. 17120 Dallas Parkway, Suite 212, Dallas, TX 75248	(800) 776-7990	(214) 931-3777
Blue Dolphin Computers 1014 Morse Avenue, Ste. 4, Sunnyvale, CA 94089	(800) 345-0633	(800) 345-0633
Blue Star Marketing 2312 Central Avenue N. E., Minneapolis, MN 55418	(800) 950-8884	(612) 788-1404
Boss Technology 6050 McDonough Drive, Norcross, GA 30093	(800) 628-1787	(800) 628-1787
Bulldog Computer Products 610 Industrial Park Drive, P.O. Box 1190, Evans, GA 30809	(800) 438-6039	(800) 438-6039
C & C Computers 556 South Milpitas Blvd., Milpitas, CA 95035	(800) 473-6787	(408) 263-8529
Chaumont and Associates 805 Bayou Pines, Suite A, Lake Charles, LA 70601	(800) 673-2271	(800) 673-2271
Clone Computers 2544 W. Commerce Street, Dallas, TX 75212	(800) 527-0347	(214) 637-5400
CompuAdd Corp. 12303 Technology Blvd., Austin, TX 78727	(800) 627-1967	(800) 999-9901
Compu-Care Of Virginia 4701 Cox Road, Glen Allen, VA 23060	(800) 253-5562	(804) 346-9959
Computer And Control Solutions 1580 Stone Ridge Drive, Stone Mountain, GA 50085	(800) 782-3525	(404) 491-1131

Name and Address	Telephone Sales	Service
Computer Direct, Inc. 22292 North Pepper Road, Barrington, IL 60010	(800) 289-9473	(708) 382-5058
Computer Discount Warehouse 2840 Maria, Northbrook, IL 60062	(800) 487-4239	(708) 498-1426
Computer Market Place, Inc. 450 Parkway, Suite 202, Broomall, PA 19008	(800) 545-7397	(217) 359-0750
Computer Products Corp. 4657 MacArthur Lane, Boulder, CO 80301	(800) 338-4273	(800) 338-4273
Computer Sales Professional 764 Easton Street, Somerset, NJ 08873	(800) 950-6660	(201) 560-1143
Computer Square Inc. 1070 North Roselle Road, Hoffman Estates, IL 60195	(800) 284-7746 (708) 885-7600	(708) 885-7774
CompuTrend Systems, Inc. 1306-1308 John Reed Court, City Of Industry, CA 91745	(818) 333-5121	(212) 382-0018
CompuWorld 16742 Stagg Street, Unit 110, Van Nuys, CA 91406	(800) 473-0779	(800) 473-0773
Comtrade 1016-B Lawson Street, City Of Industry, CA 91748	(800) 969-2123 (818) 964-6688	(800) 969-2123
Croix Computers 6640 Shady Oak Road, Eden Prairie, MN 55344	(800) 950-0174 (612) 943-8618	(800) 950-0182
CUI 1680 Civic Center Drive, Suite 101, Santa Clara, CA 95050	(800) 458-6686	(408) 241-9170
Data Dynamics P. O. Box 4129, Blue Jay, CA 92317	(800) 843-2464	(714) 336-5333
Dataworld Inc. 3733 San Gabriel River Parkway, Pico Rivera, CA 90660-1404	(800) 736-3282 (213) 695-3777	(800) 736-3282

Name and Address	Telephone	
	Sales	Service
Dell Computer Corp. 9505 Arboretum Blvd., Austin, TX 78759-7299	(800) 627-1420	(800) 624-9897 (800) 950-1329
DerbyTech Computers 718 15th Avenue, East Moline, IL 61244	(800) 243-3729	(309) 755-2662
Dynamic Technologies, Inc. 619 Westfield Avenue, Elizabeth, NJ 07207	(800) 829-0924	(800) 829-0924
Electrified Discounters 1066 Sherman Avenue, Hamden, CT 06514	(800) 678-8585	(800) 678-8585
Eltech Research, Inc. 47266 Benicia Street, Fremont, CA 94538	(800) 234-4331	(800) 234-4331
EPS Technologies, Inc. 10069 Dakota Avenue, P.O. Box 278, Jefferson, SD 57038	(800) 447-0921 (605) 966-5586	(800) 526-4258
FastMicro 3655 East LaSalle Street, Phoenix, AZ 85040	(800) 441-3278	(602) 437-0300
First Computer Systems, Inc. 3953 Pleasantdale Road, Suite 114, Atlanta, GA 30340	(404) 441-1911	(404) 447-TECH
Flash Technology, Inc. 55 West Hoover Avenue, Suite 9, Mesa, AZ 85210	(800) 448-2031	(602) 464-9272
Gateway 2000 610 Gateway Drive, N. Sioux City, SD 57049	(800) 523-2000 (605) 232-2000	(800) 523-2000
Gems Computers, Inc. 2115 Old Oakland Road, San Jose, CA 95131	(800) 969-9910	(800) 969-1911
Harmony Computers (IBM) 1801 Flatbush Avenue, Brooklyn, NY 11210	(800) 441-1144 (718) 692-3232	(718) 692-2828
HD Computers, Inc. 3325 Kifer Road, Santa Clara, CA 95054	(800) 347-0493 (408) 720-0493	(800) 676-0164

Name and Address	Telephone Sales	Service
Hi-Quality Systems 740 Mary Avenue, Sunnyvale, CA 94086	(800) 827-5836	(800) 827-5836
Hokkins Systemation, Inc. 131 East Brokaw Road, San Jose, CA 95112	(800) 526-2328	(408) 436-3021
Homesmart Computing 14760 Memorial Drive, Houston, TX 77079	(800) 627-6998	(713) 589-2749
Innovative Technology 105 Carter Road, P. O. Box 726, Elk City, OK 73648	(800) 253-4001	(405) 243-0030
Insight Computers 1912 West 4th Street, Tempe, AZ 85281	(800) 776-7600 (602) 350-1176	(800) 488-0007
Intelec 6075 NW, 82nd Avenue, Miami, FL 33166	(800) 683-0969	(305) 594-0001
International Data Systems 12800 Garden Grove Blvd., Bldg. E, Garden Grove, CA 92643	(714) 530-8677	(714) 530-8697
Iverson Computer Corp. 1356 Beverly Road, McLean, VA 22106-6250	(800) 444-7290	(800) 677-7881
JACO Computer Products 687 North Pastoria Avenue, Sunnyvale, CA 94086	(408) 732-8800	(408) 732-8800
JCC Systems, Inc. 10675 East Rush Street, South El Monte, CA 91733	(800) 421-1771	(818) 575-8197
JDR Microdevices 2233 Branham Lane, San Jose, CA 95124	(800) 538-5000	(800) 538-5002
Jinco Computers, Inc. 5122 Walnut Grove Avenue, San Gabriel, CA 91776	(800) 253-2531	(818) 309-1108
Lane Data Systems 6202 West 34th Street, Houston, TX 77092	(800) 245-5755	(800) 245-5755
LANtek Computer, Inc. 661 Brea Canyon Road, Suite 3, Walnut, CA 91789	(800) 462-0436	(714) 594-9491
Legatech Computers 789 South San Gabriel Blvd., #D, San Gabriel, CA 91776	(818) 309-2941	(818) 309-2816

| Name and Address | Telephone | |
	Sales	Service
Logix Microcomputer, Inc. Twelve Oaks Business Park, 375 Morgan Lane, West Haven, CT 06516	(800) 248-2140	(203) 937-7725
Lucky Star International Computer Company 1701 Greenville Avenue, Suite 602, Richardson, TX 75081	(800) 966-5825 (800) 336-5825	(214) 690-4165
Lyco Computer (IBM Business Partner) P.O. Box 5088, Jersey Shore, PA 17740	(800) 233-8760	(717) 494-1670
Main Street Computer Co. 1656 Main Street, Sarasota, FL 34236	(800) 456-6240 (813) 954-9017	(813) 366-8261
Mica Computer Center 10204 Norwalk Blvd., Santa Fe Springs, CA 90670	(800) 872-6422	(213) 944-1850
Micro Express 1801 Carnegie Avenue, Santa Ana, CA 92705	(800) 642-7621 (714) 852-1400	(800) 762-3378
Micro Generation 300 McGaw Drive, Edison, NJ 08837	(800) 872-2841 (800) 872-6921	(800) 872-1284 (201) 417-1732
Microlab 23976 Freeway Park Drive, Farmington Hills, MI 48335 P. O. Box 317, Novi, MI 48376	(800) 677-7900	(313) 474-7711
Microline Computers, Inc. 46757 Fremont Blvd., Fremont, CA 94539	(415) 770-1900	(415) 770-1900
MicroLink 225 Balsam Street, Ridgecrest, CA 93555	(800) 321-LINK (619) 371-3535	(619) 371-2220
Micro National Express, Inc. Birmingham, AL 35209	(800) 879-4001	(800) 942-0838
Micro Sense 370 Andrew, Leucadia, CA 92024	(800) 544-4252	(619) 632-8621
Micro Smart, Inc. 200 Homer Avenue, Ashland, MA 01721	(800) 370-9090	(508) 872-9090
MicrOtyme, Div. Of Micro Peripherals, Inc. 4049 Marshall Road, Kettering, OH 45429	(800) 255-5835	(513) 294-6236

Name and Address	Telephone Sales	Service
Micro World Computers 9090 North Stemmons Freeway, Suite C-128, Dallas, TX 75247	(800) 825-6050	(214) 637-0522
Nationwide Computer Distributors P. O. Box 7AQ, Jersey City, NJ 07307	(800) 777-1054 (201) 659-2127	(201) 659-2977
NCR Corp. 1700 South Patterson Blvd., Dayton, OH 45479	(800) 225-5627	(800) 225-5627
Network PC, Div. Of WAA, Inc. 5020 NW 39th Street, Lincoln, NB 68524	(800) 873-9235 (402) 470-3446	(800) 666-3440
Northgate Computer Systems 7075 Flying Cloud Drive, Eden Prairie, MN 55344	(800) 548-1993 (800) 322-3200	(800) 446-5037
Onyx Computer Inc. 30799 Pinetree Road, Suite 303, Cleveland, OH 44124	(800) 486-5005	(216) 591-0489
Pacific Computer, Inc. 9945 Lower Azuza Road, Temple City, CA 91780	(800) 346-7207 (818) 442-9073	(800) 346-7207
PC Brand, Inc. 954 West Washington Street, Chicago, IL 60607	(800) 722-7263	(800) 662-7379
PC Turbo Corp. 515 South Spanish Lane, #D, Walnut, CA 91789	(714) 595-3232	(800) 445-8786
Peregine Computers 110 East Canal Street, Troy, OH 45373	(800) 326-7015	(800) 729-6721
Professional Computer Services 205 Highway 54, W. Elderado Springs, MO 64744	(800) 633-1647	(800) 633-1647
Pro Max Computer 165 Kenneth Street, Hackensack, NJ 07601	(800) 875-5599	(201) 488-0770
Ralin Wholesalers, Inc. P. O. Box 450, Orchard Park, NY 14123	(800) 752-9512	(716) 674-6267

Reason Technology
290 Coon Rapids Boulevard,
Minneapolis, MN 55433   (800) 542-2049   (612) 780-4792

Rite MicroSystems
3415 South McClintock Drive,
Tempe, AZ 85282   (800) 437-0386   (800) 437-0386

Rose Hill Systems
4865 Scotts Valley Drive,
Scotts Valley, CA 95066   (800) 248-7673   (800) 767-6378
                                           (408) 438-3871

Royal Computer
14840 Valley Blvd., #A,
City Of Industry, CA 91746   (818) 333-7628   (818) 333-7628

S1 Computers
18162 East Colima Road,
Roland Heights, CA 91748   (818) 964-2298   (818) 964-2298

Sai Systems Laboratories, Inc.
911 Bridgeport Avenue, Shelton, CT 06864   (800) 331-0488   (203) 929-4959
                                           (203) 926-0374

Scottsdale Systems
15555 West University Drive,
Tempe, AZ 85281   (800) 777-2369   (800) 777-2369
                                           (602) 966-8609

Shecom Computers
22755-G Savi Ranch Parkway,
Yorba Linda, CA 92686   (800) 366-4433   (714) 637-4800

Smart Systems, Inc.
621 Montrose Avenue,
South Plainfield, NJ 07080   (201) 756-2525   (201) 756-2525

Soft Hard Systems
6325 DeSoto Ave, #F,
Woodland Hills, CA 91367   (818) 999-9531   (716) 834-2125

Solid Tech, Inc.
2014 Route 22 East, Scotch Plains, NJ 07076   (201) 322-8922   (201) 322-8922

Standard Computer Corp.
12803 Schabarum Avenue,
Irwindale, CA 91706   (800) 662-6111   (800) 662-6111

St. Croix Computer Corp.
6640 Shady Oak Road, #300,
Eden Prairie, MN 55344   (800) 950-0174   (800) 950-0182

Summit Micro Design 485 Macara Avenue, Suite 901, Sunnyvale, CA 94086	(408) 739-6348	(408) 739-6348
SunnyTech Inc. 17 Smith Street, Englewood, NJ 07631	(800) 367-1132	(201) 569-7773
Sunnyvale Memories, Inc. 1400 Dell Avenue, Campbell, CA 95008	(800) 262-3475 (408) 378-0210	(800) 262-3475 (408) 378-8378
Sunwell International Corp. 1923 Hartog Drive, San Jose, CA 95131	(408) 436-9797	(408) 436-1106
Swan Technologies 3075 Research Drive, State College, PA 16801	(800) 468-9044	(800) 468-7926
SysRudder Technologies, Co. 241 James Street, Unit B, Bensenville, IL 60106	(800) 783-6598	(708) 616-8989
System PowerHouse, Inc. 911 Bunker Hill, #180, Houston, TX 77024	(800) 999-3918	(713) 827-7162
Tandon Corp. 405 Science Drive, Moorpark, CA 93021	(800) 800-8850	(800) 487-8324
Tangent Computer, Inc. 197 Airport Blvd., Burlingame, CA 94010	(800) 223-6677	(800) 223-6677
Telephone Product Center 12603 Hoover Street, Garden Grove, CA 92641	(800) 383-3199	(714) 898-8626
Thoroughbred Microsystems, Inc. 616 Bark Cove Drive, Owensboro, KY 42303	(800) 635-9762	(800) 548-8772
Touche Micro Technologies 8205 South Cass Avenue, Darien, IL 60559	(708) 810-1010	(708) 810-1010
Treasure Chest 4668 Portrait Lane, Plano, TX 75024	(800) 245-3040	(214) 233-2880
Trendex 1875 Century Park East, Suite 2633, Los Angeles, CA 90087	(800) 338-0939 (213) 277-4168	(213) 551-3139
Tri-Star Computer Corp. 707 West Geneva, Tempe, AZ 85282	(800) 678-2799	(800) 688-TECH
True Data Products 115 South Main Street, P. O. Box 347, Uxbridge, MA 01569	(800) 635-0300	(508) 278-6556

Ultra-Comp 11988 Dorsett Road, Maryland Heights, MO 63043	(800) 435-2266 (314) 991-1988	(800) 828-1766
United Computer Express 724 7th Avenue, New York, NY 10019	(800) 448-3738	(212) 397-1081
United Systems Technologies Indianapolis, IN 46250	(800) 899-2999	(800) 899-2999
USA Flex 135 North Brandon Drive, Glen Ellyn, IL 60139	(800) 872-3539	(708) 351-7172
USA Micro 2888 Bluff Street, Suite 257, Boulder, CO 80301	(800) 654-5426	(800) 537-8596
US Computer Merchants 4685 South Ash Avenue, Suite H-5, Tempe, AZ 85282	(800) 888-8779	(800) 888-8779
US Turbo Systems and Components, Inc. 1819 North Floradale Avenue, South El Monte, CA 91733	(818) 579-2405	(818) 579-1446
UTI Computers 3640 Westchase Drive, Houston, TX 77042	(800) 237-4961	(800) 237-4961
Warehouse 54 520 South 52nd Street, Tempe, AZ 85281	(800) 735-0054	(800) 735-0054
Zeos International, Ltd. 530 5th Avenue, N.W., St. Paul, MN 55112	(800) 423-5891 (612) 633-4591	(800) 228-5390

For up-to-date (and, hopefully, assistance in finding the lowest) computer systems pricing, a 900 (pay by the minute) number is available from The Computer Connection, Princeton, MA 01541, telephone (900) 258-7283.

Index